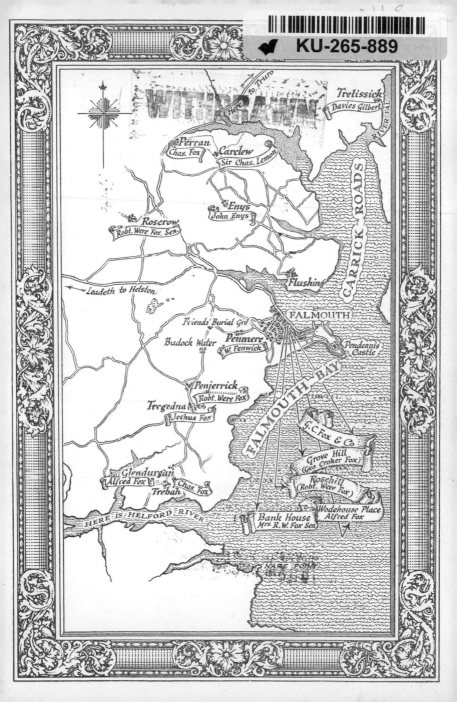

WITHDRAWN

to Truro

Trelissick
Davies Gilbert

RIVER FAL

Perran
Chas. Fox

Carclew
Sir Chas. Lemon

Enys
John Enys

Roscrow
Robt. Were Fox, Sen.

CARRICK ROADS

Leadeth to Helston

Flushing

FALMOUTH

Friends' Burial Grd

Penmere
W. Fenwick

Budock Water

Pendennis
Castle

Penjerrick
Robt. Were Fox

FALMOUTH BAY

Tregedna
Joshua Fox

G. C. Fox & Co.

Grove Hill
(Geo. Croker Fox)

Glendurgan
Alfred Fox

Trebah
Chas. Fox

Rosehill
(Robt. Were Fox)

Wodehouse Place
Alfred Fox

HERE IS HELFORD RIVER

Bank House
Mrs. R. W. Fox, Sen.

NARE POINT

Caroline Fox

Biography

CAROLINE FOX

by

WILSON HARRIS

*With five illustrations
and a map*

Constable

London

PUBLISHED BY

Constable and Company Ltd.

LONDON

First published 1944

Printed in Great Britain by T. and A. CONSTABLE LTD.
at the University Press, Edinburgh

Contents

5

Illustrations

6

A Chronology

1819   *Caroline Fox born.*

1832   *Formal education under John Richards begins.*

1835   *First entries in diary as published.*

1836   *Attends British Association at Bristol.*

1837   *At Grasmere; talks with Hartley Coleridge. British Association at Liverpool.*

1838   *Paris and London. Dr Bowring at Falmouth.*

1840   *John Sterling and John Stuart Mill at Falmouth; Ashantee Princes at Falmouth. London; Carlyle's Lectures on Heroes.*

1841   *Sterling at Falmouth; British Association at Plymouth; Professor Owen at Falmouth.*

1842   *Sterling at Falmouth. London; first visit to the Carlyles; visit to Wordsworth; to Coldbath Fields prison with Elizabeth Fry.*

1843   *To Norwich; call on George Borrow. To London; call on Carlyles. Sterling leaves Falmouth.*

1844   *London; call on Carlyles. Death of Sterling. To Lakes; talks with Wordsworth and Hartley Coleridge.*

1846   *London; painted by Samuel Laurence; talks with F. D. Maurice, the Carlyles, the Mills. Switzerland. London; visit to Landseer.*

1847 *Dublin.   London;   talks   with   Baron   de   Bunsen   and Carlyles.   J. C. Adams at Falmouth.*

1849 *London;   talks   with   Guizot.   Henry   Hallam   at Falmouth.*

1851 *London; attends lectures by Thackeray and Faraday.*

1852 *Dublin; visit to Lord Rosse's observatory at Parsonstown.*

1853 *Attacked by a bull.*

1854 *At Torquay; talks with Kingsley.   Dean Milman at Falmouth.*

1855 *Death of Barclay Fox in Egypt.*

1857 *At British Association at Dublin; meets Livingstone.*

1858 *Death of Caroline's mother.*

1859 *Whewell at Falmouth.*

1860 *At Paris;   Ary Scheffer's studio.   Tennyson and Palgrave, Holman Hunt and Val Prinsep at Falmouth.*

1863 *France and Spain.   Meets Garibaldi at Par.*

1866 *Hyères and Mentone; last meeting with Carlyle.*

1868 *John Bright at Falmouth.*

1871 *Death of Caroline.*

CAROLINE FOX

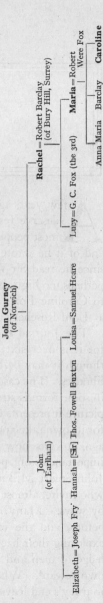

THE FOXES OF FALMOUTH

Francis Fox=1646 Dorothy Kekewich

Francis Fox=1636 Tabitha Croker
(of St Germans)

George Fox=1725 Anna Dobell
(of Par)

George Croker Fox=1749 Mary Were
(of Falmouth)

Robert Were Fox=Elizabeth Tregelles

Alfred Charles Joshua three sons died without issue three daughters

Robert Were (the 2nd)=Maria Barclay

Caroline (1819-1871)

George Croker Fox (the 2nd)=Catherine Young
(of Grove Hill, Falmouth)

George Croker Fox (the 3rd)=Lucy Larcay
(of Grove Hill)

Robert Were

Robert Barclay=Jane Backhouse
(1817-1855)

Anna Maria (1816-1897)

FOXES AND GURNEYS

John Gurney
(of Norwich)

Rachel=Robert Barclay
(of Bury Hill, Surrey)

Maria=Robert Were Fox

Lucy=G. C. Fox (the 3rd)

Anna Maria Barclay Caroline

Elizabeth=Joseph Fry Hannah=[Sir] Thos. Fowell Buxton Louisa=Samuel Hoare

John
(of Earlham)

Note.—These tables are incomplete, and designed only to indicate certain particular relationships.

A*

Foreword

A few years ago I lent a friend whose literary judgements deserve respect Caroline Fox's Journal, of which, like most people, he had never heard. Before he got to the end of it he wrote to say he had known nothing comparable since he read Sir Walter Scott's *Journal*. That is high praise, perhaps too high, but not much higher than has been accorded to Caroline Fox's work at different times by such authorities as Lord Rosebery and Cardinal Newman and John Morley.

The Journal is almost unknown to the present generation, for it is over sixty years since its only two editions appeared, though it may be found, of course, in many public and private libraries. The case for making it available to the public of today in some form is strong, for, apart from the attractiveness of the picture it presents of a cultured community, seeking knowledge for its own sake and ensuing it in a corner of England a century ago, it casts new light, always of interest and sometimes of importance, on personalities like Carlyle and Sterling and John Stuart Mill and Wordsworth and a host of lesser figures, who invite, almost compel, digressions into all sorts of engaging by-ways. Many of Caroline's friends were unknown to me before, and the effect of cultivating their acquaintance and exploring their background has been to enlarge my own knowledge of men and things substantially. Such an exercise is its own reward. When travel is so pleasant, indeed, arrival at the journey's end leaves something of a blank.

Foreword

How the Journal should be treated is, no doubt, an open question. It could be reprinted as it stands, with an introduction and whatever notes seemed necessary. There was much to be said for that. But I came to the conclusion that, in the first instance at any rate, it was not the best method. A great deal of explanation would be needed, for contemporary references and allusions to the events of the 1840's are very far from being obvious to the average reader in the 1940's, and a surfeit of footnotes is an irritation. Some, moreover, of the entries in the Journal deal with matters of small consequence to the world of today, or indeed to the world of yesterday. They are not to be described as chaff—nothing that Caroline wrote is quite that—but they are not the best wheat, and since there is more than enough of the best wheat to provide material for as long a book as anyone will be disposed to read, it seems wise to concentrate on that. The Journal, while it necessarily reveals much of Caroline's mind and character, gives no complete picture of her. No really complete picture can be presented, for the facts are lacking. All that has been possible has been to trace her origins and sketch the little society in which her lot was cast, to tell whatever can be found to tell about her life, to explain the circumstances in which her Journal was written and published, and then to arrange in separate chapters the records of her contacts and conversations with writers and poets, scientists and explorers, preachers and painters and men and women distinguished in varying degree in other vocations. What Caroline has to say about Carlyle, for example, seems to me to gain considerably if the accounts of her various visits to him are assembled in a single chapter, with some explanation of the circumstances and the background, instead of being left in the form of separate entries scattered over something like thirty years.

For the rest, the book explains, and I must hope justifies, itself. Caroline, of course, was a Friend. So am I, though not, I fear, as good a Friend as she was. She regularly used what to her was the familiar Quaker phraseology. In that, when occasion calls for it, I have followed her, for its appropriateness in such a setting is manifest; while it may be esoteric it is not at all obscure. Caroline, moreover, had her idiosyncrasies in such matters as punctuation and the use of capitals; in quoting I have with rare exceptions let her have her way, though it is not always my way. I should add that wherever, in quotations from the Journal, square brackets [ ] occur, the matter within them represents interpolations or explanations of my own.

The acknowledgements I should rightly make are multitudinous: to my wife for constant interest, assistance and salutary criticism; to my daughter, Anne Kitchin, for detecting errors in proof; to Mrs Waldo Trench Fox, of Penjerrick (in the absence of Mr Waldo Trench Fox on service abroad), for giving me access to the unpublished journal of Barclay Fox, Caroline's brother, most valuable for addition to and elucidation of many of Caroline's own entries; to Mrs John Holdsworth, of Bareppa (whose mother, Mrs Thomas Hodgkin, was a daughter of Alfred Fox, Caroline's uncle), for much family information, and permission to quote from letters written by Caroline to Mrs Hodgkin; to the Misses Olivia and Stella Fox, of Rosehill, Caroline's old home; to Mr Cuthbert Fox, of Glendurgan, the present head of the ancient family firm of G. C. Fox and Co.; and to Mrs Naomi Channell, a granddaughter of Caroline's brother. I am greatly indebted also to Mr John Nickalls, Librarian at Friends' House, London, and to Mr W. Tregoning Hooper, of the admirably equipped Public Library at Falmouth. As for the London Library, I can only say that but for its limitless resources, chief among them the incredible omniscience of Mr Frederick Cox, this book could never have been written.

WILSON HARRIS.

ABINGER,
   January, 1944.

12

Chapter I
The Foxes of Falmouth

Some hundreds of babies of either sex were born in Britain on May 24th, 1819, but only two of them are relevant here. Both of them were girls. One saw the light in the village of Kensington, a few miles from London; one in a modern Georgian house (it had only been built nine years earlier) in the prosperous Cornish port of Falmouth. One was given several names, but only one that is of consequence, Victoria; the other a single name, Caroline. Both, as they reached maturity, kept diaries recording the day-to-day incidents of their lives. One of the journals was published in the writer's lifetime (under the title *Leaves from the Journal of Our Life in the Highlands*, followed by *More Leaves*); the other, *Caroline Fox, Her Journals and Letters*, not till its author had been dead eleven years, and then in nothing like its entirety, for its editor was tied by rigorous restrictions imposed by the writer's family. There the parallel ends, for though Caroline necessarily heard much of Victoria there is no reason for supposing that Victoria ever heard anything of Caroline, nor did the fact of having been born on the same day as the Sovereign under whom thirty-four of her fifty-one years were to be lived appear to stir Caroline's interest greatly. She did, however, write on her forty-third birthday : 'I trust that our poor Queen has had the same atmosphere of lovingkindness spread round her to help her through her first solitary birthday'—the Prince Consort having died in the previous December.

It would be difficult to find anything today quite like the

cultured and philanthropic Quaker circle in which Caroline Fox grew up. Caroline Stephen, sister of Sir Leslie Stephen (who herself joined the Society of Friends in middle life), writing as long ago as 1882, spoke of it as something that was even then already passing away. The general picture has been made familiar by Augustus Hare in his *Gurneys of Earlham*—a picture of comfortable families, with some prosperous business like banking or brewing as their basis, related in varying degrees of closeness to one another, all living within easy visiting distance, all gathering regularly at the First Day Meeting (or Meetings) for Worship, and probably enough on Fourth Days too, faithful stewards of their substance, giving readily to those in need and adding the grace of sympathy and understanding to their charity, quiet but effective participants in every social crusade, well versed in the literature, and often in the science, of their own day and of the past. Just such a community did the Foxes of Falmouth constitute in Regency days. Their own roots in Quakerism were struck deep. The first of their forebears of whom there is reliable record is one Francis Fox, who moved west from Wiltshire during the Civil Wars, and marrying a Dorothy Kekewich [1] of Exeter in 1646 went on farther west still, to settle at a house called Catchfrench, belonging to the Kekewich family, in the parish of St Germans in Cornwall. A legend indeed exists of more distinguished origins. A Fox of the twentieth century, who constructed an elaborate and valuable family tree, traced the descent of the second Francis Fox's wife Tabitha Croker back through four generations of Crokers, two of Yeos and two of Granvilles—characteristic west-country names all of them—to Lady Mary Courtenay, daughter of Lady Margaret de Bohun, daughter of Princess Elizabeth, daughter of Edward I and Eleanor of Castile. That is as may be. It is enough here to concentrate on the fortunes of Francis Fox the first.

[1] So at least runs the generally accepted tradition; later researches suggest that it was a Dorothy Croker that Francis Fox married.

About this founding father the statement is made (in a privately printed volume, *The Descendants of Francis Fox of St Germans*) that he and his wife and three sons ' joined the Society of Friends soon after its first establishment in Cornwall.' That arouses interesting speculations, pointing, if not to a certain, at least to a very probable, conclusion. Quakerism in 1646, when Francis Fox was married and went to Catchfrench, was a new and unfamiliar faith, if at that time it could be called a faith at all. Francis Fox had certainly then never heard of it, for its founder, George Fox, born in 1624, only began his preaching in 1648, and for some years after that his journeys were confined to the Midlands, where he had been born and brought up, and the North of England. But in 1655 he travelled by way of Plymouth into Cornwall, holding his first meetings in that county in the parish of Menheniot. His own *Journal* describes (in almost authentically Pauline language) how ' from thence [Plymouth] wee passt Into Cornwall to Menheniot parish and there came to an Inn: and att night wee had a meetinge att Ed: Hancockes. . . . And I turned y^m to ye light of Christ by which they might see there sinns and see there saviour Christ Jesus . . . and many was convinced y^t time there and come under Christs teachinge: and there is fine gatheringes in ye name of Jesus thereaways to this day.'

Was—the question inevitably presents itself—Francis Fox of Catchfrench one of the little company who gathered from the farms and cottages around to hear his namesake (there was no relationship between the two) at Ed: Hancockes att Menheniot? Catchfrench is described as situate in the parish of St Germans, but it is almost precisely half-way between that village and Menheniot, if anything a little nearer to the latter; the distance from either place would be about three miles. Given, then, the facts that Francis Fox joined the Society of Friends soon after its first establishment in Cornwall, and that George Fox, the founder of the Society, preached within three miles of his house, the presumption that Francis

The Foxes of Falmouth

Fox became from that moment a follower of George is very strong, though we are not required necessarily to believe that he joined the still unorganised Society there and then. But if not, he joined it very shortly, and thereby became the ancestor of nine generations of Cornish Friends, whose substantial if unpretentious homes were dotted a hundred years ago over the narrow peninsula on which Falmouth stands and on the slopes or by the waterside of the fertile country to the west.

And not round Falmouth alone, for one branch of the family had settled at Plymouth and formed a notable circle there. With unfailing regularity, as I remember them fifty years ago, they drove in to Morning Meeting on First Day from their homes either on the outskirts of the town itself or some three or four miles out—the Francis Edwards from Uplands, the Reynoldses from Westbrook, the Charles Alfreds from Widey, the George Edwards from Hillside, with one or two unmarried sisters living singly or in couples nearer in. Just such a circle ringed Falmouth round another half-century earlier. It was larger than the Plymouth circle, its members were more apt to maintain both a town and a country house, and, Falmouth being a smaller centre (the population in 1841 was just under 7000), it held a relatively more dominant place in the community—if that word may properly be used of citizens so incapable of domination. There they were, firmly and tranquilly established, at Bank House and Roscrow, at Wodehouse Place and Glendurgan, at Grove Hill and Rosehill and Perran and Penjerrick and Tregedna and Trebah, comfortable, solid Friends in their comfortable, solid houses. And in their gardens—for to any Falmouth Fox the garden rivalled the house in importance.

The Foxes of the generation preceding Caroline's made a deep impression throughout West Cornwall by their public spirit, their business ability, their philanthropy, the variety of their interests and their unostentatious but uncompromising integrity. 'Seldom,' wrote the *West Briton* of April 28th, 1878,

16

in connexion with the death of Charles Fox, of Trebah, 'does it fall to our lot to notice such diversity of pursuit, and yet such oneness in essential points of character, as marked the four brothers who formed this uncommon group—Alfred Fox, hard-working, upright, conscientious man of business; Joshua Fox, the kind-hearted lover of his race and of all living things, the true child of nature; Robert Were Fox [Caroline's father], the man of science, with rare store of learning and observation; Charles Fox, the literary man, with a vast fund of diligently accumulated learning and information.' A bare mention is sufficient for three other brothers, two of whom were drowned in boyhood; the third was something of a recluse, and figured little in the family circle.

Close-knit as that circle was, it would be a profound mistake to think of it as limited either by kinship or by creed. Reference to Caroline's Journal, or Barclay's, would indicate how strongly both condemned any narrowness of that kind. The easy intimacy of all the Fox families with such orthodox Anglicans as the Lemons of Carclew, or the Enyses of Enys, or the Suttons of Penwerris, shows how healthily catholic were their associations. But they remained essentially a family circle none the less, with family affections, family traditions, a family understanding and a quiet family pride. And of course there were family legends—they could not but flourish and multiply in such a soil—but they concern Caroline little, and it is enough to quote one here as sample. It is related that at Charles Fox's home at Trebah, where a parrot was a privileged member of the household, the servants were one morning filing gravely in to family prayers (or, as Friends say, 'reading') when the following interchange ensued:

THE PARROT: 'Charles Fox, Charles Fox, kiss the cook.'
CHARLES FOX, stern but impassive: 'Remove that bird.'
THE PARROT, *in exitu*: '*Sorry* I spoke.'

Devotions then proceeded.

A word here on Uncle Joshua (as he was to Caroline), for we shall not meet him much again. He had gone his own way in early life, and it was not the accustomed way of the Foxes. He was, as the *West Briton* justly observed, a lover of all living things—among them, rather unfortunately, a French dancer. So, at least, legend has it, and except that there is little evidence that she was French and less that she was a dancer, the legend needs no correction. But she lived in Paris, even if she was of Irish extraction, and if there was no evidence that she was a dancer there was none that she was not; for any one determined to indulge in the luxury of being shocked it was much more satisfactory to be shocked at a French dancer than at an Irish midinette. Uncle Joshua, let me hasten to add, discharged all the legal, if not the ecclesiastical, formalities of marriage and came home with his bride to settle at Tregedna, near Penjerrick. In due course three daughters were born, of whom the first two were named imperially Josephine and Marie Louise respectively. Uncle Joshua was, of course, disowned by the Society of Friends, not for marrying an alleged dancer—it would have been the same if he had married a deaconess— but for marrying out of the Society. More than that, he was banned from the parental home — till one day his own house was burned down. Then the deep-rooted hospitality of the clan incontinently burst its bonds and the homeless evacuees were received at Bank House with open arms.

Caroline says little of Uncle Joshua, but the two references she does make to him illuminate different sides of his eccentric and attractive personality. First the mildly sardonic. 'Uncle Joshua,' his niece writes in 1841, 'remarked that the majority of fashionable women keep themselves in tolerable health by talking: they would die otherwise for want of exercise.' The other is more characteristic. 'We were delighted,' she says three years later, 'to watch Uncle Joshua in his sweet companionship with Nature; the little birds are now so intimate and trustful that they come when he calls them and eat crumbs out of his mouth. It is a charming and beautiful sight.' He was in fact a lover of all kinds of animals. His skill in taming birds was legendary, and so in another sense were his blood-hounds, which probably never manifested, or thought of manifesting, a tithe of the ferocity attributed to them. Fishes too he tamed successfully. But as Uncle Joshua grew older his eccentricities grew also. Left a widower at Tregedna, he preferred for some reason to be visited after dark—and on foot, for the white gravel of the Tregedna drive must never be violated by wheels. A kinsman who paid one such visit has left an instructive picture of his reception. He and his mother, a niece of Uncle Joshua's, arrived at the front door and duly knocked (the bell had long been out of action). Someone, I suppose, opened. 'Then, out of the darkness, on the top stair, a strange form loomed, holding a candle in one hand, and peered over the banisters. Grey-bearded, brown-wigged, without coat or waistcoat and with untucked red shirt flapping above the trousers, the figure advanced to meet us.' Uncle Joshua, it is to be feared, had run to seed. But let him be remembered as he was in his earlier life, not in his latter days. Good Quakerism may not have been his forte, but, disowned by the Society or not, he sleeps today beside his row of brothers in the Quaker burial-ground at Budock, and perhaps not less peacefully than they.

In one of the Fox houses, Rosehill, just below the ridge of the Falmouth peninsula, with garden sloping south towards the sea, Caroline Fox was born in May 1819 on a day made memorable, as already mentioned, by another birth. There is no need to trace in detail the generations that separated her from Francis Fox of Catchfrench. The first of her ancestors who matters is Francis's great-grandson, George Croker Fox, for he it was who, penetrating farther west than any of his predecessors, founded, first at Fowey and then, in 1759, at Falmouth, the ship agency business on which the fortunes of all the Falmouth Foxes originally depended. It was—or rather is, for it continues and prospers today, with Foxes still at the head of it—a notable firm in many respects. So long as there was an American Consul at Falmouth (the post was discontinued some forty years ago, when larger jurisdiction was given to the consul at Plymouth) that office was held throughout, except for a single year's interval, by a Fox of G. C. Fox and Co. Edward Fox acted for two years, a little informally in the first instance, but the first actual patent of appointment was issued in 1794 in favour of Robert Were Fox the first, and bears at its foot the signature of the then President of the United States, George Washington. The second patent marked the appointment of Robert Were Fox the second, Caroline's father, and is signed by James Madison as President and James Monroe as Secretary of State. The firm's activities were extensive. Their nature is indicated in part by two entries in Barclay's journal on successive days in September, 1841:

'Express from Uncle A[lfred] at Mev[agissey] brought the news of his having bought all the fish there under cure at 70/- per hh [hogshead].'

' "Seagull," from Mexico, with $800,000, of which $450,000 for us.'

There were also important mining ventures, and the foundry at Perran on an inlet of the Fal.

To return for a moment to George Croker Fox (the first), from whom the line of Falmouth Foxes sprang, it is material that he married in 1749 Mary Were of Wellington, for it explains why Caroline's grandfather and father were both allotted Were as a second Christian name. A lamentable deficiency of imagination in this matter of names, or possibly an undue subservience to family tradition, is characteristic of Quakerism, and not only in bygone generations. Thus, to the discomfiture of the historian, George Croker Fox, the founder of the family business, having begotten a son, unhesitatingly named (not, of course, christened) him George Croker, and he in turn in due time added a George Croker the third to the list. That, however, did not immediately affect Caroline. Her descent was from George Croker Fox the second's younger brother, Robert Were Fox, who raised the shipping business and its allied enterprises to great prosperity in the days of the French wars, when merchantmen running up-Channel were glad to minimise risks by unloading at the first British port available. Robert Were Fox had several sons, and needless to say named the eldest of them, Caroline's father, Robert Were. (The 'Robert,' it may be mentioned, survived in the direct line for three generations more, till Robert Barclay Fox died in 1934 without issue.)

Between the two Robert Were Foxes a dividing-line may conveniently be drawn. Hereafter it is with the second only that we need be concerned, and the name, whenever mentioned, will indicate him and not his father. Much might be said of him, but enough is said succinctly in the *Dictionary of National Biography*. An F.R.S. and a regular attendant at meetings of the British Association (a fact to which Caroline, who often accompanied him, owed some of her most interesting contacts), he was a scientist of much more than local note, for though many of his inventions were connected with Cornish tin-mining, his dipping-needle, or magnetic deflector, which was used to great advantage in the Polar expeditions of Nares and Ross, carried his name into much larger fields. In 1814 Robert Were Fox married Maria Barclay, of Bury Hill, near Dorking (where Barclays still live); her sister Lucy had four years earlier married his cousin, George Croker Fox the third. Through her mother Caroline was connected with some of the most prominent and respected members of the Society of Friends, for Maria Barclay was descended from the Robert Barclay who was author of the Quaker classic *Barclay's Apology* (apology, of course, in its original sense of defence or explanation), published in Latin in 1676, and subsequently in English.[1]

Through her mother Maria Barclay was linked up with the whole Earlham circle of Gurneys and Buxtons and Hoares; Elizabeth Fry was her first cousin; so was Joseph John Gurney, the well-known Quaker writer and speaker. The bonds of affection and spiritual sympathy between Caroline and her mother were so close that some reference to the latter's religious experience is requisite. At an early age she felt impelled to change in certain respects the way of life to which she had been accustomed. Dancing in particular caused her exercise of mind, on the ground that it ill befitted a rational creature ' to dance away a whole evening and converse only on the most trifling subjects.' She was drawn more and more to orthodox Quaker practice, to which till that time she had sat a little loose, and conformed to it first of all in declining to wear mourning, then in the use of the plain speech, 'thee' and 'thou' and 'thy,' and finally in the adoption of the Friends' dress (which Richmond's portrait of Elizabeth Fry has made familiar), with the by no means unbecoming bonnet as its most conspicuous feature. Five years after Maria Barclay's marriage to Robert Were Fox, of whom she had no doubt seen much during visits to her sister at Falmouth, Caroline was born.

Of the sixteen years between that date and the first entry in Caroline's Journal we know far too little. But one fact which every piece of information from whatever source conspires to emphasise is that the unity and family affection that prevailed in the family circle at Rosehill and Penjerrick was remarkable even for a Quaker household of that day. The elder daughter, Anna Maria, was born in 1816, and the only son, Robert

[1] The full title deserves quotation : ' An Apology for the true Christian Divinity, as the same is held forth, and preached, by the people, called in scorn, Quakers ; being a full Explanation and Vindication of their Principles and Doctrines, by many arguments deduced from Scripture and Right Reason, and the testimonies of famous authors, both ancient and modern, with a full answer to the strongest objections usually made against them.'

Barclay, in 1817. Anna Maria possessed different qualities from her sister's, but she manifested the same striking precocity, as witness the part she took in the founding of the Falmouth Polytechnic. Caroline's birth came two years after Barclay's. Whether her affection for her sister or the devotion of the two sisters to their brother was the stronger emotion it would be hard to determine; in such feelings there is no nicely calculated less or more. Barclay's premature death in Egypt in 1855 was with one possible exception the greatest grief in Caroline's life, for deeply devoted though she was to her mother, she recognised when that life ended that it had been lived to its full span happily and richly and that its close came at the appointed time. Barclay was only thirty-eight when he died; in his case grief was deepened by the sense of unfulfilled possibilities.

Chapter II

Caroline

Caroline's development was necessarily conditioned to some extent by her surroundings. Communications being what they were in the third and fourth decades of the nineteenth century, communities like that at Falmouth tended to be largely self-sufficient. The Great Western Railway, it is true, was opened in 1835, the year in which Caroline's Journal begins, but it only ran then as far as Bristol. It was not till 1859, when Brunel's Royal Albert Bridge over the Tamar at Saltash was completed, that the main line came to Cornwall (on May 14th of that year the Plymouth–Falmouth coach made its last run), and the branch line from Truro to Falmouth was not constructed till two years later. Dr Thomas Hodgkin, the historian, describes[1] the mail-coach dashing through the narrow streets of Falmouth when he first visited the town in 1848.

But to this one all-important reservation must be made. If visitors by land were relatively rare, visitors by sea were relatively frequent.[2] What made Falmouth, which dates no further back than 1613, was its choice in 1688 as the home port for the Packet Service which carried His Majesty's mails the world over. It is reliably stated that in the twenties of last century no fewer than forty Packet Services were linking Falmouth with foreign countries, mainly in North and South

[1] In an article on Anna Maria Fox in the *Friends' Quarterly Examiner*, First Month, 1898.
[2] The relation is between the number of passengers carried by one stage-coach a day (if as often) in 1844 and the daily complement of several express trains and others in 1944.

24

America. The Packets, which continued to use the port till 1850, carried passengers as well, and many of these, since no time-tables either of arrival or of departure could be dependable in days of sail, often had to wait days or even weeks at Falmouth, spending money there for the benefit of its tradesmen and giving to such of its citizens as the Foxes opportunities gladly seized for contacts with travellers of literary or scientific or other attainments. Such voyagers might reach Falmouth, if outward bound, by coach or chaise, but many came by sea from Bristol to some North Cornwall port like Hayle or St Ives, and thence by road, or else direct from Plymouth by the coastal steamer *Drake.* Whatever the mode of arrival, no small proportion of them took advantage of the hospitality readily extended by Bank House or Wodehouse Place or Rosehill, whose owners were always well posted in all shipping matters through the activities of G. C. Fox and Co.

It was in such surroundings that Caroline spent her girlhood, and to them no doubt she owed the remarkable maturity of knowledge and judgement manifest in her Journal from the first. An attractive picture of the Rosehill household is left by a slightly junior and slightly awestruck relative, Samuel Middleton Fox, a grandson of Caroline's uncle, Alfred Fox, of Wodehouse Place and Glendurgan. 'When as a small boy,' he writes,[1] 'paying a timid visit, I saw a copy of Guido's "Aurora" hanging in the dining-room, bound copies of the *Athenaeum* on the shelves and knick-knacks from Rome on the table; when I heard the second part of Goethe's *Faust* discussed at the luncheon-table under a print of Raphael's "Sposalizio della Madonna," a new world of wonder opened before me.' Whether or not her young kinsman rated that world too high, it was the world that surrounded Caroline Fox. One would give a great deal for a faithful portrait of Caroline herself in her early twenties. Her Journal, of course, reveals her to a certain extent; that could not be otherwise. But in the severe process of editing that

[1] *Friends' Quarterly Examiner*, Seventh Month, 1882.

it has undergone, much that was characteristic of her, it can hardly be doubted, has disappeared. Her brother Barclay's journal makes disappointingly little reference to her. What she herself in her self-reproachful moments no doubt regarded as failings, if not as vices—a sharp tongue, with both a temptation to and a gift for sarcasm—are mentioned by one or two of the closer friends of the family rather as sources of entertainment than as qualities to be deplored. Caroline Stephen, who never knew her personally, but knew her sister Anna Maria well, wrote: 'Her [Caroline's] chief difficulties seem to have arisen from the abundant vivacity of her mind. As a young girl especially her snare lay in the tendency to make too free and satirical a use of her sharp wit; and even in later life this tendency was not brought into full captivity to the law of kindness without a struggle.' She adds, in some mitigation of this not very damning judgement, the testimony of one who knew Caroline well, that 'the mother's will and wishes were always a sacred law to Caroline, and in the heyday of her young self-assertion and intense love of fun and wilful wild mischief she was steadied and touched by her mother's word of regret or disapproval, when nothing else in the world would have reached her.' To that may be further added a sentence or two by Dr Hodgkin. 'I think it was in the year 1843,' he wrote,[1] 'probably in the midst of visits to Hare, Carlyle and Maurier, that they [Anna Maria and Caroline, the latter being then 24] came to Tottenham to visit my father, who had recently married their second cousin, Anna Backhouse, as his second wife. I remember how we children, brought up in the calm, sedate atmosphere of Tottenham Quakerism, were astonished by the vivacious, sparkling talk of these Cornish cousins.' Brilliant Caroline undoubtedly was. The depth and sincerity of her Quakerism is equally beyond question; something will be said of that in the next chapter. But it is a satisfaction to know that she was essentially human, and not completely devoid of some

[1] *Friends' Quarterly Examiner*, First Month, 1898.

of the more attractive human weaknesses. A few more human touches in regard to such mundane matters as dress, food, incidents of travel, all of which are almost entirely ignored in the Journal, would be welcome. We should have been glad too to hear rather more about her autographs, of which she must have amassed a remarkable collection, thanks to the good offices of many of her literary friends.

Of her life as a whole her Journal is, of course, the record, and practically the only record. The story of her friendships, as rearranged and re-presented here, is drawn almost wholly from it, though with some contributions, particularly where it is a question of sketching-in the background, from other sources. Very little, unhappily, is to be discovered about her education. Her Journal makes no reference to it at all, but it can be inferred from one or two entries here and there that she knew French and probably German, while in Italian she and Anna Maria were proficient enough to translate several tracts into that language. And she could not have been her father's daughter without getting a good grounding in science. Fortunately her brother Barclay's journal fills in some of the gaps in the picture. The foundation of the three children's education was no doubt laid by their gifted parents, and there can be no question that it was well and truly laid. But at the beginning of 1832, when Caroline was twelve, Barclay fourteen and Anna Maria fifteen, more systematic arrangements seem to have been initiated. A schoolroom was fitted up at Rosehill, and on January 12th Barclay writes: 'I commenced my studies with John Richards today.' This pedagogue—who was not yet nineteen and something of a polymath, to judge by what Barclay says of the range of his tuition—was clearly responsible for all three children, and in addition there is frequent mention of a French teacher, one Alfiston, and a drawing-master named Jordan. Caroline is soon in evidence. On January 17th 'J. Richards has begun to teach Carry mathamatics' [*sic*], and nine days later—a reassuring piece of intelligence this—'Carry was turned out of the schoolroom today for laughing.' Other references to 'themes' on history and poetry, and the introduction to chemistry, indicate a curriculum of at least normal breadth.

Such formal instruction was necessary, of course, but doubtless the best education of all came from the daily routine of life in that cultured family circle. The domestic economy of the various Fox households must have been of a remarkable elasticity, for any member of any family seems to have been liable to drop in for any meal (including breakfast) at the table of any other without any sort of warning, and to have been sure to find some outside visitors as well there. Here, on the latter point, is one entry in Barclay's journal: '4 gentlemen dined here today, viz. Geo. Pelley, cos. to Emma Pelley, who married cos. A. Reynolds; Captn Darby, who is going off on a 5 years' voyage as soon as the wind will permit; Captn Robinson, Captn of a fine American East Indiaman; and Captn Bawl, Captn of an American brig which put in here yesterday much injured by the storm.' There must have been conversation worth listening to at that dinner-table. A more ordinary gathering, indicating what was regarded as a quiet meal in the Rosehill household, is thus described: 'Sterling dined with us in quiet. The Tregednites [i.e. the Joshua Foxes from Tregedna, probably four in number] and W. Hustler and Juliet our only other guests.' No day could pass without providing some material for a receptive mind to absorb.

Then there were such outside interests as—pre-eminently— the Polytechnic, to which Caroline makes such frequent reference. Her association with it, indeed, is fundamental, for she is credited not only with giving the institution its name but for implanting the word 'Polytechnic' for the first time in the English language. That is a high claim to advance for a girl of fourteen (not that Caroline ever advanced it herself), but some colour is given to it by the Oxford English Dictionary, which cites the first use of the word in such a connexion as

Caroline

applied to Quintin Hogg's Polytechnic in Regent Street in
1838; by that time the Falmouth Polytechnic, named by
Caroline, had been in prosperous existence for five years.[1]
It had, indeed, thanks to a royal warrant granted by William IV
in 1835, become the Royal Cornwall Polytechnic Society.
All three Fox children had their shares in the inception of this
admirable institution, which still holds a considerable place in
the intellectual life of Cornwall. The real originator seems to
have been Anna Maria, then aged seventeen. The development
of the mining industry (copper and tin) in the Gwennap district,
east and south-east of Redruth, in the early years of the century
had led to the establishment by the Fox firm of the famous
Perran foundry, on the Restronguet Creek, off the estuary of
the Fal, to construct machinery of various kinds for the mines—
and later for South Wales and different parts of the Continent.
The factory workmen were a highly intelligent set of men,
fertile in suggestions for improvements of methods, and it was
both for their encouragement and their instruction that Anna
Maria, whose own ideas had been enlarged by visits with her
father to British Association meetings, conceived the plan of
the Polytechnic, in which she received from the first the warm
and active support of her father and uncles and her brother
Barclay. Evidence of the practical value of the institution is
provided by the fact that the first substantial prizes offered were
for improved methods of raising and lowering men in the pits
(there was at that time nothing but a series of ordinary ladders
from ledge to ledge in the shaft) and for safer means of blasting.
Both produced valuable results. The Polytechnic, conceived
by Anna Maria, named by Caroline and actively supported by
Barclay, has for a hundred and ten years played a large part in
the life of Falmouth, as it did for as long as she lived in Caroline's.
A Fox is President of it today (1944).

[1] But the O.E.D. gives the date 1805 against ' Polytechnic,' William Taylor
having written of a Polytechnic School in the *Annual Review* for that year ; and
the Ecole Polytechnique at Paris had existed since 1794.

For the rest, there were always visits paid and visits received, in chariots and gigs and carts and rummies, there were horses to ride—'Carry,' writes Barclay, 'being mounted on too powerful a horse was run away with, but no lives were lost'—an almost unlimited variety of walks, those from Falmouth to Penjerrick or Falmouth to Glendurgan the most frequent, plenty of books to read and plenty of indoor games, notably charades and 'twelve nouns,'[1] to keep the large circle entertained. There was, of course, finally, the Quaker side of Caroline's life. She was just fifteen when she went with the rest of the family to Yearly Meeting in London for the first time (we have to rely on Barclay for particulars of that, for Caroline's Journal as we have it only begins a year later), and

---

[1] 'Twelve nouns' is of some interest. Whether the game still survives anywhere I do not know, but it was clearly popular in Falmouth in the 1830's. The dozen substantives are apparently contributed by different members of the circle, and the winner is the writer of the best passage embodying them all in the order given. This would hardly be worth mentioning but for a paper I have found at Penjerrick, a hundred years old, written in still unfaded ink in Caroline's clear, decided script. It is undated, and runs as follows:

'Twelve Nouns
in old times (by C. F.)

Cambridge, Stereoscope, Coal, the Leviathan, the 10th, Carew, Table, Punjaubi, Tower, Australia, the Moon, Young's *Night Thoughts*.

'Just before I left Cambridge I took a quiet dinner with the Master of Trinity to concoct with him a new stereoscope. "Depend upon it," said he, "there's nothing like polished coal for reflecting the image of the Leviathan. Now, mark my words"—so I took out my pocket-book and recorded that Dr Whewell had made this remark on the 10th of December, 1857. "That's right, Carew," said he, "you're worth talking to. Did you ever hear me sing a Punjaubi melody?" No, I said, I had never had that pleasure; would he favour me? "With all my heart," said he, "and give you a lecture on its theory," and then he struck up a dashing air called "The Tower of Australia." It was a wonderful language, and I hope authentic. Then he burst forth, "By the way, have you seen my researches in the Moon? The subject was suggested to me by Young's *Night Thoughts*, and I think you will grant that I have carried the matter pretty far. You know of course that I have utterly exploded the [? existence of] man there and everywhere else excepting in our own planet. But come, my dear fellow, let's look after this stereoscope. I want to show how thoroughly wrong people are about it and most other things."'

This strangely surviving relic of some firelit winter evening at Rosehill or Penjerrick spans the intervening century a little movingly. So at least it seemed to me as I came on it between the leaves of a copy of the printed Journal.

shorter visits to Quarterly or Monthly Meeting at Truro or Redruth or Penzance or St Austell or Liskeard were frequent— nor were the visits devoted exclusively to religious exercises. In addition, Friends travelling in the ministry were constantly being put up at Rosehill, some of them apt to seek embarrassing religious opportunities with the young of the household. Caroline may have lived her life in a remote corner of England, but it was anything but a cloistered life.

Caroline never married. Whether she may have thought of it who can say? What may reasonably be surmised regarding that is touched on later.[1] She read, she talked, she undertook many charitable works about Falmouth, the Sailors' Home near Bank House on the water-front being perhaps her chief concern.[2] And she travelled, to London, to the Lakes, to Ireland, to Paris, to Switzerland, to Spain, to the Riviera. Everywhere she met, naturally, with no trace of self-consciousness, the foremost figures of the day in literature and science —more rarely in politics. Among the books she speaks of reading, most of them as soon as they were published, are Carlyle's *Sartor Resartus*, *Chartism* and *Past and Present*, Tieck's *Tales*, Dickens' *Master Humphrey's Clock* and *Christmas Carol*,[3] various works of Emerson, Harriet Martineau's *Deerbrook*, *Wilhelm Meister* (whether in the original or in Carlyle's translation is not stated), Kinglake's *Eothen*, Bacon's

[1] p. 85.
[2] Barclay Fox writes (January 28th, 1841) : ' This morning, looking out of my window, which commands that of the servants' hall, I saw a picture which would have equally suited Wordsworth or Wilkie—Caroline teaching a poor girl to read who was poor indeed, being blind and deaf and almost dumb. The window formed the frame of the picture, and the light fell on their faces, showing the strong contrast of earnest intelligence in the one and the puzzled vacant expression of the other, which artists and poets so delight in. They were poring over a tablet on which C. had worked in large stitches the Lord's Prayer and was guiding her hand over the letters and words, which the other spelt and pronounced in her half-articulate way, now getting thoroughly aground and turning up her sightless eyes with a distressed look, and then returning to her task, and now highly pleased when C's approving pat on the hand told her she was right.'
[3] Though *A Christmas Carol* was only published in the third week of December, 1843, Caroline writes on January 9th, 1844, that she has been reading it aloud to some boys.

31

Essays, Mrs Gaskell's *Mary Barton* and *Life of Charlotte Brontë*, Thackeray's *Vanity Fair*, Maurice's *Theological Essays*, Kingsley's *Westward Ho!*, Dean Stanley's *Palestine*, Reade's *It's Never Too Late to Mend*, About's *La Question Romaine* (certainly in French), Mill's *On Liberty* and the Life of F. W. Robertson. To *The Essays of Elia* she was specially devoted, and according to her editor 'the works of Coleridge exercised upon her a peculiar fascination.'

Some of her literary judgements are interesting. At the age of twenty-two she had a high appreciation of Dickens (who had then written only *Pickwick*, *Nicholas Nickleby* and *Oliver Twist* of his major works). 'I am exceedingly enjoying Boz's *Master Humphrey's Clock*, which is still in progress,' she wrote in 1841. 'That man is carrying out Carlyle's work more emphatically than any; he forces the sympathies of all into unwonted channels, and teaches that Punch and Judy men, beggar children and daft old men are also of our species, and are not, more than ourselves, removed from the sphere of the heroic. He is doing a world of good in a very healthy way.' Eight years later she made what, if that conclusion may be drawn from the Journal's silence, was her first acquaintance with Thackeray, whom she clearly appreciated much less. The entry here, under date November 4th, 1849, reads: 'Finished that brilliant bitter book *Vanity Fair*; it shows great insight into the intricate badness of human nature, and draws a cruel sort of line between moral and intellectual eminence, as if they were most commonly dissociated, which I trust is no true bill?' Less than a month later she is commending, as she might be expected to, 'W. E. Forster's manly, spirited answer to Macaulay's libels on William Penn; he has most satisfactory contemporary evidence to adduce in favour of the fine old moral hero.'

Two other assessments deserve mention. In 1845, a year after publication, Caroline was reading 'a brilliant book by a nameless man, *Eothen, or Eastern Travel*. Full of careless, easy, masterly sketches, biting satire and proud superiority to common report. It is an intellectual egotism which he acknowledges and glories in. He has remarkably freed himself from religious prepossessions, and writes as he feels, not as he *ought* to feel, at Bethlehem and Jerusalem.' Finally, there is a surprisingly hostile criticism of John Stuart Mill's *On Liberty*. But consideration of that belongs elsewhere.[1]

In her general reading, though not, I think, in her appraisements, which were essentially her own, Caroline must have gained considerable guidance from the *Athenaeum*, which was founded in 1828,[2] and no doubt derived an added interest for her from the fact that it had been edited for a short time by her friend John Sterling. Of other papers and periodicals she says next to nothing, but it is clear that she kept herself well abreast of current affairs. The *Edinburgh Review* would seem to have had an established place in the Rosehill household (but that, of course, was only a quarterly), and at different times Caroline refers to something she has seen in *The Times* or the *Daily News* or *Punch*. It is probable that some papers were taken in at the Polytechnic.

A good deal of light will be shed on Caroline's life in the following pages as the record of her many and notable friendships is traced, but it will be convenient to summarise at this point the chief events in it. While she never lived anywhere but at the two Cornish homes Rosehill and Penjerrick, she travelled considerably, both in England and abroad. The most regular journeys were to London in May for Yearly Meeting, which, as every good Friend knows, or knew, begins on the first Third Day after the third First Day in Fifth Month. Crowded though the Yearly Meeting programme is, and always has been, Friends from the provinces managed usually to fit in some secular meetings or exhibitions, primarily the

---

[1] See p. 163.
[2] By James Silk Buckingham, a native of Flushing, just across the harbour from Falmouth.

Royal Academy—not, certainly, in those days the play. Caroline, for example, during the second May visit which she records, attended the last two of Carlyle's lectures on Heroes and Hero-Worship. That year, indeed, 1840, was in many ways the most memorable of her life, for in February she first met John Sterling, in March John Stuart Mill, and in May Thomas Carlyle. She was still under twenty-one. Four years earlier, in 1836, she had been with her father to the British Association meeting at Bristol; in 1837 to Grasmere, where Hartley Coleridge took charge of her, and then to the British Association at Liverpool; and in 1838 to Paris and London.

The London visit of 1842 was rich in contacts—with Carlyle, Wordsworth, the Mills, Professor Owen, F. D. Maurice and Elizabeth Fry among others. In 1843 London was combined with a stay among the Gurney relatives in Norfolk; there Caroline saw, apart from various Buxtons, the Bishop of Norwich (father of the better-known Dean Stanley), George Borrow and Amelia Opie. In 1844 came London again, and Windermere and Wordsworth; in 1846 London and Geneva; in 1847 London and the de Bunsen circle (Baron de Bunsen was for thirteen years Prussian Ambassador to this country), Julius Hare, and George Richmond, the painter. In 1849 an unforgettable day with Guizot is recorded; in 1851 Caroline attends on successive days Thackeray's lecture on the English Humorists and Faraday's on Ozone; in 1852 she is at the British Association's meeting at Dublin; in 1853 she attends in London on May 4th a 'Bible meeting' at which Harriet Beecher Stowe, whose *Uncle Tom's Cabin* was published two years earlier, is present but does not speak, and on May 8th witnesses a presentation to Louis Kossuth.

In 1853, too, occurred an incident which must be dealt with at rather greater length, Caroline's adventure with the bull. It made a deep impression on the family circle (incidentally eliciting from Barclay a deplorable poem of thanksgiving), and since her life might well have been ended at the age of thirty-four the episode is not to be too summarily dismissed. Her editor perhaps puts it a little high when he refers in his introductory memoir to 'her almost miraculous preservation when pursued by a bull in 1853, when she lay insensible on the ground, the fierce animal roaring round, but never touching her.' Caroline's own account of what happened is straightforward, dispassionate and restrained—altogether a piece of writing that does her credit. It deserves to be quoted in full.

'*March* 10.—As we turned the corner of a lane during our walk a man and a bull came in sight, the former crying out "Ladies, save yourselves as you can," the latter scudding onwards slowly but furiously. I jumped aside on a little hedge, but thought the depth below rather too great,—about nine or ten feet; but the man cried "Jump" and I jumped. To the horror of all the bull jumped after me. My fall stunned me, so that I knew nothing of my terrible neighbour, whose deep autograph may be now seen quite close to my little one. He thought me dead, and only gazed without any attempt at touching me, though pacing round, pawing and snorting, and thus we were for about twenty minutes. The man, a kind soul, but no hero, stood on the hedge above, charging me from time to time not to move. Indeed, my first recollection is of his friendly voice. And so I lay still, wondering how much was reality and how much dream; and when I tried to think of my situation I pronounced it too dreadful to be true, and certainly a dream. Then I contemplated a drop of blood and a lump of mud, which looked very real indeed, and I thought it very imprudent in any man to make me lie in a pool—it would surely give me rheumatism. I longed to peep at the bull, but was afraid to venture on such a movement. Then I thought, I shall probably be killed in a few minutes, how is it that I am not taking it more solemnly? I tried to do so, seeking rather for preparation for death than restoration to life. Then I checked myself with the thought, It's only a dream, so it's really quite

profane to treat it in this way; and so I went on oscillating.
There was, however, a rest in the dear will of God which I love
to remember; also a sense of the simplicity of my condition—
nothing to do to involve others in suffering, only to endure what
was laid upon me. To me the time did not seem nearly so
long as they say it was; at length the drover, having found some
bullocks, drove them into the field, and my bull, after a good
deal of hesitation, went off to his own species. Then they have
a laugh at me that I stayed to pick up some oranges I had
dropped before taking the man's hand and being pulled up the
hedge; but in all this I acted as a somnambulist, with only
fitful gleams of consciousness and memory.'

How far the bull seriously contemplated an assault, and what
the degree of danger really was, is a little difficult to decide on
the basis of this account. If Mr Pym made the most of it
Caroline certainly made the least, and her manifestly sincere
and dispassionate description of her emotions testifies to a
quiet courage in full keeping with all that is revealed of her
character throughout her book. But new light on that is cast
by an original letter which I found slipped into a copy of the
Journal at Penjerrick. It is from Sir Richard Vyvyan, of
Trelowarren, near Falmouth, at this time M.P. (high Tory)
for Helston, and runs thus :

'2 Grafton Street,
March 21, 1853.

Dear Miss Caroline Fox,—Yesterday Sir C. Lemon
informed me of your escape from a great danger, and added
that one of my bulls was the cause of your being in such peril.
This morning I read for the first time the paragraph in a Cornish
paper of last week, which, without naming you, gave a fearful
account of the accident. I most cordially congratulate you on
being *providentially* saved, and if the animal was one of the
bulls sold from Trelowarren I cannot find words to express my
sorrow that anything which had belonged to me should have

placed you in so deadly a predicament, which Sir Charles described as much worse than that reported in the newspaper.

At first I was in hopes that there was some mistake about the bull having been driven from Trelowarren to Falmouth; but I am afraid on looking over the bailiff's cattle-book for March, where I find a large Durham bull noticed as still being there on the first of this month, although he had previously reported its being sold in February,—that it is the brute in question, and that although it had not the character of being ferocious the long drive to Falmouth may have made it dangerous when under the charge of the butcher or his servant to whom it was not accustomed. Henceforward this shall be a lesson to the bailiff and he shall never allow a bull to be driven away without a stipulation that it shall be properly restrained on the road, whatever may be its reputed good temper. Had the humblest pauper been exposed to the hazard which you have undergone I should have been deeply grieved. Judge then of my mortification and *horror* that you should have been in peril of your life on this occasion.

Believe me, dear Miss Fox, Very sincerely yours,
R. R. VYVYAN.'

This puts a definite complexion on the incident, and suggests that Mr Pym's assessment of the degree of danger may not have been far wrong. It might have been thought that Caroline would have made some reference to the receipt of such a letter—if Caroline had not been Caroline. It is characteristic of her that she never mentions it.

To return to more normal happenings: in 1854 she met Charles Kingsley at Torquay and Martin Tupper, author of *Proverbial Philosophy*, at Bury Hill. In 1857 the British Association met again at Dublin; Caroline was there with her father, who was reading a paper, and heard, and apparently met, David Livingstone among others. In 1859 she spent the winter in Rome and Naples, and in the following year was summoned to Pau, where Jane Fox, her brother Barclay's widow, had died suddenly. In 1863 her father went on a mission to Spain to plead for the freedom of Matamoros and other Protestants who had been sentenced to long terms of imprisonment by the Spanish Government, and Caroline and her sister accompanied him. In 1866, in spite of failing health, she visited Venice and the Paris Exhibition. From this time she was more and more tied to home by illness—she suffered from chronic bronchitis—and on January 12th, 1871, she died peacefully in her sleep. She was then fifty-one. Her father lived till 1877, and her sister Anna Maria, her senior by three years, till 1897. Her brother Barclay had died in 1855 and her mother in 1858.

She lies in the Quaker burial-ground at Budock, about equidistant from her home at Rosehill and her home at Penjerrick. The walled graveyard, as I saw it last in the fading light of an October day in which rain and sun had alternated like April, was impressive in its simplicity and peace. The trees were still green, and if for lack of labour the grass had been left to grow as it would, that was preferable to any trimmed and disciplined formality. The graveyard is divided into two portions, an older and a newer, by a plain rough-cast wall, grass-topped and pierced by a gateway under an arch of Cornish granite. All the headstones are of slate, rounded to an arc at the top—none departing from that single pattern—and all bear a simple inscription of name, date of death and age—that, and never more. Caroline's stone at the head of her mound is almost in the centre of the older enclosure. On its upper half it bears the words:

CAROLINE FOX

DIED

12·1·1871

AGED 51

So it stood for nearly twenty-seven years, till the time

came for another inscription to fill the lower half. That
runs:

ANNA MARIA FOX

DIED

18·11·1897

AGED 81

The grass that had grown up over the lowest line had to be
trodden down before that could be deciphered. It was the
same with the stone over the next grave, where the name of
Maria Fox, Caroline's mother, 'Died 4 of 6th month, 1858,
Aged 70 years,' comes first, with that of her father, Robert
Were Fox, 'Died 25 of 7th month, 1877, Aged 88 years,'
below it. On the graves around them the names of Fox and
Tregelles (Robert Were Fox the elder married Elizabeth
Tregelles) far outnumber any others. Caroline sleeps with
her own people.

Chapter III
Caroline's Journal

aroline Fox's Journal was published in 1882,[1] eleven years after her death, by the firm of Smith, Elder, in an inconveniently large quarto volume of some 350 pages, priced 21/-, bearing on its binding the title 'Caroline Fox, Her Journals and Letters,' but on the title-page the legend :

MEMORIES OF OLD FRIENDS
being extracts from
The Journals and Letters
of
CAROLINE FOX
of Penjerrick, Cornwall
from 1835 to 1871.

Edited by HORACE N. PYM.

'All, all are gone, the old familiar faces.'

The book attracted considerable attention. John Bright secured it immediately it appeared and wrote in his diary: 'Much interested in reading "Memorials" etc of Caroline Fox, of Falmouth. Charming book, records of a mind intelligent and good.' Cardinal Newman, as will be seen later, was reading it almost as soon. It received the distinction, in the week of publication, of a review of four columns, not much less than 4000 words, in the *Spectator*. The article, like most reviews in those days, was unsigned, but investigation shows it to have been by Julia Wedgwood (author of *The Moral Ideal*,

[1] Though it bore that date, the actual day of publication was December 10th, 1881.

a *Life of Wesley*, and various other works). The *Saturday* gave it two columns. The *Athenaeum* seems not to have noticed it in the first instance, but when a reprint appeared a year later it published an appreciative paragraph on 'Mr Pym's charming work,' observing that 'the popularity of this book is a good sign of the taste of the reading public.' This second edition differed from its predecessor in form by consisting of two convenient volumes instead of one ponderous one, and in content by the acquisition of fourteen letters, of no great interest or importance, from John Stuart Mill, not to Caroline herself but to her brother Barclay. Since 1883 the Journal has not been reprinted, but second-hand copies of the original editions are sometimes obtainable.

The origin of the Journal is of some interest. Robert Were Fox was a wise father, and according to Dr Thomas Hodgkin he offered each of his daughters the inducement of a guinea (whether a single payment or an annual subvention is not indicated) if they would keep diaries regularly. Their brother Barclay apparently needed no such stimulus, but with it or without it he too kept a journal, which still exists, unpublished. Caroline left her Journal to her sister Anna Maria, with instructions that on the latter's death it was to be destroyed, as it most unhappily was. A great-niece of Caroline's tells how as a child of twelve she was an accomplice in the sacrilegious task, helping to carry out armfuls of red-bound volumes (similar, no doubt, to Barclay's surviving nine) for incineration on the terrace at Penjerrick after Anna Maria's death in 1897. What happened to Anna Maria's own journal I cannot discover, but there is reason to believe that it too has been destroyed.

How comes it, then, that anything of Caroline's Journal has survived at all? Thanks for that are due to Horace Pym, a London solicitor, who married twice into the Fox circle, his first wife being Julie Backhouse, niece of Barclay Fox's wife, and his second Jane Fox, Barclay's daughter. He was not a member of the Society of Friends, and there is no reason to think he had any special interest in Quakerism, but he read Caroline's Journal in manuscript as one of the family, and prevailed on Anna Maria Fox to allow him to prepare a collection of extracts from it for publication. This, it is safe to assume, was a step never contemplated by Caroline herself, and all her reactions would unquestionably have been against it. But Anna Maria fortunately did not feel that she was gravely transgressing her sister's wishes by authorising publication under strict limitations, and satisfaction that so much has been saved can be balanced against regrets that so much has been lost.

For it is unhappily certain that much, probably the major part, of the Journal has perished. Dr Hodgkin speaks of the published portion as 'a small percentage,' and family tradition confirms the estimate. The editor, moreover, was by no means allowed unrestricted freedom of selection. He was to confine himself to such passages as could be regarded as of public interest; entries on family affairs were to be treated as confidential and left where they were. Mr Pym discharged his task to the best of his ability, but he could hardly identify himself with Caroline's Quaker outlook and his literary gifts were not considerable. His introductory memoir falls far short of what the subject of it deserved, and the explanatory footnotes are few, and usually jejune. But any deficiencies of that order are outweighed by the supreme merit of having rescued a fraction at least of Caroline's writings from destruction.

It is clear that no ordinary rules of criticism can be applied to a volume produced under such conditions. Most particularly must the argument from omission be excluded, for there is no means of knowing in any given case whether the omission was Caroline's or her editor's. The Journal in its entirety may or may not have reflected her faithfully as she was; it is impossible that these severely conditioned extracts from it should. Certain of her characteristic qualities—a remarkable capacity for calm and balanced judgement, marked felicity of expression, skill and accuracy in putting the day's harvest of experiences

and impressions on paper (witness her striking summaries of
two of Carlyle's lectures on Heroes) it is easy to recognise and
appreciate. But there hardly emerges from the published
Journal the Caroline of whom her contemporaries have left
some picture. There is practically nothing, for example, of
the 'decided tendency to sarcasm, not ill-natured, but pungent
enough to make her rather formidable to the general run of her
acquaintance' of which Dr Hodgkin speaks. In the same way
Julia Wedgwood, who clearly knew Caroline personally,[1] said
of the Journal: 'Many of those who only knew Caroline
Fox here would have been glad of more unreserve as to her own
feelings, and some of those who knew her otherwise will feel
perhaps that the latent fire of an impassioned and enthusiastic
nature is too much hidden here by shrewd remark, lively
recollection and humorous anecdote.' There is reason to
accept that judgement.

To many questions of importance concerning the Journal
no answer can be given. We do not know when it was begun,
or what relation the published part bears to the whole, or by
what eyes that whole was seen in Caroline's lifetime. Since
her father encouraged her to keep a journal it is reasonable to
suppose that he expected to see and comment on it; and a
grief-charged sentence written just after the death of Barclay
Fox—'I could fill volumes with remembrances and personal
historiettes of interesting people, but for whom should I record
them now?'—shows that the book was open to Barclay at
least. But Caroline was not writing to be read, even by those
closest to her, much less by a wider circle who knew her little
or not at all. There can be no complaint if she fails to tell
us much that we should like to know—how, for example, she
travelled from Falmouth to Grasmere (Wordsworth himself
displayed curiosity about that) or where the family stayed
during its periodical visits to London. These were details

[1] No doubt through the Sterling family; Miss Wedgwood was a great friend
of Sterling's daughter Julia, who spent the latter part of her life at Falmouth.

that would not enter into the scheme of a Journal concerned only with its writer's activities and contacts and reflections— or else details which the editor was not imaginative enough to assess at their proper value. They are the kind of point on which Barclay Fox is always explicit.

How Horace Pym as editor interpreted the trust reposed in him can only be inferred. It must be remembered that he was preparing the Journal for publication not more than ten years after Caroline's death, when many of the persons who figured in it were still alive, or had been so recently that it was necessary to consider the feelings of their relatives. That fact makes the destruction of the original manuscript the more deplorable, for it is clear that much that had been rightly withheld in 1882 could have been published without injury to anyone's susceptibilities twenty or thirty or, still more, fifty years later. But to labour that reflection would be to argue with the irrevocable. The Journal is burnt, and there is no more to be said. Nor, so far as I have discovered, are there any other documents to throw much light on Caroline apart from her brother's journal (which, in fact, says surprisingly little about her), a few letters quoted by Caroline Stephen in two articles in the *Friends' Quarterly Examiner*, and a number of others, which I have been permitted to see, addressed to Caroline's cousin, Mrs Thomas Hodgkin, in the 1860's. Another unanswered question is whether, as Dr Hodgkin's statement rather suggests, all three children began keeping journals at the same time. If so, the date can be fixed, for Barclay's first entry is on January 1st, 1832. Pym's first selection from Caroline's Journal is for March 19th, 1835. At that time she was older than Barclay when he first took up his quill ('pit of stomach to edge of desk; point of quill to face of paper; such has been the work today,' he wrote a few years later). But it is clear that this was not the beginning of Caroline's Journal. When it did begin, and how, we shall never know.

It is reasonable to assume—though very far from certain—that Pym left the general proportions of the Journal much as they originally were. If that is so, the allocation of space is significant. The volume covers close on thirty-six years, and consists in the original quarto edition of 343 pages. That means an average of rather less than ten pages to a year. Actually the year 1840 alone occupies sixty-three pages; the eight years 1840-47 fill more than half the book. Towards the close the entries are very scanty, much of the last sixty pages being devoted to extracts from letters from Caroline to her friends. It was between 1840 and 1844, the twenty-first and the twenty-fifth years of her own life, that the world had most to offer to Caroline in interests and stimulus and the joy of friendship, and in those years that there was most within her to overflow on to paper.

Something has been said already of the impression the Journal made on leading reviewers and on public men like John Bright. That may be supplemented by judgements passed on it by two masters of literary judgement, one a Prime Minister of Great Britain, the other a Cardinal of the Church of Rome. Speaking at Falmouth in November 1905, Lord Rosebery, in the course of a remarkable tribute to Quaker tenets and Quaker literature, spoke of Caroline Fox's Journal as 'one of the most delightful books I ever read, and which leads you into the atmosphere of pure, intellectual and devout life.' A Prime Minister to be, in the biography of his wife, Margaret MacDonald, mentioned that 'in 1886, in addition to the ordinary reading of a girl of sixteen, she was studying Stanley's *Jewish Church*, Froude's *Studies*, *The Memoirs of Caroline Fox*, Carlyle's *French Revolution*.' [1]

Cardinal Newman, as his biographer, Wilfrid Ward, relates,[2] was sent a copy of Caroline's Journal by an Evangelical friend, Mr G. T. Edwards, in 1882, soon after its appearance. His

[1] *Margaret Ethel MacDonald*, by J. Ramsay MacDonald, p. 51.
[2] *Cardinal Newman*, by Wilfrid Ward, vol. ii. p. 333.

letter of thanks for the volume is a curious mixture of appreciation and reservations. 'I had not heard of the book,' he writes (from The Oratory, Birmingham, on September 17th, 1882), 'nor of the lady who is the subject of it. It is full of matter, and to those who have a curiosity about stars in literature, interesting matter. She has a talent for description of character, and a great sense of humour. What is most remarkable is her union of taste for society with a deep religious sense. And what is most perplexing to me is her boast and glorying in a Quaker's truthfulness and her insensibility to truth in matters of faith.'

This would appear to have evoked some reply from Mr Edwards, in consequence of which Newman writes again a few days later (on September 23rd) in terms which reveal a singular incapacity to recognise the possibility of combining spiritual with intellectual activity. 'I have,' he says, 'a natural dislike of literary and scientific society *as such*, or what Hurrell Froude (whom I agreed with in this) used to call "the aristocracy of talent," and for this reason perhaps I am not quite fair to the remarkable and beautiful Life which you sent me. . . . It is something of a wonder to me that a mind so religious as Miss Fox's should feel pleasure in meeting men who either disbelieved the Divine mission or had no love for the person of One she calls "her Lord and her Saviour."' Here, it is interesting to note, the letter as quoted by Ward ends. A copy which I have obtained from another source contains the additional sentence: 'Our Lord tells us that no man can serve two masters —how can this religious lady be friends at once with Him and with Carlyle, Mill and the like?'

That did not quite conclude the correspondence. In November Newman returns the book to its owner with a letter, in which he remarks: 'I am very much struck and won as to C. F's inner mind by this private record of her thoughts and feelings. Don't think me flippant when I say that she was too good for a Quaker and that she ought to have been a Catholic.' Then follows an exposition of the rightness of the

Catholic position and the wrongness of Caroline's in regard to sacraments. The letter ends: 'We have a more wonderful, soothing time of silence than the Quakers. It is the silent half-hour, spent, *solus cum solo*, before the innermost. No, C. Fox never understood what we hold. She might have been a Catholic if she had.' It would seem that at this point Newman's letters were shown to Caroline's sister Anna Maria, and that she was at pains to remove what she thought were misconceptions on the Cardinal's part. That emerges clearly from a further letter in December, in which Newman, after explaining why he felt that Caroline had misunderstood Catholicism, concludes: 'Pray thank C. Fox's sister for the kind interest she has taken in removing my criticisms, which sincerely troubled me as made in the case of so excellent and remarkable a person.'

It would be too much to expect the author of the *Apologia* and the author of the *Journal* to see eye to eye on matters of faith. But that a man of Newman's discrimination should have described Caroline's book as 'remarkable and beautiful,' and its writer as 'excellent and remarkable,' is a noteworthy fact. How unimaginable it would have seemed to Caroline that her unassuming day-to-day record of the great and small things of her life should find such a commentator.

I cannot but add to these one more appreciation—from the outstanding literary critic of his day. In 1891 John Morley wrote in his diary: 'In the evening read again Caroline Fox's Journal—especially the part about Mill. It was like visiting the scenes of one's childhood, and friends of whom one has for long lost sight. Interesting, exciting, and at the same time soothing, to find myself once more in this luminous atmosphere of abstract questions and disinterested answer, of curiosity about deep problems and detachment as to solutions and persons. Yet abundant sociability, affection and genial friendliness. Well might Voltaire in his memorable visit to England (1726) fix upon the Quakers for our admiration and even reverence, not a common mood with him.'

It would be an interesting exercise, if time and space permitted, to trace the parallels between Caroline's comments on various personalities and public events and those to be found in other nineteenth-century diaries like Scott's (e.g. on Davies Gilbert [1]) or Greville's. Examples are Greville's references to two scientists whom Caroline encountered—'Met Dr Buckland and talked to him for an hour, and he introduced me to Mr Wheatstone, the inventor of the electric telegraph, of the progress in which he gave us an account' [2]; to Joseph Wolff,[3] the missionary; and to the controversy between Brougham and a Mr Handley at an Exeter Hall anti-slavery meeting.[4]

Some of Caroline's omissions are surprising. She says nothing of the death of Sterling's wife and mother in 1843; or of Sterling's own death in 1844; or of her brother Barclay's marriage in the same year; or of her own dangerous illness in 1848; or of her mother's death in 1858. She displays no interest in such matters as changes of government, and while she is stirred to something like excitement over events in France in 1848 she makes no reference at all to the Chartist agitation of that year in England, culminating as it did in the anti-climax of the march to Westminster and the presentation of the great petition in April. These omissions must have been her own, for there is nothing here that her editor could have felt called on to suppress.

[1] See p. 257, note. [2] *The Greville Memoirs*, Part II. vol. i. p. 79.
[3] *Ibid.*, pp. 88-9. [4] *Ibid.*, p. 99.

Chapter IV
Caroline's Faith

Caroline Fox was a simple and sincere Christian. In the Society of Friends, to be born of Quaker parents is to enter forthwith into full membership of the Society. There is nothing corresponding to confirmation or 'joining the Church' in adolescence, and nothing like baptism, infant or adult. Caroline therefore grew up not merely in a Quaker household but as a Friend herself from the first, without any serious thought—it may be doubted, indeed, whether the possibility ever occurred to her—that she could be anything but a Friend. What did that mean? In the lesser field, that of form, it meant that she regularly attended the Sunday, or rather First-Day, Meeting for Worship, probably evening as well as morning, held on a basis of silence, though with full liberty to any who felt a genuine concern to speak or engage in prayer; that she used among Friends, and to some extent in other circles, the plain speech, 'thou' or 'thee' instead of the customary 'you.' She may or may not have worn the plain Friends' dress. Whether she ever 'spoke in meeting' herself the Journal does not indicate. In the larger field, that of belief, it meant a profound conviction that life is essentially spiritual; that outward observances may be a hindrance rather than an assistance to the worship of God, Who is spirit, and to be worshipped in spirit and in truth; that such worship calls for no intermediary in the form of an ordained minister or for any outward sacrament, even the sacrament of Holy Communion; that, in the words of George Fox, the founder of Quakerism, 'there is in every man a spark

49

of the divine,' which the spirit of God can fan to a pervasive fire.

That faith, or broadly that, Caroline held for the most part unquestioningly, though not for a moment casually or thoughtlessly. During her early and formative years the Society of Friends as a whole tended to be distinctly evangelical. It was a time when the Clapham Sect was flourishing, and though that movement did not touch Quakerism directly, the contact between Evangelicals like Wilberforce and many Quaker circles, like the Gurneys of Earlham and their Barclay and Buxton relatives, was sufficiently close to create a certain sympathy in the matter of religious beliefs. The fact that a distant kinsman of Caroline's, Joseph John Gurney, was the leading defender of Scriptural Christianity in the controversy then current in the Society of Friends between revelation through the Scriptures and revelation through the Inner Light no doubt had some influence on Caroline. It might be supposed that Falmouth was geographically too far out of the main stream of Quaker life to be much affected by discussions that were stirring the Society as a whole. But that would be a wrong assumption. Every year some Friends from Falmouth would be going up to Yearly Meeting in London (Caroline's own family made a practice of going every other year) and coming home to report what they had seen and heard. And there were weekly and monthly Quaker periodicals—the existing *Friend* dates from 1843—through which all schools of thought in the Society could find expression.

Holding what was broadly the orthodox faith of the Society of her day, Caroline was never narrow or intolerant. Many of her friends round Falmouth were Anglicans, and there is never a word in her Journal to suggest that she claimed that her vision of the ultimate Truth and Reality was clearer than theirs. When John Sterling's friend and hers, Dr Calvert, was quietly sinking to his end he used words which she quotes with obvious agreement: 'Conversation turned to church matters, and the importance of even children going regularly, were it only to cherish those reverential feelings which unite one with all in worship. Long after he himself gave up going to church on account of his health he continued to take the sacrament, because that is a ceremony on the force of which none dares to dogmatise; the wisest and best are divided concerning its true meaning, so that each may take it according to his own conscience.' That was in 1841. Between four and five years later, when Caroline was twenty-six, she opened her Journal for 1846 with a brief but suggestive declaration of faith: 'I have assumed a name today for my religious principles —Quaker-Catholicism—having direct spiritual teaching for its distinctive dogma, yet recognising the high worth of all other forms of Faith; a system in the sense of inclusion, not exclusion; an appreciation of the universal, and various teachings of the Spirit, through the faculties given us, or independent of them.'

That, it may be objected, is too nebulous to be particularly helpful. The reply is that Caroline was not trying to be helpful. She was writing for no eye but her own, and she was trying to put into words something that words can only imperfectly convey. In fact, our knowledge of her spiritual life is limited. Her editor was not free, even if he had desired it, to quote at length on such a subject from her manuscript journal; it is surprising indeed that he has let light into that secret chamber at all. We may be glad that he has, but often where light might reasonably be looked for it is lacking. It might have been thought, for example, that Caroline's eighteenth birthday, or her twenty-first, would be a time of some self-examination, to be noted, however restrainedly, in the Journal. If it was so noted the entry has been withheld, but in July 1841, when she was a little over twenty-two, she did, apparently without any extraneous motive, put an extended statement of her faith on paper. It is a piece of unsparing self-analysis, ending in a humble yet assured affirmation. If an essential, indeed *the* essential, side of Caroline's personality is to be understood, a quotation of some length is necessary.

'As I think it may be a profitable employment,' she wrote, 'and at some future time when faith is at a low ebb may recall with greater distinctness the struggle through which a spark of true faith was lighted in my soul—I will attempt to make some notes of the condition of my mind in the summer and autumn of 1840. [The Journal, it may be noted, is almost completely silent about this period; between Caroline's return to Falmouth in the first week of August from one of the regular visits to London and the end of the year there are only three entries, none later than August 29th.]

'I felt I had hitherto been taking things of the highest importance too much for granted, without feeling their reality; and this I knew to be a very unhealthy state of things. This consciousness was mainly awakened by a few solemn words spoken by Dr Calvert on the worthlessness of a merely traditional faith in highest truths. The more I examined into my reasons for believing some of our leading doctrines, the more was I staggered and filled with anxious thought. I very earnestly desired to be taught the truth, at whatever price I might learn it.

'Carlyle admirably expresses my state of mind when he speaks of "the spasmodic efforts of some *to believe that they believe.*" But it would not do; I felt I was playing a dishonest part with myself, and with my God. I fully believed in Christ as a Mediator and Exemplar, but I could not bring my reason to accept Him as a Saviour and Redeemer. What kept me at this time from being a Unitarian was that I retained a perfect conviction that though *I* could not see into the truth of the doctrine it was nevertheless true; and that if I continued earnestly and sincerely to struggle after it, by prayer, reading and meditation, I should one day be permitted to know it for myself. A remark that Hender Molesworth one day made to me was often a gleam of comfort to me during this time of distress and warfare. He said that he thought "a want of faith was sometimes permitted to those who would otherwise have no trials; for you know," he added, "a want of faith is a very great trial." I did not tell him how truly he had spoken.

'The first gleam of light, "the first cold light of morning" which gave promise of day with its noontide glories, dawned on me one day at Meeting, when I had been meditating on my state in great depression. I seemed to hear the words articulated in my spirit "Live up to the light thou hast; and more will be granted thee." Then I believed that God speaks to man by His Spirit. I strove to live a more Christian life, in unison with what I knew to be right, and looked for brighter days; not forgetting the blessings that are granted to prayer.'

Steadily Caroline's questioned and tested faith took deeper root. At some later date an exposition of the tenth chapter of Hebrews by the Rev. John Stevenson (Rector of Cury, between Helston and the Lizard, and a friend of the Fox family) made a considerable impression on her, and that was deepened a few days later by reflections on Teufelsdröckh's triumph over fear, which 'came forcibly and vividly' over her in the course of a walk home from Penrose, a mile or two south of Falmouth. As a result 'the truth came before me with a clearness and consistency and brightness indescribably delightful; the *reasonableness* of some Christian doctrines which had before especially perplexed me, shone now as clear as noonday; and the thankfulness I felt for the blessed light that was granted was intense.'

Her final comments prove how strengthening an experience her sincere and fearless searching of her spirit had been. 'I by no means regret,' she wrote, 'the perplexities and doubts and troubles through which I have passed. They have increased my toleration for others, and given me a much higher value and deeper affection for those glorious truths which make up the Christian's hope, than I could have had if they had only been passively imbibed.'

> '*Perplexed in faith but pure in deeds,*
> *At last he beat his music out* '—

Caroline's Faith

Tennyson's words were not written, at any rate not published, when Caroline faced her questionings and resolved them, but it is hard to think of anyone to whom they would apply more fitly.

The statement of which the main portions are here quoted did not, it is of some importance to note, form part of the Journal; it was found in Caroline's desk, a repository even more remote from alien eyes, after her death. In November of the year in which she wrote it the Journal itself contains a lengthy reflective passage, rather philosophical than definitely religious, suggesting that Caroline was, without realising it, revolving the problem of determinism. 'This morning,' she says, 'I began to disbelieve in accidents; does not everything, both in mind and matter, act definitely, every event have a necessary cause? In Nature events are called accidental which are the direct consequences of some pre-established law of being, known or unknown; in mind, the result of a conflux of causes, equally definite and certain, though often mysterious and unfathomed. Thus a carriage is overturned by some infringement of the laws of matter generally discoverable enough. A man is led to adopt a particular line of conduct consequent on his peculiar constitution, modified by his education, association, line of thought and outward surrounding circumstances. Suppose he were to get drunk and neglect his family. This proves his animal instincts strong and his social ones weak, a deficient moral sense and an abused understanding, the intensity of all heightened by bad association. Suppose he at length recognises his mistaken mode of life. Self-love, respect for the good opinion of his fellows, brightening intellectual vigour or the power of religion—may any of them be a sufficient motive to induce him to change his mode of life; and it is an irrefragable law of mind that moral efforts become easier by repetition. That which first discovered to him his altogether false position did so because exactly addressed to his perceptions and consciousness; whilst another might have passed it by, and been roused

54

by quite a different cause. In all cases the cause is sufficient to produce the effect.'

Caroline then proceeds from the general to the particular, taking Luther as a good illustration of the working of her doctrine. It would be interesting, but unfortunately is not possible, to trace her reflections to their origin; as she observes, every effect has its cause. She had, by this date, seen a good deal of Sterling and John Stuart Mill, and the conversation in the Penjerrick household was on a higher average level than most middle-class families in provincial England in the first half of the nineteenth century attained. But the passage quoted indicates serious reading as well as serious thought, and Caroline unfortunately tells us nothing about that. The only books, indeed, which she specifically mentions having read before this date are Carlyle's *Chartism* and Dickens' *Master Humphrey's Clock*, though the reference to Teufelsdröckh shows that *Sartor Resartus* must also be included.

There are no entries on religious matters comparable with these in length, but at the end of this same year, 1841, and on the New Year's Day that opens the next, Caroline reveals the trend of her deeper thoughts. The New Year's entry is sufficient here:

'*Falmouth, January* 1.—What an era is every New Year's Day, if well considered. Another stage in our journey, a shifting of the scene without interrupting the continuity of the piece, but rather essential to its representation as a Whole, a Unity; the winding-up of our watch that it may tell us the time to-morrow; a fresh page in our Book of Existence, on which much may be written; by itself a fragment, but how important to the order of narration and to the train of thought, shaping, colouring, modifying, developing; how much does a quiet year silently affect our condition, character, mode of thought and action; explain mysteries of outward and inward life, and trace some of the sequences in the phenomena of Being.'

There is nothing here, it may be observed, very different from what many diarists have written on many New Year's Days through the centuries. Perhaps not. But it may still be claimed that the sincerity of the thought and the clarity of the words that clothe it is something not encountered at every turn of every street in a girl of twenty-two.

But the imperfections of our knowledge of Caroline's spiritual pilgrimage are emphasised at this point. Her editor writes: 'In the years 1844 and 1845 came a time of great sorrow, and a considerable blank occurs in the Journals of these and some of the succeeding years; what she wrote at this time containing, save so far as is extracted, nothing but a most sacred record of great personal suffering and inward struggle.' Even if the veil which covers those years could be withdrawn it should not be. As to the nature of Caroline's sorrow there can be no certainty, but there is one surmise that seems more probable than any other; John Sterling died in September 1844. Caroline's very silence about the event (she makes no reference to it till Wordsworth, in ignorance, asks how Sterling is) is a measure of the depth of her feeling. In any case there is no reason to believe that her trouble was due to any religious perplexity, except the perplexity that arises from the great mystery of death, and that in itself, as her reference to other death-beds shows, made little trial of her faith.

Rather, indeed, the contrary. One of Caroline's testimonies to a departed friend merits quotation, for her assessment of him involves an unconscious revelation of certain qualities in her own character. Samuel Rundall, a Liskeard Friend, powerful in the ministry and usually acceptable, died in 1848 at the age of eighty-four. Caroline writes of him in May of that year: 'Old Samuel Rundall had ended his weary pilgrimage, with his old wife sitting by his side: "he departed as one who was glad of the opportunity." He, far more than any I have seen, carries one back centuries in the history of opinion and feeling. He was a perfect Quaker of the old George Fox stamp, ponderous, uncompromising, slow, uninfluenced by the views of others, intensely one-sided, with all the strength and weakness of that characteristic; a man to excite universal esteem but no enthusiasm; simple and childlike in his daily habits, solemn and massive in his ministry; that large voice seemed retained to cry with ceaseless iteration "The Kingdom of God is within you." Last of the Puritans, fare thee well! There was a certain Johnsonian grandeur about him, and one would have lost much insight into a byegone time and an obsolete generation by not having known him.' There is shrewdness as well as sympathy in this appreciation—and considerable understanding, in spite of the gulf that separates twenty-nine (Caroline's age in May 1848) from eighty-four.

There are in Caroline's life, as in so many others, moments when special events—danger or serious illness—have deepened the consciousness of the reality of the eternal. She was thirty-four when the well-known adventure with the bull befell her. It caused her family and her friends more concern than she felt herself, and her description of her emotions is tranquilly unemotional, but absence of fear is plainly the result of the practice of the presence of God. It had been the same in 1843, when she was seriously alarmed, needlessly as it turned out, by a sudden haemorrhage. 'It proved only from the throat,' she wrote then, 'but I for half an hour took it entirely as a signal of death, and shall, I believe, often look back with satisfaction to the solemn quietness which I felt at that time. I finished Aunt Charles's note, and then lay down alone, and felt altogether rather idle about life, and much disposed to be thankful, or at any rate entirely submissive, whatever might be the result.' In 1866, five years before her death, in the last entry of any consequence in her Journal she mentions another illness. An attack of bronchitis which she speaks of as 'sharp,' but which may have merited a stronger description, again brought her face to face with sobering possibilities, but again she shows herself capable of quenching fears and doubts in faith. 'Never less lonely than when thus alone—with God,'

57

she writes of long sleepless nights, and adds: 'Surely I know more than ever of the reality of that declaration, "This is Life Eternal, that they might know Thee the only true God and Jesus Christ whom Thou hast sent."'

But these quotations may give an unjustified impression if they suggest that Caroline's faith in the unseen tended to degenerate into mere pietism. At the end of the last passage quoted there is a revealing sentence: 'I write all this now, because my feelings are already fading into commonplace, and I would fain fix some little scrap of my experience'—indicating that the solemnities of a moment are not the norm of common life. That comes out more clearly in a letter written on her forty-third birthday, four years earlier, in 1862. After a word of acknowledgement of the enrichment of her life she goes on: 'I enjoy things frightfully and think very little about the future, either the celestial or terrestrial future. I have a bump on my head which says "retrospect," and I am tolerably true to my bump. No, in my best, my very best, moments, I am a mere woman of business, not an interesting mystic. My highest ambition is that the day's work should keep pace with the day, whether it be to do or to suffer, and I make a pretty splutter inwardly over the opportunity recklessly wasted, the work given one to do perpetually neglected or else done in one's own slovenly fashion. Ah no, I have uncommonly little of the mystic element of meditation or communion in me.' No one familiar with the Journal could accept this as a picture of the whole of Caroline's life, nor would she have seriously claimed it was that, but it is a picture of a part of it, and without this picture our ideas of her would be one-sided.[1]

The last of Caroline's words to be published are dated just a

[1] With this may be contrasted, rather as a matter of interest than for any value as evidence, an extract from Barclay Fox's journal for July 24, 1841 : ' Rumball [the phrenologist] examined the six young ladies . . . and gave them each credentials . . . Caroline's very good, but he gives her a practical tendency rather than a speculative, which is false.'

week before her death, and they may fitly close this chapter. They form part of a letter to her friend Elizabeth Carne.

'*Penjerrick, January* 5, 1871.—And now, dear, thank thee so much for that earnest pamphlet. Thank thee for so bravely speaking out the conviction, which was doubtless given thee for the good of others as well as thy own, that nothing short of communion with our present Lord can satisfy the immense need of man. How true that we are so often fed with phrases, whilst our patient Master is still knocking at the door. I trust that the seed thou hast been faithfully sowing may lodge in fitting soil, and bring forth flowers and fruit, to the praise of the Lord of the garden, and to the joy of some poor little human creature with whom He deigns to converse.' Within seven days the closing sentence of the letter—'In hopes of a happy meeting whenever the fitting time may come'—had acquired an unintended meaning.

It has taken only a few pages of this volume to span Caroline's spiritual history from 1841 to 1871, but the material available is scanty. What there is falls into a regular and peaceful pattern. Enough of her self-searching is revealed to spare her from the reproach that attaches to the unexamined life, but inwardly as well as outwardly her days are seen for the most part to have passed tranquilly. If she ever prayed for 'the ornament of a meek and quiet spirit, which is in the sight of God of great price,' she plainly did not ask in vain—though, for application to Caroline at least, I like better the adjectives as Moffatt renders them, 'a gentle, modest spirit.' Of this side of Caroline there will be little sign in the chapters that follow; they are concerned with the changes and chances of her outward rather than her inward life. But her friendships and her pleasures, and the expansion of her warm and vivid personality, will only be understood aright if her daily encounters and experiences are seen against that unchanging and immovable background of the eternal before which the shadow-show of the temporal is played.

Chapter V
John Sterling

Sterling's place in English literature is singular. If Carlyle
had not written his Life he would be unknown today,
for Archdeacon Hare's Memoir was hardly calculated
to confer immortality on him. No one now reads *Strafford*,
a tragedy, or *Arthur Coningsby*, a novel, or *The Onyx Ring*,
a tale. And Carlyle, who wrote Sterling's Life, admitted
that, apart from one consideration, there was no good ground
for writing it. 'Sterling's performance, and real or seeming
importance in this world,' he affirmed, 'was actually not of a
kind to demand an express Biography, even according to the
world's usages. His character was not supremely original;
neither was his fate in the world wonderful. What he did was
inconsiderable enough; and as to what it lay in him to have
done, this was but a problem now beyond possibility of settlement.' But—Julius Hare, in editing Sterling's *Essays and
Tales*, had prefixed to them a 230-page Life of their author,
which in Carlyle's judgement misrepresented Sterling so
seriously in certain respects that he felt impelled to present a
different picture. Hare, it seems, had foreseen this possibility
and tried to guard against it. At any rate, Caroline writes on
December 3rd, 1847: 'Long letter from Julius Hare detailing
difficulties in the Sterling Memoir, which we had foreseen and
could well enter into. He seems almost forced to publish more
than he would wish, in order to leave Mill and Carlyle no
pretext for an opposition portrait.' Carlyle did find a pretext,
if Mill did not. It consisted in the claim that Hare, with his
Anglican bias, had not done justice to the evolution of Sterling's

JOHN STERLING

ROSEHILL

religious opinions. Whether Carlyle, by no means devoid of bias in another direction, did full justice to them either is not a question that need be argued here, but it is a matter on which Caroline's reports of her conversations with Sterling throw considerable light.

Sterling, it is clear, was no ordinary person. 'Sterling's bright ingenuity, and also his audacity, velocity and alacrity, struck me more and more,' Carlyle wrote at an early stage in their acquaintance; while Archdeacon Hare, who was Sterling's tutor at Cambridge as well as his vicar at Hurstmonceux, says of him in his undergraduate days: 'I have been told by several among the most intelligent of his contemporaries that of all the speakers they ever heard he had the greatest gift of natural eloquence. On this I never had adequate means for forming a judgement; but his conversational powers were certainly among the most brilliant I have witnessed. In carrying on an argument I have known no one comparable to him.' To that may be added an example of the impression made on a more ordinary and a younger man, Caroline's brother Barclay. 'His eloquence,' Barclay Fox wrote in April 1841, 'was like a clear cascade. His knowledge seems almost universal. You name a writer or an event and he can tell you all the details. His mind is European, his liberality unbounded. His insight of character is like an infallible instinct, his imagination rich to overflowing. To know him is a privilege the highest might be proud of; to know what he knows is an affluence few could bear.' That Caroline, at an impressionable age, should be impressed profoundly by such a man is not astonishing.

His life was brief, and it was not till four years before his early death at the age of thirty-eight that Caroline first met him. But he figures more largely in her Journal than any other single person, and of the warmth of her regard for him there can be no question; the precise degree of warmth there is no need to try to determine, and no means in any case of determining. There are, it is true, silences from which some inferences might

John Sterling

be drawn. It is remarkable, for example, that the Journal
—in its published form—leaves Sterling's death unrecorded and
makes no mention of the double blow that robbed him of
his wife and his mother within forty-eight hours in 1843. But
here is a case where the tendency to make normal deductions
must be checked. It would not be safe to assume that Caroline
wrote nothing on a subject that must have moved her deeply; it
is at least as probable that the editor of her Journal omitted the
entry, perhaps rightly, as too intimate and personal. There is a
tradition that Caroline was 'in love with' Sterling, and her
sister Anna Maria with his friend Dr Calvert, but no weight
can attach to it as such, and it is barely worth recording.
Reference has been made already to a passage in the introductory
Memoir to the effect that 'in the years 1844 and 1845 [Sterling
died in September 1844] came a time of great sorrow, and a
considerable blank occurs in the Journals of these and some of
the succeeding years; what she wrote at this time containing,
save so far as is extracted, nothing but a most sacred record of
great personal suffering and inward struggle.' These words
are open to any interpretation that may be put on them. But
this must always be remembered. When Caroline first saw
Sterling, early in 1840, she was twenty; he was thirty-three,
and had been married, so far as is known quite happily, for
nine years. She practically never saw him as a widower, for
immediately after his wife's death in 1843 he moved from
Falmouth to the Isle of Wight, and remained there till he died
in the following year. There is no evidence whatever that his
feelings for Caroline were other than those of perfectly normal
and open friendship, and if on her side they grew involuntarily
warmer it is most unlikely that Sterling was ever allowed to
become conscious of that.[1]

There is not much to be said of Sterling's family. While
his father, Captain Edward Sterling, had a varied career, he
was best known as one of the chief leader-writers of *The Times*

[1] But see pp. 85 *seqq.*

in the great days of Barnes and Delane. But his son had been born long before that, when Edward Sterling was trying farming in Bute. He tried it with indifferent success there, and with little better in Wales, whither he moved for a few years. Then the family lived in Paris for some nine months, but left it precipitately in 1814 on hearing that Napoleon had left his exile in Elba and landed at Antibes. John Sterling was sent to two or three schools in and around London, but his education only acquired interest when in 1824, at the age of eighteen, he went up to Trinity College, Cambridge, where Julius Hare, his future biographer, was his tutor. F. D. Maurice, who became his particular friend and subsequently his brother-in-law, James Spedding, the future Baconian scholar, Charles Buller, Monckton Milnes and others were among his contemporaries.[1] He and Maurice both migrated to Trinity Hall, but Sterling went down in 1827 without taking a degree. Settling in London, he became a devotee of Coleridge, who was then living with Dr Gillman at Highgate, and in 1829 he joined Maurice in editing the recently founded *Athenaeum* for a short time. A year later he became involved with General Torrijos, a political refugee, and helped to organise an unsuccessful expedition to overthrow the existing Spanish Government.

From then onwards the course of his life was largely determined by the state of his health. It was for his health that in 1830, with the wife he had just married, he went out to some family estates in St Vincent in the West Indies, where they were both almost killed by a hurricane. In 1833 he came back to England, took a belated degree at Cambridge, re-established acquaintance with Julius Hare at Bonn during a visit to Germany, decided to take orders and became Hare's curate at Hurstmonceux in Sussex. That, however, lasted only for

[1] In his *Trinity College* (Cambridge University Press, 1943) Dr G. M. Trevelyan speaks of Arthur Hallam, Charles Buller, F. D. Maurice and Sterling as having much to do with the early history of the private debating-society known as The Apostles.

seven months, the severance being due, according to Hare, to reasons of health alone, according to Carlyle to religious doubts; Sterling's references to the event in his talks with Caroline support Hare's explanation. Henceforward most winters had to be spent out of England on account of lung trouble, and it was during a stay at Madeira in 1837 that Sterling met Dr John Calvert, who became and remained his closest friend. In 1838 he founded in London a body that came to be known as the Sterling Club. The list of proposed members, including as it does the names, among many others, of T. Carlyle Esq, C. L. Eastlake Esq, Copley Fielding Esq, Alfred Tennyson Esq and the Rev. Connop Thirlwall, is some indication of the standing of the founder, who figures, by the way, as *the Rev.* John Sterling.

In 1840 Sterling and Calvert decided on another winter in Madeira, and both, travelling separately, got as far as Falmouth, where they were to embark, no doubt in one of the famous mail packets. But the weather was stormy, the start delayed and the prospects of the voyage through the Bay of Biscay unpropitious—so much so that both travellers changed their plans suddenly and decided to winter at Falmouth instead of Funchal. So began the acquaintance, which soon ripened into warm friendship, between Sterling and Caroline Fox. It was destined to be a brief association. On February 8th, 1840, Caroline entered in her Journal: 'Barclay has been much pleased with a Mr Sterling, a very literary man, now at Falmouth, who was an intimate friend of S. T. Coleridge during the latter part of his life'; [1] and on the following day:

[1] Barclay's own version of this deserves record : ' Had a call from a very superior intelligence in the person of a consumptive clergyman called Sterling, who came on behalf of a Mrs Mill to enquire about her forfeited passage-money. She with her daughter and son (Henry Mill) arrived just too late for the packet, the latter being ordered there for his health, a blessing he is never likely to see by all accts. Called on the family with S. Saw the two ladies, who are ladylike. Looked for lodgings for them in the aftⁿ. S. is a person with whom you cannot converse 5 minutes without being struck by his vigorous intellect and fluency of expression. He was well acquainted with Coleridge, and was his bedside companion during his last days.'

'Mr Sterling called—a very agreeable man, with a most Lamb-like liking for town life.' Rather more than three years later, on May 30th, 1843, she mentions that Sterling dined with the family, evidently at Penjerrick, and adds: 'he went off in the rain in very good spirits, looking quite like his old self' (a reference no doubt to the fact that it was less than six weeks since his wife and his mother had both died). He never came back to Penjerrick or Rosehill, but she must have met him, though she never mentions it, when he stayed for a day or two with Barclay Fox at Perran in July. She saw him once more, in London in October of that year in company with one of the Mills, W. E. Forster and others, but there was nothing more than a general conversation.

Caroline and Sterling were therefore only in frequent touch for something under four years, and for by no means the whole of that period, for Sterling was not living at Falmouth continuously. His first stay there was from early in 1840 (Caroline, as stated, saw him first on February 10th) to the beginning of April of the same year; his second from April 1841 to January 1842; his third from June 1842 to May 1843—some twenty-two months altogether. There is no reference in Caroline's Journal to anything but rare and casual letters in the intervals.

To the warmth of the association between Sterling and the Foxes generally Carlyle is the best witness. 'At Falmouth,' he writes, in reference to his friend's first arrival there in 1840, 'he had been warmly welcomed by the well-known Quaker family of the Foxes, principal people in that place, persons of cultivated opulent habits, and joining to the fine purities and pieties of their sect a reverence for human intelligence in all kinds; to whom such a visitor as Sterling was naturally a welcome windfall. The family had grave elders, bright cheery younger branches, men and women; truly amiable all, after their sort: they made a pleasant image of home for Sterling in his winter exile.' 'Most worthy, respectable and highly cultivated people, with a great deal of money among them,' writes Sterling himself in the end of February, 'who make the place pleasant to me. They are connected with all the large Quaker circle, the Gurneys, Frys etc., and also with Buxton the Abolitionist. It is droll to hear them talking of all the common topics of science, literature and life, and in the midst of it: "Does thou know Wordsworth?", or, "Did thou see the Coronation?", or, "Will thou take some refreshment?" They are very kind and pleasant people to know.' In another passage a few pages later Carlyle emphasises the relationship in its reference to 'his new small circle of acquaintance, the ready and constant centre of which was the Fox family, with whom he lived on an altogether intimate honoured and beloved footing.' A little later still, referring to an inaugural lecture which Sterling gave at the Polytechnic, Carlyle observes: 'Doubtless his friends the Foxes were at the heart of that lecturing enterprise, and had urged and solicited him. Something like proficiency in certain branches of science, as I have understood, characterised one or more of this estimable family; love of knowledge, taste for art, wish to consort with wisdom and wise men, were the tendencies of all: to opulent means superadd the Quaker beneficence, Quaker purity and reverence, there is a circle in which wise men also may love to be.'[1] That is a tribute that comes with some authority, and all evidence from every source endorses it.

Of a friendship which Caroline prized so highly she may well have said more in her Journal than her editor thought proper to publish. Some indeed of the omissions are too striking not to be significant, in view of the length at which every ordinary conversation with Sterling is chronicled. Early in 1843, Carlyle relates, Sterling, who was then living at Falmouth, fell dangerously ill as the result of bursting a blood-vessel in lifting a heavy table. Neither of that, nor (as already mentioned) of the deaths of Sterling's wife and mother, nor of his own death, does Caroline say a word in her Journal as published. Her silence, it cannot be

---

[1] All citations from Carlyle's *John Sterling*, Part III. chap ii.

doubted, must be ascribed to depth, not to lack, of feeling; that inference is inevitable whether she wrote nothing on such sorrows or whether her editor held that it would be desecration to give to the world what was meant for no eye but her own.

It would be an equal desecration to seek to probe and assay her feelings regarding Sterling. They are sufficiently indicated by the general tenor of her many references to him. Here and there a sentence seems perhaps to lift a little more of the veil than it was meant to lift, but in fact they amount to little more than an appreciation of Sterling's intellectual qualities. It is not difficult to imagine what Sterling's advent meant to Caroline. She was a little under twenty-one when she saw him first, and he clearly brought a new element into her life at a time when a mind that was maturing beyond the common standard of its years was in full expansion. Cultured as the Falmouth circle was within its limits, it was necessarily, in those days of undeveloped communications, a small society. In Sterling there arrived a figure from a larger world, not old enough to seem separated from Caroline by a gulf of years, yet old enough to be accepted as a leader and a guide, a man who had read widely, travelled considerably, written books, mixed with men like Mill and Carlyle and Julius Hare, all of whom would be known by repute to the Fox circle. In the Rosehill household the primary interest would naturally be scientific. For Caroline, at any rate, Sterling made it literary.

So he and Caroline talked, as Caroline had never talked or been talked to before—of life in all its rich and varied aspects, of religion, of travel, of books, particularly of poetry, of painting and sculpture, of people, sometimes of politics. It was not a case of a new world being opened up for Caroline, for her own culture was above the average for her age and the times she lived in. But where doors had been half-open before they were thrown wide now, and where a few halting steps had been taken in this path or that there was confident progress under guidance which in a warm and unaffected friendship it was as natural to accept as to offer. Of her feelings toward Sterling, Caroline, as has been seen, says next to nothing. In default of that it is worth while trying to see him externally as she saw him. The characterisation she gives is the outcome of a monition skilfully turned against the monitor.

'After a busy morning at Falmouth and Flushing,' she writes on May 20th, 1841, 'Sterling offered to take us back to Penjerrick in his car. [This has an almost startlingly modern ring; the reference appears to be to a two-wheeled vehicle of some sort.] He said "You must see many eminent persons; why don't you make notes of their appearance as well as of their conversation?" The idea being good, I'll try my hand.— John Sterling is a man of stature, not robust but well-proportioned; hair brown and clinging closely round his head; complexion very pale, eyes grey, nose beautifully chiselled, mouth very expressive. His face is one expressing remarkable strength, energy and refinement of character. In argument he commonly listens to his antagonist's sentiments with a smile, less of conscious superiority than of affectionate contempt (if such a combination may be)—I mean what would express "Poor dear, she knows no better." In argument on deep or serious subjects, however, he looks earnest enough, and throws his ponderous strength into reason and feeling: small chance then for the antagonist who ventures to come to blows. He can make him and his arguments look so small; for, truth to tell, he dearly loves this indomitable strength of his; and I doubt any human being bringing him to an acknowledgement of mistake with the consequent conviction that the opposite party was right. Sterling possesses a quickness and delicacy of perception quite feminine, and with it a power of originating deep and striking thoughts, and making them the foundation of a regular and compact series of consequences and deductions such as only a man, and a man of extraordinary power of close thinking and clearness of vision, can attain unto. He is singularly uninfluenced by the opinions of others, preferring on the whole to run counter to them than make any approach to a compromise.'

This was written early in the second period of Sterling's residence in Falmouth, when he had just decided to take a house there. When he first arrived in 1840, and Caroline's acquaintance with him began, he was alone, and remained so (except for Calvert) for the whole three months of that stay, his family only joining him when he returned in the following year. He could not but be heartened by the welcome he received at Rosehill and Penjerrick, particularly perhaps—particularly, indeed, beyond a doubt—from the lively, alert, responsive girl whose reactions to the life into which she was entering more fully every day could not fail to arouse the deep interest, if not the deep emotions, of a man of Sterling's temperament. What might have been if he had lived and returned to Falmouth after his wife's death is a matter on which no surmise is of any value and random speculation something of a despite to the memory both of Caroline and of him.

Caroline was during her years of contact with Sterling a convinced, though by no means a narrow or exclusive, Friend, and she must have noted with satisfaction the interest Sterling displayed in Quakerism while at Falmouth. He had never been in close touch with Friends before; his own religious beliefs had, no longer than six years earlier, been such as to warrant his taking Orders in the Church of England. How far they had evolved since then is a moot question. Carlyle and Julius Hare speak with different voices on the point, and neither is an entirely reliable guide. It does not appear that Sterling often attended Friends' meetings while in Cornwall, but he certainly studied the literature of the Society with some diligence. But the first indication of that dates only from January 1842, almost at the end of his second stay at Falmouth. He spoke then of 'the great importance of making allowance for inward as well as outward conditions. "Some are naturally so constituted as to make certain trains of thought and feeling which appear to you natural and necessary impossible to them. If you admit this principle you will get at wide results." Contrasted the outward facts which bind most Christians together, such as a Church, and ordained minute ceremonies, and the inward fact of spiritual Communion, the belief in which has united the Society of Friends since the days of George Fox. He, however, thinks this invisible bond will not for ever keep the latter together as a separate Body, and is, I think, disposed to wish that by a general amalgamation with other bodies their high and peculiar doctrines may be more widely disseminated and felt.'

Caroline, for all her breadth of mind, probably disagreed with him there, but when Sterling was back at Falmouth in July of the same year he made it clear that his views on Quakerism were not greatly modified; nor, on the other hand, were Caroline's. That emerges from her record of a conversation on July 21st. 'He is devouring,' says Caroline, 'the new and greatly improved edition of Maurice, whose notion of Quakerism is that it is all included in the belief of the Church of England, and therefore that George Fox mistook his calling when he separated himself and followers into a sect. Sterling would fain abolish all sects, and desires that all might concentrate their light into one pure Crystal. But I fear that this Crystal will never be discovered but in Utopia—or Heaven.' The talk may have had its effect in quickening Sterling's interest in the Society, for less than a week later Caroline mentions that 'John Sterling is interesting himself much about George Fox, whose life he means to write. He sadly misses his earnest, prophetic spirit in the present day, and thinks Carlyle the only one who at all represents it.' In the course of the next month she reports that 'Sterling has finished George Fox's Journal, which has interested him much, though he does not find it as remarkable as he had expected—less originality and out-flashing of the man's peculiar nature. He is greatly amused at Fox's placid conviction that he has never committed a fault or made a mistake; also his undoubting belief in the most astounding judgements pronounced and executed around him on his account. Thus—"A Judge treated me very cruelly; accordingly God smote him with a fever, so that he died the next day!"' That, limited as Sterling meant it to be limited, is not an unfair criticism of Fox, but it would apply to a good many prophets with a passion for their mission. Sterling never wrote George Fox's Life. Family afflictions and his own impaired health checked all serious literary activity (except on the unfinished *Coeur-de-Lion*) from this time on. It is a pity, for the play of so original and critical a mind as Sterling's on the life and teaching of the austere founder of Quakerism would inevitably have resulted in a stimulating study.

What Sterling's conversation meant to Caroline I have tried to indicate. The estimate she herself put on it is shown by a sentence in her Journal for July 13th, 1840: 'Methinks Sterling's Table Talk would be as profitable reading as Coleridge's,'—and when account is taken of the advantages of lucidity over obscurity it probably would. At any rate, Caroline's opinion is strongly supported by a remark John Stuart Mill made to her a couple of months earlier about Sterling, to the effect that 'though his writings are such as would do credit to anybody, yet they are inferior to his conversation; he has that rare power of throwing his best thoughts into it, and adapting them to the comprehension of others.' Caroline has done the inestimable service of reporting Sterling's talk more fully than Carlyle or Hare or anyone else, though she regretfully admits that when he was in a circle of his intellectual equals he far outran her powers as chronicler. In talking to her alone he adapted his conversation without a shadow of condescension to the measure, necessarily limited in a girl of twenty-one, of her knowledge and comprehension—though Caroline seized so quickly on a new idea that in fact no great effort of adaptation was needed. He gave her no bad sample of what college talk at midnight can be at its best; no better compliment could be paid her.

To summarise further Caroline's summary, and indicate the main trends of her talks with Sterling at different times, is no easy task. There were few subjects on which Sterling could not speak with knowledge, and generally with authority. On people—people whom Caroline had heard of but never expected to see, though as things turned out she often did—he constantly had stories to tell or judgements to pronounce. One anecdote, not entirely new (though it may have been then) is worth telling as Caroline reports Sterling to have told it. He was talking of 'Philip van Artevelde (Taylor [1]), Irving, Coleridge and Charles Lamb being together; and, the conversation turning on Mahomet, Irving reprobated him in his strongest manner as a prince of impostors, without earnestness and without faith. Taylor, thinking him not fairly used, defended him with much vigour. On going away Taylor could not find his hat, and was looking about for it, when Charles Lamb volunteered his assistance, with the query, "Taylor, did you come in a h-h-hat or a t-t-t-turban?"'

He was interesting on Coleridge and Carlyle, both of whom he knew intimately. Regarding the former, he 'spoke of the womanly delicacy of his mind; his misfortune was to appear at a time when there was a man's work to do—and he did it not. He had not sufficient strength of character, but professed doctrines which he had ceased to believe, in order to avoid the trouble of controversy. He and Carlyle met once; the consequence of which was that Coleridge disliked Carlyle, and Carlyle despised Coleridge.' In that connexion the rival verdicts of Sterling himself and Carlyle on Coleridge are sufficiently apposite to quote. 'I was in his company about three hours,' wrote Sterling, 'and of that time he spoke during two and three-quarters. It would have been delightful to listen as attentively, and certainly easy for him to speak just

[1] i.e. Sir Henry Taylor (1800-1886), author of *Philip van Artevelde*.

72

as well, for the next 48 hours.' 'I have heard Coleridge talk,' wrote Carlyle, 'with eager musical energy two stricken hours, his face radiant and moist, and communicate no meaning whatsoever to any individual of his hearers—certain of whom, I for one, still kept eagerly listening in hope.'

About Carlyle Sterling was constantly talking. 'On Carlyle,' writes Caroline, quoting Sterling soon after she had first met him, 'his low view of the world proceeding partly from a bad stomach. The other day he was, as often, pouring out the fullness of his indignation at the quackery and speciosity of the times. He wound up by saying "When I look at this I determine to cast all tolerance to the winds." Sterling quietly remarked, "My dear fellow, I had no idea you had any to cast." Sterling would define Carlyle's religious views as a warm belief in God, manifested in everything that is, whose worship should be pursued in every action. He religiously believes everything that he believes, and sees all things so connected that the line of demarcation between belief in things spiritual and things natural is not by any means distinct.' Another view of the prophet, less profound but equally revealing, emerges in the mention of a recent expedition with Carlyle to Hampton Court. 'Carlyle was in gloomy humour and finding fault with every-thing, therefore Sterling defended with equal universality. At last Carlyle shook his head and pronounced "Woe to them that are at ease in Zion."'

A few days later comes more information about Carlyle, this time about an American visitor whom I have failed to identify. 'The American Regenerator of his species, of whom he talked to us, has been with him; he finds that his nostrum for the ills of life is a simple agricultural life and a vegetable diet. They had him at their house, gave him various strange accommodating dishes, but as he could not make Carlyle a believer in vegetables he left him in despair.' To this may be added Sterling's account (the story is fairly familiar by this time) of how Carlyle got his entry into the world of literature on the

C*

nomination of Edward Irving; Irving had been asked to contribute to the *Gentleman's Magazine*,[1] but on looking into it he discovered the expression 'Good God!'; this so scandalised him that it was out of the question for him to write for such a paper, but it did not prevent him from recommending a young friend called Carlyle, who had no such scruples. Finally Carlyle in his domestic aspect: 'Sterling dwelt with delight on Mrs Carlyle's character—such hearty sympathy in the background, and such brilliant talent in front; if it were merely "eternal smart" with her it would be very tiresome, but she is a woman as well as a clever person. She and her husband, though admiring each other very much, do not in all things thoroughly sympathise; he does not pay that attention to little things on which so much of a woman's comfort so much depends.' Either Sterling or Caroline appears here to have cultivated the art of charitable understatement to some effect.

These quotations, of course, are merely sidelights. A fuller picture of Carlyle is given in a later chapter devoted to him, on the basis of Caroline's own conversations at Chelsea. But even in sidelights there can often be useful illumination.

We hear little of Sterling's views on politics, partly because he was not a very ardent politician, partly because Caroline was less ardent still. The Corn Laws formed one of the only two current issues in that field on which he clearly declared himself. Caroline briefly mentions that he discussed the subject one day in 1840 with her father, who was much more Conservative than Sterling, and that in 1841, when he was a supporter of the Liberal candidate for the division, he 'talked excellently on the Corn Laws; he would amend them at once and for ever. Statistics are mightily in his favour respecting the rise and fall of wages with the price of bread; in Ireland and Holland the result is precisely the converse of what the landholders here predict.' The other topic which prompted a

---

[1] So Caroline. It was, in fact, the *London Magazine*.

declaration of Sterling's views was education. He diplo-
matically substituted it for the Corn Laws in the conversation
in which he and Robert Were Fox had found themselves at
variance on the latter subject. 'He talked extremely well,'
says Caroline, 'about popular education. It is not those who
read simply but those who think who become enlightened.
Real education had such an effect in restraining and civilising
men that in America no police force is employed where education is general. In a Democracy it is all-important, for as that
represents the will of the people you must surely make that will
as reasonable as possible.' This in the 1940's of course seems
obvious enough (except the American reference), but it was by
no means that in 1840, when popular education as such had
been hardly so much as thought of, the only move in that
direction being represented by the Bell and Lancaster schools.

On books generally and poetry in particular, on art and
sculpture, Sterling had guidance to offer that was eagerly
welcomed. In February 1840, for example, in the course of
a walk which Caroline took with Sterling and Clara Mill, the
conversation centred on the education of the mind and how to
train it to reflection. 'For this,' she recalls, 'he would recommend the study of Bacon's Essays, Addison's papers and
Milton's tract on Education, and Pensées de Pascal. From
these you may collect an idea of the true end of life; that of
Bacon was to heap together facts, whilst Pascal's was to make
conscience paramount. He considers Bacon's the best book
in the English language.' Later on he is found expatiating on
Emerson, a copy of whose essays he had just secured. 'It
would answer your purpose well,' he told Caroline, 'to devote
three months entirely to the study of this one little volume;
it has such a depth and originality of thought in it as will require
very close and fixed attention to penetrate.' Two days later
he showed Caroline Emerson's book 'and drew a parallel
between him and Carlyle; he was the Plato and Carlyle the
Tacitus. Emerson is the systematic thinker; Carlyle has the

75

clearer insight, and has many deeper things than Emerson.'
Tacitus hardly sounds right in this context, but Caroline
was habitually accurate in her chronicling. Sterling, moreover, rather liked unexpected comparisons. In writing to
Anna Maria in April 1841 'He compares the contemporary
genius of Michael Angelo and Luther; something of the
Coleridge *versus* Bentham spirit; both fine, original and clear,
though opposite and apparently contradictory poles of one
great force.'

On the poets of the day he held decided views. Byron, he
thought, 'possessed a fine mind and very deep emotions, but
altogether diseased, such ostentatious vanity running throughout;
he never forgot his rank, and had that peculiar littleness of
extreme sensibility to the least and lowest ridicule from even
the obscurest quarter.' Wordsworth: 'the first of the modern
English poets.' Shelley: 'the complete master of impassioned
feeling, and such an instinctive knowledge of music—harmony
ever waited his beck, and loved to cherish and crown her
idolatrous son.' These views were elaborated a few months
later. Caroline, Clara Mill and Sterling joined in another
walk, in the course of which Sterling 'reviewed the poets,
with occasional illustrations, well painted. Shelley's emotions
and sympathies not drawn forth by actual human beings, but
by the creations of his own fancy, by his own ideal world,
governed by his own unnatural and happily ideal system. This
species of egotism very different to Byron's, who recognised
and imprinted George Gordon, Lord Byron, on every page.
Shelley fragmentary in all his pieces, but has the finest passages
in the language. Wordsworth works from reflection to impulse;
having wound up to a certain point, he feels that an emotion
is necessary and inserts one—the exact converse of the usual
and right method. Coleridge had no gift for drawing out the
talent of others, which Madame de Staël possessed in an eminent
degree. She was by no means pleased with her intercourse
with him, saying spitefully and feelingly, "M. Coleridge a un

grand talent pour le monologue."' Spiteful or not, it was a sentiment which everyone who knew Coleridge would endorse.

The next day there was more literary talk. It began on eloquence, 'of which he thinks Jeremy Taylor the greatest master; he had enough genius to ennoble a dozen families of the same name. It is very odd that so few of our great men should have left any sons—Taylor, Shakespeare, Milton, etc. [great company for the author of *Holy Living* and *Holy Dying*]. Talked over Coleridge—*The Friend* his best prose work; a terrible plagiarist in writing and conversation.' Shelley was not mentioned on this occasion, but he was constantly recurring. A drawing of him elicited the comment, 'What an absence of solidity in the expression of that face.' To avert the face made things no better, for 'Shelley's head was most strangely shaped—quite straight at the back.' So the talk meandered on. Transition from the author of *Alastor* to Trench on the Parables is a little abrupt, but Sterling thought the latter a very interesting work, and said so.

On art and sculpture Sterling was equally qualified to speak, as one or two of his observations to Caroline indicate. One day in 1840 the subject of sculptors came up. Sterling pronounced a series of dogmatic verdicts. 'Canova an accurate depicter of a certain low species of nature, voluptuous, addressed to the comprehension of the animal part of our nature. Flaxman the head of English art. Chantry's [*sic*] power in physiognomy wondrous in busts and likenesses, but no poetry or composition; he can't arrange a single figure decently. Stothard gave the design for the Lichfield Cathedral monument. Thorwaldsen one of the greatest geniuses and clearest intellects in Europe. When engaged over his Vulcan one of his friends said to him, "Now you must be satisfied with this production." "Alas!" said the artist, "I am." "Why should you regret it?" asked his friend. "Because I must be going downhill when I find my works equal to my aspirations."'

He was an ardent collector of engravings, which he frequently turned over with Anna Maria and Caroline. An evening in July 1841 at Sterling's house was spent 'in looking at Raphael's heads from his frescoes in the Vatican. . . . Sterling's critique was most interesting. He spoke of them being far inferior in grandeur to Michael Angelo's, but then Michael Angelo's were perpetual transcripts of himself. Now Raphael was able to look quite out of himself,[1] alike into the faces of his fellows and their opposites, and to render them truly on the canvas. He called Cruikshank the Raphael of Cockneydom.' That may be supplemented by a fragment of conversation between Sterling and Mill, with both of whom Caroline was visiting the Temple Church in 1842. 'It was much,' she wrote, 'to listen to him and John Mill on Italy and the thoughts it inspired. Sterling has advanced to the conviction that Correggio is after all *the* painter; he alone achieved the Impossible: the others are all attempts more or less successful. Raphael you can carry away in the understanding, but you must always return to Correggio to drink afresh at that delicious fountain of pure feeling. Mill remarked quietly "I am greatly confirmed by what Sterling has just said. I have for some time come to the same conviction about Correggio."'

Sterling, who had studied at Bonn, was well read in German literature, and had much that was interesting to say about it at different times. Schiller, he told Caroline once, 'was the only person who could bear to have all his words noted down. Of him Goethe said to a friend of Sterling's "I have never heard from him an insignificant word."' A month after that, Caroline found him enthusiastic about *Wilhelm Meister*, 'which he considers worth any ten contemporary works. He contrasts it with Novalis, who was young, untutored and passionate, and transcribed his crude self with his ardent aspirations and unequal

---

[1] ' *Reaching, that Heaven might so replenish him*
Above and through his art.'
Browning (on Raphael) : *Andrea del Sarto.*

78

attainings. *Wilhelm Meister* he would rather characterise as the Gospel of Experience. It abounds with indecorums, but contains no immoralities; he ventures not to recommend it to young ladies, but would wish all young men to study it earnestly.' He seemed to have read everything that Goethe wrote, and expounded to Caroline his conception of the idea of *Faust*. Of *Tasso* and *Iphigenia* he says : 'the latter is by far the greater work, but fewer people could have written *Tasso*, it displays such dainty, delicate touches, just letting us into the secret of the Princess's feeling, but not playing with it. Also the exact tone of a Court which it gives is inimitable by any who have not lived there on the same terms as Goethe.' Of Goethe generally, on another occasion: 'The more Sterling examines, the less he believes in his having wilfully trifled with the feelings of women; with regard to his selfishness, he holds that he did but give the fullest, freest scope for the exercise of his gift, and as we are the gainers thereby he cannot call it selfishness.'

German philosophy was even more familiar to Sterling, for it was what he had studied specially at Bonn. Caroline could hold her own in that field too, and it must have been an interesting walk and conversation (in July 1842) which she summarises in her diary for that day. 'Capital walk,' she says, 'with John Sterling. He gave a very interesting chronological sketch of German Philosophy, showing how one man and his system were the almost necessary deduction from the preceding. Leibnitz began the chain of those Germans who addressed themselves to think; then a long interval, at the end of which Kant appeared and taught the supremacy of reason as exhibited in the Divine works, and, above all others, in the nature of man. Fichte carried this still further, and dogmatised on his view of Truth to the exclusion of tolerance towards all other thinkers. A witness told Sterling of an interview between Fichte and Schelling, which concluded by the former declaring that a man who could believe there was any revelation in the dead Nature around him, and not that it dwelt only in the brains of the few wise men, was not a fit companion for any reasonable being! with which appalling words, exit Fichte. Schelling's mission was to proclaim the living tuneful voice of Nature, and to teach that she was animated by a higher principle than material existence. Fichte viewed the Universe as a mere logical process in the Divine mind.' Such an epitome is no doubt vulnerable to criticism. But it is after all only an epitome. The conversation must have taken an hour at least, if most of the walk was devoted to it, and what Sterling said at length was probably much less arbitrary than as it appears in brief.

About religion Sterling talked less frequently, except, for some reason, Roman Catholicism, which he could view dispassionately from without. That topic, indeed, came up the second time Caroline ever saw Sterling, in February 1840. After a party of Foxes, with Sterling and Derwent Coleridge, had been to the Perran foundry to see a 14-ton beam for a steam-engine cast, the two visitors and Caroline moved off to Penjerrick, where, 'sitting over the fire, a glorious discussion arose between Coleridge and Sterling on the effect of the Roman Catholic religion; Sterling holding that under its dynasty men became infidels from detecting the errors and sophistry and not caring to look beyond, whilst women became superstitious because, in conformity with their nature, they must prostrate themselves before some higher power. Coleridge contended that women were naturally more religious, and able to extract something good from everything. We had to drive off and leave this point unsettled.' Just a fortnight later, after a walk from Falmouth to Penjerrick, they were back on the subject again. 'His talk was of the Jesuits, who are governed by a Superior always obliged to reside in Rome. The present incumbent is a Dutchman. The order has risen to the height of veneration in Rome from their devoted conduct during the cholera, nursing the sick indefatigably as an act of faith and effect of their principles. All the scholars at their schools have daily registers kept of every particular in their character and conduct, which is annually sent to the Superior; thus those who would join the brotherhood are often astounded at the knowledge he shows of their private history; and this knowledge is a powerful agent in his hands. No deep or original thinkers have ever sprung from this Order, freedom of thought is so at variance with their principles and discouraged by their Superiors; their clever men are generally great bibliologists, and addicted to the physical sciences.'

On the last day of the February in which Sterling had arrived in Falmouth there was a conversation that went a little deeper. 'Some of our subjects were the doctrine of Providential interference and the efficacy of prayer as involved in this question. His view of prayer is that you have no right to pray for any outward manifestations of Divine favour, but for more conformity of heart to God, and more desire after the imitation of Christ. He would not, however, dogmatise on this subject, but would that everyone should act in this matter (as in every other) according to conscience, he views sincerity as the grand point; and a sincere, however erroneous, search after Truth will be reviewed with indulgence by the Father of Spirits. Spinoza is an illustrious example, a truly good, conscientious, honest man, who recognised a Deity in everything around him, but omitted in his system the idea of a presiding and creating God. A long, interesting and eloquent summary of the opinions of the Pusey party [this was less than seven years after the famous Assize Sermon]—the question first arising was "Where shall we find an infallible rule of conduct?" The answer was, "In the life of Christ." Then, "Where is this most clearly developed?" "In the gospel, and the writings of those immediately succeeding that period." This brought them to the Fathers, who, though abounding in error, are thus made the infallible exponents of the Christian religion.' Dr Pusey and Dr Newman might possibly not have accepted this as a precise reflection of their views, but it is near enough to the facts to form a diagnosis of some interest. As to Sterling's thoughts on prayer, not many people would be disposed to stigmatise them as heterodox today, but in 1840 there was much less room for them between the Clapham Evangelicals and the 'Pusey party.' And they were probably something rather new to Caroline.

Such talk, indeed, was perhaps the greatest influence in Caroline's life, apart from her own inner communings. She was less than twenty when she saw Sterling first. She was just over twenty-five when she saw him last—at Perran, at the beginning of July 1844. Later in that month, when he had got back to the Isle of Wight, he sent her some lines to put in her copy of Schleiermacher's *Dialogues*. They are brief enough to quote, and worth quoting.

> '*This, our World, with all its changes,*
>   *Pleases me so much the more,*
> *That wherever Fancy ranges,*
>   *There's a Truth unknown before.*
>
> *And in every land and season,*
>   *One the life in great and small;*
> *This is Plato's heavenly Reason,*
>   *Schleiermacher's All-in-all.*
>
> *Head and heart let us embrace it,*
>   *Seeking not the falsely new;*
> *In an infant's laugh we trace it,*
>   *Stars reply, Yea, Life is true.*'

On September 18th Sterling died. When Caroline got the news we are not told; it would take two or three days to reach Falmouth. By the 28th or earlier she was at Windermere. The journey thither would be leisurely, and she may not have received tidings that would have cut so deep before she left home. But she knew by the beginning of October, for on the sixth of that month Wordsworth, whom she was seeing at Grasmere, asked how Sterling was. 'Dead,' they told him.

'Dead!' he exclaimed; 'that *is* a loss to his friends, his country and his age.'

There is only one mention of Sterling more, but there must have been constant thought of him. When, for example, in March of 1845 Caroline was reading *Wilhelm Meister*, she could not but remember how he had estimated it as 'worth any ten contemporary works.' And in her Journal for that year she had copied a poem by him from a recent *Blackwood's*. It is called *Serena*, and addressed 'to a friend of my youth.' Was Serena Caroline? Did she believe she was? It is hard to say, but I am inclined to think not. Much of the description—for example:

> *'Though years have left their mark,*
> *How calmly still thine eyes their beauty wear;*
> *Clear fountains of sweet looks, where nothing dark*
> *Dwells hidden in the light unstained as air,'*

might well have been written of her. But unless the motif which runs through the whole, the memory of a boyhood's friendship, is a mere literary artifice, the inspiration of the poem must be sought elsewhere. Caroline was no friend of Sterling's youth. He never saw her till he was over thirty-three, and they knew each other for little over four years. It was probably more for the authorship than for the theme that Caroline embodied the poem in her Journal. Having done that, for a time she left its pages almost blank. It was on October 6th that Wordsworth asked about Sterling and was told that he was dead. Caroline wrote a few lines two days later, and nothing more that year. The whole of her entries for 1845 fill less than three pages. There may have been more which her editor felt was not for the public eye. There may have been no more. In either case the inference is the same. But if she

> *'stooped*
> *Into a dark, tremendous sea of cloud,*
> *It was but for a time.'*

The dawn of 1846 shows her on normal terms with life, wounded it may be, but displaying no outward scar.

Five years after Sterling's death she heard a striking tribute paid to him. Henry Hallam, the historian, to whom she was talking at Carclew, asked her if she knew anything of a man of whom he had heard much, though he had never met him— Sterling. The question was natural, for Hallam was aware, of course, that Sterling had lived at Falmouth. He went on to speak of 'the peculiar affection and loyalty which all who had ever known him at all intimately seemed to cherish towards him, and their criticism on Hare's Memoir—that it portrayed a mere bookworm always occupied with some abstruse theological problem, rather than the man they delighted in for his geniality and buoyancy of feeling.' (Of Carlyle's Memoir he could not speak, for it was not yet published.) The conversation must have quickened Caroline's pulse.

Two more testimonies which she quotes at different times indicate the impression Sterling made on his contemporaries. In 1842, more than two years before Sterling's death, John Stuart Mill, in a letter dwelling on his character and intellectual position, added: 'Sterling fancied himself idle and useless, not considering how wide an effect his letters and conversation must produce; and indeed the mere fact of such a man living and breathing amongst us has an incalculable influence.' And on the last day of 1846 Herman Merivale, whom Caroline met at Carclew, 'spoke of John Sterling with enthusiastic admiration, as one quite unlike any other, so deeply influential in the earnest eloquence of his conversation. At Cambridge he had a most loving band of disciples, who after he left still felt his opinion a law for themselves.' As Merivale's younger brother Charles (subsequently Dean Merivale, the historian) had been a fellow-member of The Apostles with Sterling at Cambridge, this estimate was based on accurate knowledge.

* * *

Here this chapter, as originally written, ended, and it seems best on the whole to let it stand as it is, in spite of the fact that a few lines here and there ought properly to be modified in the light of what I can now add. What has been said of the relations between Caroline and Sterling embodied all the material which, so far as I knew, was available on that subject. But since then I have, as I have more than once mentioned, been given access to Barclay Fox's unpublished journal, and some of its entries in the years 1843 and 1844 cast new light on a period and a relationship in Caroline's life on which new light was much to be desired. The conclusions to which they point do not impose themselves irresistibly. Something is still left to conjecture. But the general opinion, I think, will be that a sufficient answer is given to questions hitherto unanswered.

The relevant entries begin at the end of May 1843. On the 29th of that month Barclay, returning to England from a long continental tour, found a letter from his mother waiting for him, telling of Mrs Sterling's recent death—an event to which Caroline, it will be remembered, made no reference in her Journal. The letter went on to tell 'how the girls have suffered from their close and active sympathy with the bereaved husband, and assiduous care of the children. Poor C. [Caroline] has been recruiting at Wadebridge.' Little can safely be inferred from this, for no appreciable distinction is drawn between Caroline's feelings and Anna Maria's. But a little more than a month later Sterling came from the Isle of Wight, where he had just settled, to stay at Falmouth, paying several visits to Perran, where Barclay was living since he had taken up the management of the foundry there. He arrived on July 6th and stayed several days. On the Sunday he went to Meeting at Falmouth and must have seen Caroline there; she and Anna Maria, moreover, spent at least one evening at Perran while Sterling was there. There is no reference in Caroline's Journal to Sterling's visit to Falmouth at all.

Six months later, in January 1844, Mrs Sterling having at

that time been dead nearly nine months, occurred a curious episode which may or may not have come to Caroline's ears. Barclay, going to Truro on business, took the opportunity of making some investigations regarding 'a preposterous report of Sterling's second marriage.' The story, it appears, was that he had married a Falmouth girl who had gone with him as maidservant to the Isle of Wight. Barclay interviewed the girl's mother, who knew nothing to confirm the report, and in the end it could be traced to nothing more convincing than a vague rumour that some Cornish girl had married her master. Since the girl who went to Sterling's service, Pamela Williams, was perfectly well known, the story of her marriage would undoubtedly have been confirmed if there had been any foundation for it.

That, then, was cleared up, but three days later comes an entry to which much more importance must be attached. Barclay, with a strange simplicity, used occasionally a not very occult code, consisting merely of spelling a few words backwards. That does not defy interpretation, and when on January 21st (1844) he begins his entry with 'Sgnilrit's rettel. Sc rewsna' it needs no superhuman sagacity to discover (in spite of the curious mis-spelling of Sterling's name) that what is meant is 'Sterling's letter. C's answer.' What was the letter, what the answer? The comment which immediately follows goes some way towards confirming the natural conjecture. 'It is a safe rule,' Barclay writes, 'in inward struggles and perplexities to give sentence in favour of the side which inclination opposes. To-day I watched with no common interest such a struggle and victory, and have no doubt that the result will ultimately be self-approval.' That was on January 21st. On the 22nd, 'Wrote Sterling;—*rather* an important letter.' On the 26th simply 'Letter from Sterling!' On the 28th, indicating that Caroline's victory was still to win, 'Poor C.! She bears up nobly, but not without praying and struggling.' On the 31st, 'S.'s final letter to C.' The entry for the next day, February 1st, begins with a word which I have failed to decipher. It is more like 'scene' than anything else, and the words immediately following are 'Poor C.,' but anything like a scene in the ordinary sense of the word would be so utterly alien to Caroline's character that I can only conclude that whatever the word may be it is not that. It is not very material in any case; the 'Poor C.' tells its own tale. Then follows silence for several weeks, till March 25th, when a letter of congratulation arrives from Sterling on Barclay's engagement (to Jane Backhouse of Darlington). On March 31st comes the entry: 'Interesting chat with my father in the evening about C.; our views agree entirely—he gave me S.'s letter (self-justificatory) to read—an able production and well answered!'

Barclay's references to Caroline are brief, and for a particular reason; he was at this time so engrossed with his recent engagement and impending marriage that he could write of little else. But in April there was a chance of all doubts about Sterling and Caroline being dispelled. In the middle of that month, Barclay, then in the North of England, heard that Sterling was dying, and hurried south to see him. When he got to Ventnor he saw to his relief that the blinds were not drawn, but Sterling's sister-in-law, Mrs F. D. Maurice, who was in charge, said the doctor had forbidden the patient to see anyone, and Barclay left without Sterling knowing he had been there. But Sterling rallied after all, and lived till September. Early in May Barclay got a very depressed letter from him, ending with the injunction: 'Think of me as of one dead'; the next day a letter from F. D. Maurice told of another violent haemorrhage. This must have caused Caroline great distress, for it would hardly be kept from her, and it may account for an entry, on May 22nd, which a single letter makes baffling. It is put within the square brackets which Barclay for some reason habitually used for his references to Caroline at this time, and runs: ['Poor, poor, C. P.—What a mournful lesson! What an afflicting dispensation!']. There would be no difficulty about that but for the inexplicable 'P.' It is entirely in keeping with previous entries, and no one would doubt that it referred to Caroline. But there is no question about the 'P.' It is perfectly clear in the manuscript. We are left, therefore, with the choice between assuming that the letter slipped in through some aberration on Barclay's part, and concluding that the entry does not refer to Caroline at all—though there is nothing anywhere in the journal to provide a clue to the identity of any 'C. P.'

There is little more that is relevant to add. In July Barclay had two letters of no special interest from Sterling, and Caroline had measles. During most of August Barclay was away in the north, and on getting home at the end of the month he noted that 'C. looks better.' On September 11th he and his two sisters left Falmouth, he for Darlington, they for the Lakes. At Bristol, which they reached the next day, he observed that 'C. is evidently in better health and spirits.' He got back to Falmouth on the 20th, and on the 22nd Robert Were Fox received a letter from Ventnor telling of Sterling's death. Caroline must by that time have been at Grasmere, and no doubt got the news in the next letter from home.

So John Sterling passes out of the Foxes' life. Barclay's entries remain to be interpreted, and the interpretation is not difficult. It seems clear that some nine months after his wife's death Sterling wrote and asked if Caroline would marry him. It is equally clear that she answered that she could not. What is less clear is whether she was in love with him; but in view of what Barclay says of her distress and the struggle she went through it can hardly be doubted that she was. Why then did she answer as she did? That, again, is not difficult to answer. There was the lesser reason of health; Sterling in January 1844, when he wrote to her and she replied, was virtually a dying man. There was the greater reason of the gulf between their religious beliefs. To marry out of the Society and be disowned would have distressed Caroline and all her family greatly. But there was more than that. Sterling was not merely not a Friend; he would at this time almost certainly not have called himself a Christian, fundamentally religious, and even spiritual, though he was. That obstacle, to Caroline, would have been fatal. These considerations supply the key to the only word that seems to need explanation. Why did Barclay describe Sterling's letter to Robert Were Fox as 'self-justificatory'? What had Sterling to justify? It is not a crime for a widower of thirty-eight to ask a woman of twenty-four to marry him. That is true. But when the man of thirty-eight knows that he can only have months to live, and that consumption is a contagious disease, when he is conscious, too, of deep differences between his own beliefs and the woman's, and the weight she attaches to hers, then the need for some defence of his proposition emerges clearly. But that is of little relevance. Caroline did not marry Sterling. She never married anyone. It is a satisfaction to have the questions that her own Journal inevitably prompts answered so conclusively by Barclay's.

Aunt how many 19th men of letters & poets were also Clergymen —

Chapter VI
Sterling's Friend

I f John Sterling would be virtually unknown today but for Carlyle, John Mitchenson Calvert would be virtually, or wholly, unknown but for Sterling, It was as Sterling's friend that Carlyle wrote of him, as Sterling's friend that Caroline Fox first knew him, and it is due to those two that his memory has been perpetuated. Sterling first met him in Madeira, where both men were wintering for their health, in 1838, and wrote home that he had moved his lodgings, 'and now come to live with a friend, a Dr Calvert,' whom he described as 'about my age, an Oriel man, and a very superior person.' Carlyle has given a comprehensive picture of him.

'Among the English in pursuit of health,' he wrote, 'or in flight from fatal disease, was this Dr Calvert; an excellent ingenious cheery Cumberland gentleman, about Sterling's age [he was, in fact, five years older], and in a deeper stage of ailment, this not being his first visit to Madeira: he, warmly joining himself to Sterling, was, as we have seen, warmly received by him; so that there soon grew a close and free intimacy between them; which for the next three years, till poor Calvert ended his course, was a leading element in the history of both. Companionship in incurable malady, a touching bond of union, was by no means purely or chiefly a companionship in misery in their case. The sunniest inextinguishable cheerfulness shone, through all manner of clouds, in both. Calvert had been travelling physician in some family of rank, who had rewarded him with a pension, shielding his own ill-health from one sad evil. Being hopelessly gone in pulmonary disorder, he now moved about among friendly climates and places, seeking what alleviation there might be; often spending his summers in the house of a sister in the environs of London; an insatiable rider on his little brown pony; always, wherever you might meet him, one of the cheeriest of men. He had plenty of speculation too, clear glances of all kinds into religious, social, moral concerns; and pleasantly incited Sterling's outpourings on such subjects. He could report of fashionable persons and manners in a fine Cumberland manner; loved art, a great collector of drawings; he had endless help and ingenuity; and was, in short, a very human, lovable, good and nimble man, —the laughing blue eyes of him, the clear cheery soul of him, still redolent of the fresh Northern breezes and transparent Mountain streams.'

There is something, though not much, to add to that. Calvert's epitaph, composed by Sterling and recorded by Caroline, shows that he was born in 1801, and was therefore thirty-nine when he first came to Falmouth. He was son of Wordsworth's schoolfellow and friend William Calvert of Penrith, and nephew of that Raisley Calvert who by his bequest of £900 enabled Wordsworth to escape the drudgery of a legal or clerical career and remain first and foremost a poet. Caroline, who mis-spells the uncle's name, though she had seen it in writing, mentions immediately after Calvert's death that his brother-in-law, Mr Stanger, 'showed us a letter of condolence from Wordsworth, in which he says that the bequest of Dr Calvert's uncle, Racely, was what enabled him to devote himself to literary pursuits, and give his talents, such as they were, opportunity to develop themselves.' The family of rank in which, as Carlyle says, Calvert had been family physician, was that of the second Earl Spencer, of whom Greville observes that he 'lives among oxen, not among men.' It is true that he was given a pension, but there was nothing *ex gratia* about it. Calvert had wanted to leave the earl, on the ground that it was professionally necessary for him to take up ordinary practice, but was begged to remain, on terms which provided for a pension of £500, dating from Earl Spencer's death. He told the full story of the negotiations to Barclay Fox, and it is recounted in the latter's journal. Calvert went to Rome with Sterling in the autumn of 1838 and was nursed by him through a serious illness. The next winter was to have been spent by the two friends in Madeira, but in circumstances already described in connexion with John Sterling[1] they decided to stay at Falmouth, and so began their close friendship with the Foxes.

Calvert may be thought to have no great claim to commemoration, and in fact the reference-books know nothing of him, but during the two years he was at Falmouth he had a definite place in Caroline's life, both as a friend of Sterling's and for his own sake. She tells more of him than is known from any other source, and makes it clear that he possessed qualities above the common average. She saw him first six days after she had first seen Sterling, and describes him as 'a nervous, suffering invalid, with an interesting and most mobile expression of countenance.' His talks with Caroline included some fragments of information about himself and one or two reminiscences of the Spencer family, none of them of great intrinsic importance,—this, for example, as Caroline records it: 'Dr Calvert described old Lord Spencer (whose travelling and private physician he was), looking over and burning one after another of the letters his wife had received from the most eminent persons of the day, because he thought it a crying modern sin to make biographies piquant and interesting by personalities not necessary to them; he therefore resolved to leave nothing of which his executors might make ill use. At length he came to one from Nelson, written just after a great victory, and beginning with a pious ejaculation and recognition of the Arm by which he had conquered. Dr Calvert snatched it out of his hand—it was on the way to the fire—and put it in his pocket, saying, "My Lord, here is nothing personal; nothing

[1] See p. 64.

but what everybody knows, and burn it must not." His lordship was silent. A few hours after he said "Doctor, where is that letter you put in your pocket?" "Gone, my lord." "Indeed? I was wanting it." "I thought you probably would, so I immediately put it in the post-office and sent it to a young lady who is collecting autographs.'" There is some temptation to apply the last sentence to Caroline, whom it so exactly fits; but it clearly could not refer to her, for Calvert only came in touch with her six years after Earl Spencer's death. There were, no doubt, many young feminine collectors of autographs in the 1830's.

One other anecdote of Calvert's gains its interest from the personality who was the subject of it, the third Earl Spencer, son of Calvert's patron and patient, better known throughout his political career as Lord Althorp. It appears that 'a confidential butler was discovered to have omitted paying the bills for which he had received about £2,000; this came to light in an investigation preparatory to settling a life annuity on him. Dr Calvert asked Lord Spencer, "Well, what shall you do now?" "Oh, I shall settle the annuity on his wife: I can't afford to lose £2,000 and my temper besides."'

The only further light cast on Calvert's life before 1840, the year when he came to Falmouth, consists of a few unimportant references to his time at Oriel and his illness at Rome, and some more detailed references to his stay at Madeira, where he first met Sterling. At dinner at Rosehill one summer day in 1841 he spoke with great sympathy of the peasantry in that island, utterly disregarded by the classes above them and not even attended by any doctor when they were ill; he himself, finding fever prevalent among them, used to give them treatment and sometimes money, considerably to the indignation of the practitioners who neglected them. Calvert was denounced as a quack till he silenced criticism by mentioning that he was an English M.D. and threatening to compete with the local doctors for the fees of the rich. The medical art, he reported, was in a lamentably low state in Madeira, a condition which he attributed to the fact that 'wherever Spain or Portugal had influence there pride and indolence formed barriers to all improvement.'

Caroline quotes Calvert's conversation freely. In one of her happy phrases she speaks of 'Dr Calvert's mild wisdom flowing as usual in its deep, quiet channel,' and everything she mentions concerning him justifies that description. Sterling, talking to her one day, gave his estimate of his friend, describing Calvert's character as one of pure sympathy with all his fellows, and delighting to trace the outlines of the Divine image in even the least of His creatures. What the force of Calvert's personality normally was is hard to say, for neither Caroline nor Sterling, who had known him earlier, ever saw him in anything like ordinary health. He came to Falmouth an incurable consumptive, knowing, as a medical man, what his own state was, and how soon the inevitable end might be expected. In the two years, or rather less, that he was there he gained not merely the friendship but the affection of the Fox family, and all that Caroline writes of him makes that very understandable. He was evidently fond of animals. 'Dr Calvert joined us at dinner,' Caroline wrote in June 1841, 'and we all lounged under our drooping spruce, with Balaam the ape, which I had borrowed for the afternoon, in the foreground, and the kid near by, quite happy in our companionship.' From 'Aunt Charles,' of Trebah, he got a present of a Neapolitan pig, which he had washed and shampooed every morning, but which in spite of such encouragement declined to assume any other attributes of civilisation. And as he grew weaker he bought for £5 a pony which, for reasons unknown, he named Z. It would carry him to Penjerrick when the walk there was beyond his powers.

He and Sterling would appear to have lived together during Sterling's first stay at Falmouth. After that he settled down in lodgings by himself and rapidly made congenial friends, in addition to, and of a different order from, the Foxes. 'He has formed,' says Caroline, 'an intimacy with a cheery-hearted old woman, Nancy Weeks, who busies herself with the eggs of Muscovy ducks; they exchange nosegays, and he sits for much of his evenings with her and her husband.' There is an authentic note in the reference to lodging-house art in the next sentence: 'He has stuck a portrait of Papa over a painting to which he has taken a great antipathy, and spite of the incision of four pins, his landlady quite approves of it.' Gravely ailing though he was at this time, 'he is still often able to shoot curious little birds, which he brings to Anna Maria to draw and stuff.' Taxidermy was a favourable hobby of Calvert's; Caroline somewhere comments on the singularity of dining at his lodgings off roast heron, with the stuffed integument of the bird a solemn spectator of the meal.

Calvert possessed a good deal of quiet humour, as two or three conversations and incidents mentioned by Caroline testify. Soon after his arrival at Falmouth he sat to the local portrait-painter, Cunningham (both Caroline's and Barclay's journals provide constant reminders of the importance of this profession in days before photography so largely displaced it), and took the result to Rosehill for the Foxes to inspect. He admitted that it was a good piece of painting, 'but,' he added, 'not the Dr Calvert that I shave every morning.' Even *in extremis* he could see life's humorous side. Some six weeks before his death, when he was praying for the end to come, his sister asked what the physician, who had just left him, had recommended. 'An apple,' he answered. 'Dear me,' she said, 'that doesn't seem a matter of great importance.' 'Oh, yes,' the invalid replied, 'an apple drove Adam and Eve out of Paradise, and perhaps this apple may drive me in.' A month later still, when he was thought to be actually dying, his brother-in-law, Stanger, gave him a glass of wine, to which he had surreptitiously added a dose of morphia. Calvert immediately detected the drug, and not content with refusing the draught insisted on Stanger swallowing it himself.

Most of Calvert's conversation, as recorded by Caroline, was on religion and metaphysics. It had none of the brilliance which so often marked Sterling's casual talk, but it was charged with that 'mild wisdom' which Caroline found characteristic in Sterling's friend. He and she were manifestly kindred spirits, the more so by reason of the interest he manifested in Quakerism. The first time Caroline saw him he 'described being brought up as a Friend, and he perfectly remembers riding on a little Shetland pony to be christened. He is very anxious to go to Meeting on the first favourable opportunity, to put himself in a position to prove the correctness of some of those tenets of Friends which he has been interesting in study-ing.' (The second half of the first sentence is something of a *non sequitur*, for Friends practise neither infant nor adult baptism; it must be supposed that Calvert was christened as an infant and subsequently brought under Quaker influences.)

He recurred to the subject more than once. In a passage worth quoting as Caroline wrote it, 'Dr Calvert talked of the aid metaphysics might afford to religion, and did afford in many cases; for many minds required more opportunity for the exercise of faith, and this the study of metaphysics, and demon-strative theology, afforded them. Then the Friends became our topic; he again extolled their code of laws, partly because they do not dogmatise on any point, do not peremptorily require belief in any articles. As to particular scruples, he would hold that circumstances should have the greatest effect in giving them a direction: in his own case, for instance, when living in a county where hunting is ruinously in vogue, he bore his testi-mony against it by neither riding nor lending his hunter; here he would not object to do either. So in George Fox's time dress was probably made a subject of great importance; "but," he added, "Satan probably tempts the Foxes of Falmouth in a very different way to that in which he attacked their spiritual ancestors; he is vastly too clever and fertile in invention to repeat the same experiment twice."'

These were no mere casual references. Three weeks later Caroline mentions that 'Dr Calvert has been examining the principles of Friends. He thinks that as much was done by George Fox as could be done at the time at which he lived, but it is not enough for the present time; forms and words are still too apt to be accepted instead of ideas, and a new prophet is wanted to give reality to the abstract. Fox's work was to lead man from his fellow-man to Christ alone; and how great an aim was this!' No doubt it was not only the tenets but the exponents of Quakerism that attracted Calvert, as they did so many who came in contact with the Falmouth Foxes. He says, indeed, ten days later again, that 'at Falmouth he has met with two new and most interesting facts, John Mill and Grand-mamma. The satisfaction he derives from finding that the experience of the latter,—an aged and earnest Christian—tallies often with his own theories, is extreme.' Grandmamma was the widow of Robert Were Fox the elder, formerly a Falmouth Tregelles, a spirited old lady who used, so it was said, to be driven in to Meeting on Sunday mornings from her house at Roscrow in a coach-and-four. She was, at the time when Calvert was talking of her, seventy-three.

He talked of many other things, of art and politics and sometimes of his own profession; Carlyle, it will be recalled, spoke of his love of pictures and his collection of drawings. In the first long conversation Caroline had with him most of his interests were touched on. 'Dr Calvert,' she recalls, 'talked about the fine arts; he cannot remember the names of the painters, but only the principles evolved in their works. Those before the time of Raphael interest him the most, for though very defective in drawing they yet evidently laboured to enforce a genuine Idea. Since Raphael's time the execution is often exquisite, but the Idea seems to him to have vanished. He talked on politics, and sympathises most with the philosophic Radicals, who think it right to throw their weight into the scale of the weak—with those who advocate progression, yet he would be very sorry to see their measures now carried into practice. They would put power into the hands of those who would doubtless at first abuse it, but experience would gradually put things right and keep real Conservatism in existence. Of the Princess Galitzin, who gave over her moral government into the hands of her confessor, Overburg; she represents a large class in England who put their consciences into the keeping of others—a favourite clergyman, for instance,—and let reason and conscience bow before authority. This must interfere with living faith, for having a sort of intermediate agent between man and his God destroys the sense of real immediate dependence on Him.'

Like everyone of that day he was a student of Goethe, and gave Caroline a copy of *Hermann and Dorothea*; and he had interested himself deeply in the only book Darwin had then published, *The Voyage of the Beagle*. On the basis of that he 'talked of Darwin and his theory of the race being analogous to the individual man; having in the latter form a certain quantum of vitality granted for a certain period, he would extend the idea to the race, and thus would regard the Deluge, for instance, as simply the necessary conclusion of our race because it had lived the time originally appointed for it: this, though abundantly conjectural, is interesting as a theory, and probably originated with Herder.' As a physician, and a sick physician, he diagnosed his own state and observed his own symptoms with complete objectivity, and reported visible proofs of the break-up of his constitution. He was equally dispassionate in his mental self-analysis. 'He went,' says Caroline, 'into some of the intricacies of his own character—his want of self-esteem, which, though it does not hinder him from objecting to the theories of all others, prevents his confidence in his own, unless built up on indisputable, reasonable, manifest truth. Rumball, the phrenologist, has been examining his head, and he is quite willing that his character of him should be seen, because he thinks it an instructive one, just as he would have his body examined after death for the benefit of medical science.'

On the whole, Calvert's was a reflective temperament, naturally disposed to quietism. He 'does not agree with Carlyle and others who think that we all have a message to deliver. "My creed is that Man, whilst dwelling on the earth, is to be instructed in patience, submission, humility,"' and while appreciating that activity was essential to an ardent spirit like Sterling's, he could still dwell on the importance of what he called passive heroism. A good deal of his creed is summed up in views he once expressed about Luther, who, he said, was the first who revived the conviction that it was the inward principle, rather than the outward manifestation of forms or ceremonies, to which Christ claimed man's loyalty; the heart rather than the senses which should do Him homage. 'There has,' he added, 'been through all time a constant hankering after the Law as opposed to the Gospel; it has been perpetually restored in some form or other: one Form wears itself out, then a master-mind arises, teaches a pure principle, and can only transmit it by a new Form, which in its turn wears out and dies, and another takes its place. Form is in its nature transitory, but the living Principle is eternal.'

With Calvert's belief in the continuity of Principle went an equally firm belief in the wholeness of life. He spoke of that when Caroline went to call on him and his sister one day in October 1841, within nine or ten weeks of his death. 'What Dr Calvert lays stress on,' Caroline noted, 'is the general tone of mind to be prescribed, not the particular book or engagement that will do good or harm: of that every individual must judge by his own feelings and perceptions, but a quiet satisfied sense of being in your right place and doing your own duty is the best physical state imaginable. The young aspirants after eminence and fame fancy themselves made up of a pure Divine intellect and a lower animal nature, and for the higher to make any concessions to the lower is, they think, an intolerable sin; whereas in reality all parts of our nature have been alike created by Divine Wisdom, who has Himself subjected them to certain laws of co-operation, any infringement of which brings certain punishment with it. In carrying out the Divine will, in whatever direction it may be, our higher nature or intellectual and moral faculties can surely suffer no loss.' It is not surprising that Calvert should have set himself to study Quaker principles. He must have found them to resemble his own very closely; if he had lived he might well have identified himself openly with a Society in which he had been brought up, and with which so many of his new friends at Falmouth were intimately associated.

But that was not to be. On January 8th, 1842, Caroline wrote in her Journal: 'Dr Calvert's longings for death this morning were most touching. "Oh, lead me to the still waters" was his cry'; on the 9th: 'Our dear friend Dr Calvert was this morning permitted to put off the life-garment which has so painfully encumbered him, and is, I trust, drinking of those still waters after which he pined.' He was buried on the 13th, and Sterling wrote an epitaph, the last two lines of which,

> *'Reason thy lamp and Faith thy star while here;*
> *Now both one brightness in the light of God,'*

gained the distinction of special praise by Wordsworth. Characteristically, Calvert had left instructions that his death should be made no occasion of grief, and that it should be marked by dinners and minor festivities for the old people at the workhouse. Caroline has established one more claim on our gratitude by revealing and recording much that would otherwise never have been known of a patient, tranquil and beautiful spirit.

Chapter VII
The Carlyles

How much Caroline Fox knew of Carlyle before she first saw him in May 1840 can only be conjectured. Her acquaintance with the two men who were at that time his closest friends, John Sterling and John Stuart Mill, was still fresh. Sterling she had met in February of that year, and Mill in March, and Carlyle was almost the first subject of conversation in either case. She might have read *The French Revolution* or *Sartor Resartus* (which had appeared in 1837 and 1838 respectively), but there is no indication that at that time she had. But Sterling supplied her with an outline picture of the establishment at Chelsea where the Carlyles had been settled since 1834. Jane Carlyle 'plays all manner of tricks on her husband, telling wonderful stories of him in his presence, founded almost solely on her bright imagination; he, poor man, panting for an opportunity to stuff in a negation, but all to no purpose; having cut him up sufficiently, she would clear the course. They are a very happy pair.' This last judgement is Sterling's, not Caroline's, but there is nothing to show that she would have questioned it at any time; no light is cast by her journal on the strains and tensions that so often made the highly-strung couple at 5 Cheyne Row miserable.

It was in May 1840 that Caroline first saw Carlyle in the flesh. By that time the prophet had gained honour in his own country (which he had quitted six years earlier) and beyond it. He was forty-five, and had been married to Jane Welsh nearly fourteen years. His articles in the *Edinburgh* and *Fraser's* had laid the foundation of his fame, and the *Life of Schiller*, *The*

French Revolution and *Sartor Resartus* had established it im-
pregnably. At the same time Harriet Martineau had persuaded
him to take to lecturing, and with profound misgivings and
reluctance he had in 1837 delivered before a highly appreciative
audience at Willis's Rooms his first course—on German literature. The venture was reasonably lucrative, and the Carlyles
needed money. Other courses followed in 1838 and 1839,
and in May of 1840, when Caroline, then not quite twenty-one,
was in London with her family (no doubt for the Yearly Meeting of the Society of Friends), the famous series on 'Heroes,
Hero-Worship and the Heroic in History' was more than half
through. The Hero as Divinity, as Prophet, as Poet and as
Priest had been dealt with. Those Caroline missed, but she
was in time for the last two lectures, on the Hero as Man of
Letters and as King respectively. With her sister Anna Maria
she sat next to John Mill's sister Clara, and was by her introduced to Mrs Carlyle, who was sitting on Miss Mill's other
side; the result was an immediate invitation to call at Cheyne
Row any evening.

The entries the lectures inspired in Caroline's Journal have
two features of interest, the description of Carlyle's appearance
on the platform and the remarkably competent résumé the
writer gives of the lectures themselves. As to the first, 'Carlyle
soon appeared,' wrote the young and eager listener, 'and looked
as if he felt a well-dressed London crowd scarcely the arena
for him to figure in as popular lecturer. He is a tall robust-
looking man; rugged simplicity and indomitable strength are
in his face, and such a glow of genius in it—not always smoulder-
ing there, but flashing from his beautiful grey eyes, from the
remoteness of their deep setting under that massive brow. His
manner is very quiet, but he speaks like one tremendously convinced of what he utters, and who had much—very much—in
him that was quite unutterable, quite unfit to be uttered to the
uninitiated ear; and when the Englishman's sense of beauty
and truth exhibited itself in vociferous cheers he would im-

patiently, almost contemptuously, wave his hand, as if it were not the sort of homage that Truth demanded. He began in rather a low nervous voice, with a broad Scotch accent, but it soon grew firm, and shrank not abashed from its great task.'

That is admirably adequate. So are the summaries of the two lectures. A comparison with the version in the published volume shows how sound is the young diarist's grasp of essentials and how comprehensive and well proportioned her survey. It reveals, incidentally, certain differences between the lectures as delivered and as published. That Caroline's summary should differ verbally from the full text is natural enough, but when she puts in quotation-marks a particular passage which corresponds with nothing in the printed volume, it seems clear that between platform and publisher it has been revised away. Take, for example, a few sentences on Rousseau: 'The Confessions are the only writings of his which I have read with any interest; there you see the man such as he really was, though I can't say that it is a duty to lay open the Bluebeard chambers of the heart. I have said that Rousseau lived in a sceptical age; there was then in France no form of Christianity recognised, not even Quakerism.' There is, no doubt, some paraphrase here, in spite of the inverted commas, but Caroline could hardly have invented the 'Bluebeard chambers of the heart'; and the reference to Quakerism would naturally impress itself on her mind. Neither phrase appears in *Heroes and Hero Worship* as we have it today. One more example. The 'St Diderot' in the assertion that 'Napoleon was brought up believing not the Gospel according to St John but the Gospel according to St Diderot,' has an authentic Carlylean ring about it; but there is no St Diderot in *Heroes and Hero-Worship* as published. Only once have I found Caroline wanting—when she rather curiously transfers to Napoleon a remark which Carlyle in fact made of Cromwell. 'There is much pathos,' she writes, 'in the fact that many times a day his mother would say "I want to see the Emperor; is he still alive?"' What Carlyle said—what, at any rate, he has written in *Heroes and Hero-Worship*—was, 'I think always too of his poor Mother, now very old, living in that Palace of his; a right brave woman; as indeed they lived all an honest God-fearing Household there: if she heard a shot go off she thought it was her son killed. He had to come to her at least once a day, that she might see with her own eyes that he was yet living. The poor old Mother!' Even if there were no context to preclude misunderstanding, that could hardly carry conviction as a description of the Bonaparte ménage.

So far Caroline *viderat tantum*, and she did not avail herself of the invitation Mrs Carlyle had extended at the Edward Street lecture; the Foxes' programme for Yearly Meeting week, or fortnight, was no doubt well filled up in advance. But before they left for home Caroline and her brother and sister spent an evening with the Mills in Kensington Square, and the two Carlyles were among the guests. The conversation was general; Caroline consequently had no Carlylean monologue to report, as she so often had later. Sombre as usual, the sage dwelt on 'the progressive degeneracy of our lower classes,' the deplorable condition of Ireland and the not less deplorable condition of England. Then a reference to Quakerism caught Caroline's alert ear. Carlyle, in a context which perhaps escaped her—at any rate she has not indicated it—commented on George Fox's *Journal*. 'That's not a book one can read through very easily,' he said, 'but there are some deep things in it, well worth your finding.' (If Caroline had read *Sartor Resartus* at this date she would not be surprised at finding Carlyle familiar with George Fox.)

No more lavish a harvest than that did the first personal contact with the lecturer on Hero-Worship yield. But a fragment of Jane Carlyle's conversation must have gratified one of her hearers, conforming as it did in large measure with the impression formed by perhaps the youngest member of Carlyle's audience of his emotions on the platform. 'It is so dreadful for him,' said his wife, 'to try to unite the characters of the prophet and the mountebank; he has keenly felt it; and also he has been haunted by the wonder whether the people were not considering if they had had enough for their guinea.' That was all. The Fox contingent left, but at the door found their waiting postilion inebriated. So they walked home, John Stuart Mill going most of the way with them.

There was no journey to London in 1841—a British Association meeting at Plymouth being the 'away' event for that year—but the end of May 1842 found Caroline up for Yearly Meeting as usual, and before she started home again two visits to Cheyne Row (Mill's warning that 'he has a peculiar horror of lion-hunting ladies' was no doubt borne in mind) had provided her with abundance to chronicle. The conversation on both occasions seems to have been completely discursive. The visitors were received 'with affectionate cordiality,' and Carlyle, having evidently asked, or guessed, what brought them to London, 'wanted to know what we were doing at the Yearly Meeting, and what were its objects and functions, and remarked on the deepening observable among Friends.' What they were doing, in fact, among other things, was to pass resolutions, or rather 'adopt minutes,' on various matters of public concern, not always with much consideration of how the ideal should be related to the actual. That tendency did not escape Carlyle. 'When we told of the letter to the Queen [who was then, like Caroline, just twenty-three] recommendatory of peace in Afghanistan he was terribly amused. "Poor little Queen! She'd be glad enough to live in peace and quietness if the Afghans would but submit to her conditions."' 'Poor little Queen' was evidently the dominant note in Carlyle's references to his Sovereign at the moment. He recurred to it in the course of Caroline's second visit to Cheyne Row a week later. In the interval a penniless carpenter called John Francis had fired at the Queen and Prince Albert as they were driving through the Green Park. That prompted some characteristically oracular reflections. ''Tis an odd thing this about Queen Victoria. After having had a champion to say before the whole assembly of them "O Queen, live for ever!" a little insignificant fellow comes up, points his pistol at her and says "Chimera, die this minute!" Poor little Queen! I have some loyalty about me, and have no wish to see her shot, but as for her having any right to hold the reins of government if she could not manage them, all the cartloads of dirty parchment can't make that clear. There are thousands of men about her made of the same flesh and blood, with the same eternities around them, and they want to be well governed and fed. It is something to get it recognised that the ablest man should be the one to guide us, even if we never see it carried out.'

The same reservations about hereditary royalty had figured in the previous conversation. The talk had somehow got round to 'politics and bribery, and the deep and wide influence of money, which seems now the one recognisable claim to human esteem.' But that, Caroline observed sensibly, couldn't last long. 'No, it can't last,' Carlyle agreed, 'unless God intend to destroy the world at once and utterly.' Thence his mind switched towards the 'Hero as King' of his sixth lecture. 'He looks to Parliament,' Caroline reports, 'for some great vital change in our condition, and expects that ere long some sincere earnest spirit will arise and gradually acquire and exert influence over the rest. Not that he supposes it will ever again take the form of Cromwell's Revolution.' The topic stirred the speaker to satire—its object John Arthur Roebuck, that pertinacious politician who distinguished himself by hostility to any government of any colour. Roebuck, he thought, 'would very much like the place of the Lord Protector of England, Scotland and Ireland. The other day he was talking to him about bribery [here we connect up with the beginning of the conversation] when Roebuck said "Really, if you so remove temptation, you will take away opportunity for virtue." "Then," said Carlyle, "we must recognise as a great encourager of virtue

one who certainly has not got much credit for it yet—namely
the Devil." He thinks it would have a wonderful effect in
the House if Roebuck was to raise his small curious person,
and with his thin shrill voice give utterance: "Either bribery
is right or wrong: if wrong let us give up practising it, and
abuse it less: if right, let it go on without outcry." '

The other topics discussed that day were Emerson, and the
host's namesake Richard Carlile, the Devonshire Radical, who
in 1819 had been sentenced to three years' imprisonment and
a fine of £1500 for reprinting Paine's *Rights of Man* and
similar works. Carlyle and Emerson (in whom Sterling had
already interested Caroline) had at this time only met once—in
1833, when the Carlyles were living at Craigenputtock.
Emerson, on his first visit to Europe, reached England by way
of Italy and Paris, and—as Jane Carlyle once told Caroline—
'came to them first in Scotland with a note from John Stuart
Mill, and was kindly welcome in a place where they saw nothing
but wild-fowl, not even a beggar.' [1] Since then Emerson had,
at some loss to himself, arranged for the publication of several
of Carlyle's works in America, and in 1842 (the year in which
Carlyle and Caroline were discussing him) he became editor of
the New England transcendentalist journal *The Dial*—which
expired in 1844 after an existence of rather less than four years.
Caroline, who had heard much of Emerson from Sterling,
speaks of him (in 1843) as 'quietly but deeply influencing a few
both in England and America. In America he is indeed a great
phenomenon; he must live and feel and think, apart from public
opinion, on the adamantine basis of his own manhood.' The
Carlyles, she adds, like his conversation much better than his
books, which they think often obscure and involved in both
conception and execution. She herself remarked on the democratic way in which he had levelled all ranks of subjects and
holy and unholy personages. 'Why,' Carlyle answered, 'they
are all great Facts, and he treats them each as a Fact, of value

[1] Emerson gives his own account of the visit in the first chapter of *English Traits*.

rather with reference to the whole than to any preconceived theory! I was amused, on asking Webster about him the other day, to hear him say "Oh, do you mean the Socinian Minister?" You see, he has no vote in Congress, no authenticated outward influence.'

One tangible benefit which Caroline derived from the conversation was a copy of a recent issue of *The Dial*, which Emerson had sent to Carlyle 'as a good sample of the tone and struggling nature of American thought'; also an American pamphlet on capital punishment, with some of Carlyle's characteristic annotations in the margin. Caroline, like most Friends, held decided views on this subject, as many entries in her journal indicate, and she no doubt drew Carlyle out on it. 'He does not like capital punishment,' she writes, 'because he wishes men to live as much and as long as possible; he rejoices in the increasing feeling that it is a right solemn thing for one man to say to another "Give over living!" But on my characterising it as a declaration that though God could bear with the criminal man could not, he said "Why, there are many things in the world that God bears with:—He bears with many a dreary morass and waste, yet He gives to man the will and the power to till it and make oats grow out of it. But you'll make no oats grow out of men's corpses. This pamphlet-author is oddly inconsistent; with all his enthusiastic feeling for the value of human life, he is quite in favour of going to war with England, and thus willing to sacrifice thousands of brave fellows, while he would save the life of a miserable rascal like Good, who cut his wife into pieces and stuffed them into a coach-box."' That very reasonable criticism evidently gratified the critic himself, for Caroline concludes her report of his observations with the remark, 'Carlyle's laughs are famous fellows, hearty and bodily.'

There is no obvious connexion between capital punishment and Richard Carlile, on whom the talk next turned, but it is easy to see how the subject came up. Caroline, no doubt, gave

Carlyle news of his friend Sterling, who was then living at Falmouth, and had been lecturing at the Polytechnic there. Carlyle was interested in hearing of this inaugural lecture, which Sterling had given in the previous autumn, and in which he had referred to 'a recent volume of Mr Carlyle's on Heroes and Hero-Worship,' and amused to learn the horror which mention of his (Carlyle's) name aroused. 'I suppose they took me for Richard Carlile, but they say that even Richard has taken another turn and become a religious character. I remember when his father was a bookseller, and his shopmen were constantly being taken up for selling the sort of book he kept, yet there was such an enthusiastic feeling towards him, such a notion that he was supporting the right cause, that no sooner was one taken up than another offered himself from the country, and so he was always kept supplied. Edward Irving fell in with one of them at Newgate, who appealed to him as to whether it was not very hard to be imprisoned for disseminating views which he honestly believed to be true. Irving rather agreed with him, and he afterwards paraded Irving's opinion in a somewhat mortifying manner.'

It may be added that Caroline, on her first two visits to Carlyle in his own home, was considerably impressed by the effect of his digestive disabilities on his outlook on life. That was, indeed, one of the first subjects he mentioned to her. 'Of himself he says it is just the old story of indigestion; dyspepsia is a sort of perennial thing with him (how much does this explain!), he can do no work before breakfast, but is just up to viewing Life in general, and his own Life in particular, on the shady side.' That was at the beginning of the first visit; the record of the second, six days later, ends with the comment: 'Carlyle's conversation and general views are curiously dyspeptic, his indigestion colouring everything.' Caroline may, no doubt, have had certain prepossessions on that subject, for in the previous year Sterling's friend, Dr Calvert, had dwelt on it in conversation with her. He found, he said, it would not do to be much with Carlyle, his views took such hold on him (Calvert) and affected his spirits. None but those of great buoyancy and vigour of constitution should, Calvert thought, subject themselves to his depressing influences. Calvert, it must be remembered, was an invalid, and therefore perhaps unduly sensitive to such influences, but he quoted Carlyle himself as saying to him one day, 'Well, I can't wish Satan anything worse than to try to digest to all eternity with my stomach; we shouldn't want fire and brimstone then.' This, it may be observed parenthetically, was what Jane Carlyle had to live with.

Between Caroline's first visit to Cheyne Row on Saturday May 28th and her second on Friday June 3rd she had dined, on the Tuesday, with the Mills, and John Mill had some interesting observations to make about Carlyle. 'He thinks Carlyle,' Caroline notes, 'intolerant to no class but meta-physicians; owing to his entire neglect of this mode of thought he is presently [i.e. immediately] floored by Sterling in argument. Carlyle is not getting on pleasantly with his work on the Civil Wars: he finds so little standing authority; and the mode of revolutionary thought then was so different to what the present age can sympathise with; all its strivings were for immediate results, no high abstract principles apparently influenced them—except transiently.' The work on the Civil Wars, in fact, never materialised in the form suggested. Largely for the reasons given by Mill, Carlyle abandoned his original scheme and produced instead his notable edition of Cromwell's Letters and Speeches, with the necessary explanatory matter.

Mill's comments on Carlyle found their counterpart in Carlyle's comments on Mill in the course of Caroline's second visit to 5 Cheyne Row. 'Ah! poor fellow,' he commiserated, 'he has had to get himself out of Benthamism; and all the emotions and sufferings he has endured have helped him to thoughts that never entered Bentham's head. However, he is still too fond of demonstrating everything. If John Mill were to get up to heaven he would hardly be content till he had made out how it all was. For my part I don't much trouble about the machinery of the place; whether there is an operative set of angels or an industrial class—I'm willing to leave all that. Neither do I ever quake on my bed like Wordsworth, trying to reconcile the ways of Providence to my apprehension. I early came to the conclusion that I was not very likely to make it out clearly; the notions of the Calvinists seem what you cannot escape from, namely that if it's all known before-hand, why, it all must happen. This does not affect your actual work at all; if you have faith that it is all just and true, why, it won't harm you to shape any notions about it. I don't see that we do any good by puzzling our poor weak heads about such things while there is plenty of clear work before them in the regions of practicability. In the mean time I know that I have uncontrolled power over one unit in creation, and it's my business in life to govern that one as well as possible. I'm not over-fond of Bolingbroke's patronising Providence, nor of Voltaire's "If there were no God we should be obliged to invent one for the completion of the system."'

The conversation that day had begun on Swedenborg. Carlyle, says Caroline, came in in his blouse, and somehow or other someone mentioned Swedenborgianism. That started Carlyle. Swedenborg, he observed, was a thoroughly practical, mechanical man, and was in England learning shipbuilding. He went to a little inn in Bishopsgate Street, and was eating his dinner very fast, when he thought he saw in the corner of the room a vision of Jesus Christ, who said to him, 'Eat slower.' This was the beginning of all his visions and mysterious com-munications, of which he had enough in his day. He gave exactly the date—Carlyle thought it was the 5th of May 1785—when Christianity died out, that is to say when the last spark of truth left its professors, which is truly the death of anything; and that, he thought, was the Day of Judgement; not our old notions of it at all, but a sort of invisible judgement, of which he got informed in his visions.

At this point Caroline takes to direct quotation, with Carlyle's final verdict on the Swedish mystic: 'There was a great deal of truth in the man, with all his visions and fancies, and many hold with him to this day. Law got many of his notions from him. Then there's Böhme; I could never follow him in his books; it is the most distracted style of writing possible. His first vision was of a bright light stretching all across the road, which turned out to be an angel, who communicated with him ever after. George Fox and Novalis and many others were among his followers, for there's a deep truth in him after all.'

Then came a little philosophic pessimism on the subject of vocation. As to that: 'You're better judges of this than any-one else, yet you must often waste half your life in experi-menting, and perhaps fail after all. There is a set of people whom I can't do with at all—those who are always declaring what an extremely perfect world this is, and how very well things are conducted in it; to me it seems all going wrong and tending irresistibly to change—which can't but be for the worse.' After that it was natural that Caroline should ask encouragingly whether there was a single institution existing which was as he would have it, and inevitable that she should get the answer, 'Why, I can't say there is, exactly.'

She was perhaps wise in steering him off at this point into reminiscence. Having clearly read *Sartor Resartus* by this time, she asked him how his early history compared with Teufelsdröckh's. 'Why,' came the answer, 'my advent, I believe, was not at all out of the common; one extraordinary fact of my childhood was that after eleven months' profound taciturnity I heard a child cry, and astonished them all by saying "What ails wee Jock?"' The description of Entepfuhl, Caroline learned, was identical with that of Carlyle's native village Ecclefechan; the indivisible suit of yellow serge, into which he had daily to insinuate himself, was also historical.

The Carlyles

Cursory observations on various topics followed. Mrs Carlyle said her husband liked to read *Hermann and Dorothea* on a warm day; he thought Wordsworth might have written it, but there were thoughts in Goethe, and particularly in *Wilhelm Meister*, which a dozen Wordsworths could not see into; their two maids got hold of his translation of the book and were always at it, scrubbing with one hand and holding the book with the other. Then some words on the misery of the Scotch poor, which led Carlyle to express himself strongly in favour of emigration; some about his visit to Newgate with Elizabeth Fry, and a few more on how self-forgetfulness is attainable. Mrs Carlyle, says Caroline, was very affectionate— whether towards her husband or her young guests is not clear. But her health and spirits were deeply depressed by what she had gone through. That, too, is a little ambiguous, but Caroline no doubt appreciated what life with Carlyle meant. She—Mrs Carlyle—was asked which book her husband had had the greatest pleasure in writing. 'Oh,' she answered, 'he has pleasure in none, he is always so dissatisfied with what he does; but the one which gave him the greatest torment was *The French Revolution*'—and then she launched into the now familiar tale of how Carlyle had lent the manuscript of the first volume to Mill, who lent it to his friend, Mrs Taylor, whose servant accidentally burned it to ashes. Carlyle had kept neither a copy nor even his original notes and had no choice but to begin the whole thing afresh.

Host and guests parted on an agreeable note. 'There was something particularly engaging in his reprobation of a heartless caricature of the execution of poor Louis XVI, which he desired us not to look at, but introduced a beautiful one of himself smoking in his tub, which John Sterling compares to one of Michael Angelo's prophets. He stood at the window with his pipe to help us to draw a comparison.'

Caroline's contacts with Cheyne Row in the latter part of 1842 and the early part of 1843 took the form of a lively correspondence between her and Carlyle over the fortunes of the miner Michael Verran (dealt with in the next chapter), one letter from him on general matters, and reports of him from John Sterling. He was engaged on *Past and Present*, and found it, like all his writing, a considerable travail. Sterling had told Caroline towards the end of February that 'Carlyle is bringing out a thirty-pounder of a book on the Northern troubles,' and six days later she got a letter from the author himself, dwelling distressfully on his labours. Her summary of it is instructive: 'Letter from Carlyle. His present work is one that makes him sad and sickly. It is likely to be ready in about three weeks, and then he expects to be ready for the hospital. He says that John Sterling was the first to tell him that his tendencies were political, a prophecy which he feels is now being strangely verified. Terrible as it is to him to pronounce the words which he does, he feels that those and no others are given him to speak; he sees some twenty thousand in pauper-Bastilles looking for a Voice, inarticulately beseeching "Speak for us," and can he be silent? His book is on the sorrows in the North, and will probably consist of the Facts of the French Revolution connected with his theory of the present misgovernment of England.' Just a month later Sterling got back to Falmouth from a visit to London and gave the latest intelligence regarding the state of temperament at Cheyne Row. 'Carlyle,' he reported, 'very unhappy about the times, thinking everything as bad as ever, and conducted on the least-happiness-for-the-greatest-number principle; the only thing good is that people are made to feel unhappy, and so prove that enjoyment is not the object of life.'

Past and Present duly appeared, and by August Caroline was in a position to record her verdict on it. 'Finished that wondrous *Past and Present*,' she wrote, 'and felt a hearty blessing on the gifted Author spring up in my soul. It is a book which teaches you that there are other months besides May, but that with Courage, Faith, Energy and Constancy no

December can be "impossible."' She was no doubt looking
forward to expressing her appreciation of the volume to Carlyle
himself when she called at Cheyne Row at the end of October
in the course of a visit to Norwich and London. But the great
moralist, as Lord Houghton calls him, was invisible. He was
not away. In fact, he had just come back from a post-travail
trip to Wales and Scotland. Mrs Carlyle's observations on his
return perhaps explain his non-appearance to greet even so
habitually welcome a visitor as Caroline. 'Carlyle,' wrote
Jane Carlyle to her sister, 'returned from his travels very
bilious, and continues very bilious up to this hour. The amount
of bile he does bring home to me in these cases is something
"awfully grand."' In his absence Jane herself entertained
Caroline, who speaks of her as 'very brilliant, dotting off, with
little reserve, characters and circumstances with a marvellous
perception of what was really significant and effective in them,
so that every word told.' Of Carlyle she gave the kind of
report that was to be expected. He 'has to take a journey
always after writing a book, and then gets so weary with knocking about that he has to write another book to recover from it.
When the books are done they know little or nothing of them,
but she judges, from the frequent adoption of some of his
phrases in the books of the day, that they are telling in the
land.'

That diagnosis found decisive confirmation on Caroline's
next visit to Chelsea, in May 1844 (after another letter, in
January, on the subject of Verran). This time the affliction
was Oliver Cromwell. The wrestler with Cromwell was ill,
and asleep on a sofa. Awakened, he was told of the engagement
of Caroline's brother Barclay and braced himself to the coinage
of an appropriate felicitation, which took the form of the
comment, 'Well, they must club together all the good sense
they've got between them; that's the way, I suppose.' Then
to the subject of the moment. 'He groaned over Oliver
Cromwell, for his progress in that memorial is slow and painful:

all that had been said or written in his favour was destroyed or ignored when Charles II came to reign; as a Calvinistic Christian he was despised, and as a Ruler and Regicide he was hated; the people would not forgive him for having seemed to deceive them, and so they dug up his body and hanged it at Tyburn, and have been telling the most abominable lies about him ever since; lately there had been some better feeling, but the case was still very bad.' 'Upon the whole,' he summed up, 'I don't believe a truer, more right-hearted Englishman than Oliver ever existed. Wherever you find a line of his own writing you may be sure to find nothing but truth there.' There followed a general conversation on the resemblance between Cromwell and Francia, the lately deceased dictator of Paraguay. The comparison is of limited interest today, when Dr Francia means less than nothing to anyone, but Caroline's obvious capacity to hold her own in the discussion is one of the not very frequent demonstrations in her Journal that though she wrote little about the public events of the day she kept herself quite adequately posted in them.

The year 1845 was, as already indicated, a time of deep oppression of spirit for Caroline. Her Journal for that year, as published, fills less than three printed pages, and there is no entry later than June 12th. There is no evidence that she left home that year at all, and her only contact with Carlyle was through the pages of his *Wilhelm Meister*—if, indeed, it was his; Caroline may have read it in the original, but all the probabilities are that it was in Carlyle's translation, a second edition of which had appeared in 1839. Her appreciation of it need not be quoted here, for it concerns Goethe the author, not Carlyle the translator.

In 1846 the Foxes went up for Yearly Meeting as usual, and Caroline again made her way to Cheyne Row. The day before she went there she called on F. D. Maurice and took note of his dictum that Emerson possessed much reverence and little humility; 'in this he greatly differs from Carlyle.' Carlyle himself she found just getting over Cromwell. 'He looks thin but well, and is recovering from the torment of the sixty new Cromwell letters: he does not mean to take in any more fresh ones on any terms. He showed us his miniature portrait of Cromwell, and talked of the fine cast of him which Samuel Laurence has. Carlyle says it is evidently a man of that Age, a man of power and of high soul, and in some particulars so like the miniature that artists don't hesitate to call it Cromwell.' Then the conversation took other turns. The Fox sisters said they were hoping to go to Switzerland, with the idea that their brother Barclay should get fat there. The reaction to that was characteristic. 'This,' remarks Caroline, 'he thinks exceedingly unnecessary: "It's not a world for people to grow fat in."'

One of the talks of 1842 had included in its content some facts about *Sartor Resartus* and Carlyle's childhood. The same combination reappeared now, this time at Carlyle's instance, not Caroline's. For some reason not specified 'he spoke of his first vision of the Sea, the Solway Firth, when he was a little fellow eighteen inches high: he remembers being terrified at it all, and wondering what it was about, rolling in its great waves; he saw two black things, probably boats, and thought they were the Tide of which he had heard so much. But in the midst of his reverie an old woman stripped him naked and plunged him in, which completely cured him of his speculations. If anyone had but raised him six feet above the surface there might have been a chance of his getting some general impression, but at the height of eighteen inches he could find out little but that it was wet.'

The clothes-philosophy came in through the author of *Sartor Resartus*, who was always interested in Friends, asking about Yearly Meeting and the question of Friends' dress. 'I told him,' says Caroline, 'that the Clothes-Religion was still extant; he rather defended it as symbolising many other things, though of course agreeing on its poverty as a test. He said "I have often wished I could get any people to join me in dressing in a rational way. In the first place, I would have nothing to do with a hat; I would kick it into the Serpentine, and wear some kind of cap or straw covering. Then, instead of these layers of coats one over the other, I would have a light waistcoat to lace behind because buttoning would be difficult; and over all a blouse"—*ecce* Thomas Carlyle.' Judging by the punctuation the last three words represent Caroline's comment; they might as well be the speaker's climax. The conversation, it may be noted, took place in June; the attire-reformer seems rather to have overlooked the vagaries of December.

The record of the 1847 visit gives more space to Jane Carlyle's observations than to her husband's. Gloom was upon her too this time. She had been very ill, and had strange stories to tell about the experiences an opiate had induced. The doctors, she told Caroline, gave her opium and tartar for her cough, which resulted, not in beautiful dreams and visions but in a horrible sensation of turning to marble herself and lying on marble, her hair, her arms and her whole person petrifying and adhering to the marble slab on which she lay. One night it was a tombstone—one in Scotland which she knew well. She lay along it with a graver in her hand, carving her own epitaph under another which she read and knew by heart. It was her mother's. She felt utterly distinct from this prostrate figure, and thought of her with pity and love, looked at distant passages of her life and moralised as on a familiar friend. It was more like madness than anything else she had ever experienced. 'After all,' she said, 'I often wonder what right I have to live at all.'

This was sombre talk, and there was a little more of it, but then Mrs Carlyle turned to her husband's activities—or rather to the absence of them, for he was, she said, not writing at the moment but resting, reading English history and disagreeing with the age. She spoke of M. F—, an American transcendentalist, who had come to London with an enthusiasm for Carlyle. (Whether it was Caroline or her editor who felt it requisite thus to veil the lady's identity is not to be determined;

she was clearly Margaret Fuller,[1] Emerson's ardent friend, who for a time edited his paper, *The Dial*.) Mention of her inevitably brought Emerson into the conversation. But Jane Carlyle, according to Caroline, 'does not see that much good is to come of Emerson's writings and grants that they are arrogant and shortcoming.' Very differently had Sterling taught Caroline to think of the essayist.

At this point Mrs Carlyle took to reminiscence. 'She talked of her own life and the mistake of over-educating people. She believes that her health has been injured for life by beginning Latin with a little tutor at five or six years old, then going to the Rector's school to continue it, then having a tutor at home, and being very ambitious she learned eagerly. Irving being her tutor, and of equally excitable intellect, was delighted to push her through every study; then he introduced her to Carlyle, and for years they had a literary intimacy, and she would be writing constantly and consulting him about everything, "and so it would probably always have gone on, for we were both of us made for independence, and I believe should never have wanted to live together, but this intimacy was not considered discreet, so we married quietly and departed." ' This calm and very sensible reference to their marriage relations concealed wounded feelings of which Caroline probably knew nothing, for eighteen months earlier Carlyle had met Lady Ashburton—Harriet Baring—for the first time, and his undisguised admiration for her introduced into the Carlyle household a strain which lasted till Lady Ashburton's death in 1857.

Next came a lively digression on that curious personality Geraldine Jewsbury, remembered, when the novels she wrote are long forgotten, as a friend of both the Carlyles. ('The most intimate Friend I have in the world,' Jane Carlyle wrote in 1854.) Some of her memories of Mrs Carlyle will be found

[1] Carlyle's own description of her has its merits : 'Yesternight there came a bevy of Americans from Emerson, one Margaret Fuller the chief figure of them, a strange, lilting, lean old maid, not nearly such a bore as I expected.'

embedded in Carlyle's paper on his wife which made the publication of his posthumous work *Reminiscences* by Froude the centre of an impassioned controversy, but they are followed by a note by Carlyle himself indicating that few of the stories she tells are completely correct and that 'on the whole, all tends to the *mythical*.' Be that as it may, Carlyle had a warm regard for Miss Jewsbury, and so had his wife, but the portrait Mrs Carlyle drew of her for Caroline, though it does not directly call her reliability in question, makes Carlyle's subsequent strictures on her completely intelligible. Caroline thus summarises: 'Talked of her brilliant little friend Zoe (Miss Jewsbury), who declares herself born without any sense of decency: the publishers beg she will be decent, and she has not the slightest objection to be so, but she does not know what it is; she implores Mrs Carlyle to take any quantity of spotted muslin and clothe her figures for her, for she does not know which are naked. She is a very witty little thing, full of emotions, which overflow on all occasions; her sister, the poetess, tried to bring them into young-ladylike order, and checked her ardent demonstrations of affection in society and elsewhere. The sister died, so did the parents, and this wild creature was thrown on the world, which hurled her back upon herself. She read insatiably and at random in an old library, alchemy, physiology and what not, and undraped "Zoe" is the result.' On the whole a not unattractive characterisation, for a writer who does not know what decency is must be incapable of being intentionally indecent.

At this point Carlyle 'wandered down to tea looking dusky and aggrieved at having to live in such a generation.' However, he greeted his visitors cordially and began to talk about Thomas Erskine of Linlathen, a friend of both the Carlyles, Edward Irving, Dr John Brown and various other persons of interest in the literary or religious world. Mrs Carlyle said, 'He always soothes me, for he looks so serene, as if he had found peace. He and the Calvinistic views are quite unsuited to each other.'

Carlyle agreed: 'Why, yes; it has been well with him since he became a Christian.' (There is no evidence that he was ever anything else.) This tribute seemed to call for an antidote, and 'we had such a string of tirades that it was natural to ask "Who *has* ever done any good in the world?"' The reply may perhaps be taken as a graceful tribute to Caroline's Quakerism. 'Why, there was one George Fox; he did some little good. He walked up to a man and said "My fat-faced friend, thou art a damned lie. Thou art pretending to serve God Almighty, and art really serving the devil. Come out of that, or perish to all eternity."' That congenial quotation served to open the sluices. The moral had to be pointed, and it was pointed with zest. Fox's denunciations were needed in other days than his. 'This—ay, and stronger language too—had he to say to his generation, and we must say it to ours in such fashion as we can. It is the one thing that *must* be said; the one thing that each must find out for himself is that he is really on the right side of the fathomless abyss, serving God heartily and authorised to speak in His name to others.'

The prophet warmed to his theme. 'Tolerance and a rose-water world,' he affirmed, 'is the evil symptom of the time we are living in; it was just like it before the French Revolution, with one hundred and fifty a day butchered—the gutters thick with blood, and the skins tanned into leather—and so it will be here unless a righteous intolerance of the devil should awake in time. Utter intolerance of ourselves must be the first step—years of conflict, of agony—before it comes out clearly that you have a warrant from God to proclaim that lies shall not last, and to run them through or blow them into atoms. 'Tis not, truly, an easy world to live in, with all going wrong. The next book I write must be about this same tolerance, this playing into the hands of God and the devil—to the devil with it.'

Then, to close, back for a moment to the question he started from. 'Another man who did some good was Columbus, who fished up the island of America from the bottom of the sea; and Caxton—he too did something for us; indeed all who do faithfully whatever in them lies do something for the Universe.' That sounded an encouraging note to end on, but no extensive optimism could be inferred from it. Caroline indeed sounds a warning against any such assumption. 'He is as much as ever at war with all the comfortable classes,' she insists (not failing, no doubt, to reflect that it was to those classes that she belonged herself), 'and can hardly connect good with anything that is not dashed into visibility on an element of strife.' There the report of the conversation ends. The Foxes had to go. Not content with seeing them off on the doorstep, he got into the fly and drove to Sloane Square with them, 'talking with energetic melancholy to the last.' Caroline knew how to choose her words. What could express Carlyle's disposition better than 'energetic melancholy'?

That was in May 1847. In July Carlyle wrote Caroline a singularly interesting letter, to which, rather surprisingly, she makes no reference in her Journal. I am indebted to the Rt. Hon. Isaac Foot, who acquired the original from a member of the Sterling family, for permission to quote from it. Caroline, it is evident, had sent Carlyle a Cromwell medal, which he hailed with great enthusiasm. How it reached her is not explained, but it would appear that she was simply an intermediary, and that Carlyle was really indebted to 'the Dillwyns.' This, it must be assumed, refers to the family of Lewis Weston Dillwyn, who was born and brought up a Friend (which would account for Caroline's acquaintance with him), settled at Swansea in 1803 and became Member of Parliament for Glamorgan in 1832. At any rate Carlyle wrote:

'CHELSEA,
14*th July* 1847.

'DEAR MISS CAROLINE,—I am greatly delighted with my Cromwell Medal, which arrived safe yesterday, and had a warm welcome from me. It is an excellent likeness—much resembles the best Bust I know of Oliver, and the Mask of his dead Face too;—and I doubt not it is by Symons, and in addition to its other worth to me, deserves the best praises from judges of art. Many thanks to you and to your kind friends the Dillwyns, who have also been kind friends of mine on this occasion. I have sent the Piece to be carefully framed under glass; with a fit historical label pasted on the back of it; and shall often thankfully remember you all, as the brave old Face looks out at me from its place here.'

Then follows a discussion regarding the identity of the original owner of the medal (one Nicol, Nichols or Nickol), which is of no special interest except for the suggestion that he might have been one of the celebrated 'Eleven Members' and have sat for Bodmin in Caroline's own county. 'If,' added Cromwell's editor, 'it should turn out that one of the Eleven had been appointed by the Destinies to bequeath a Medal of Oliver to me, in two centuries' time, I might reckon it rather a droll turn of things!'

The letter ends with a half-apology for the vehemence of the monologue at Chelsea during Caroline's visit there in May: 'You would not find me always such an "Apostle of Intolerance" as you did on that wet night, with a dull party lying ahead, and the hackney-coachman lost! At least the opposite side too, if I say less of it, lies present with me in the mute state. But I do confess myself sick of all this sugary twaddle, and mawkish, slavish, *godless* confusion of Good and Evil,—and find *Hudson's Testimonial* more connected with *Howard's* and *Douglas Jerrold's* than you would imagine;—and indeed know always how it is that a good man has to bring "not peace into this world but a sword,"—not to *his* joy, I suppose.'

The medal discussion had better be pursued to its close. Before Caroline saw Carlyle again she got another letter from him on the subject—dated February 28th, 1849. She does briefly mention this in the Journal, but only for a reference in its opening paragraph to the Cornish sculptor Burnard. Of much greater interest is the latter part, reporting discoveries about the origin of the medal. 'At this hour, as it happens,' Carlyle writes, 'I have come upon your Swansea Medallion of Cromwell again; concerning which I have long intended asking you another little question. Namely, what is the *reverse* of the Medallion? Has it any chance to be the *Medal* of the Dunbar Battle; which is said to be somewhere in existence yet? On the whole, what is on the reverse;—what other indications of any kind are there?

'Of the original proprietor, "Colonel Nicholls," I imagine, I long since came upon a track; and (as above hinted) I am at his name this very day, muddling along at a third edition of *C's Letters and Speeches*. "Captain Nicholas, who is at Chepstow" (17 June 1648), he is twice mentioned in a letter of C's (I 350-1, 2nd edition) and him I believe to be the man—or dimly strive to believe, having never heard of him otherwise than there, and at Swansea in reference to a certain Miss Caroline Fox, once a visitor of that town. Captain Nicholas, I will guess, became Colonel Nicholas in the course of 7 years and left that Medal to the said Miss Caroline— who is hereby requested to inform me with all brevity and precision what is on the *reverse* of the same.

'Miss Caroline's sincere friend, T. Carlyle.'

The last few lines are by no means clear. What seems to be meant is that Caroline, when on a visit to Swansea (of which there is nowhere any record),[1] secured the medal, presumably from Mr Dillwyn, who was a person of considerable importance there. The suggestion that the seventeenth-century Colonel Nicholas 'left that Medal to the said Miss Caroline'

[1] Barclay Fox, however, mentions that in June 1847 Robert Were Fox met ' the femininity ' of his family at Bristol on their way home from Yearly Meeting, and took them with him to Briton Ferry, where he had business ; this town is within about ten miles of Swansea, where alone suitable hotels were likely to be found. Carlyle's reference to ' your Swansea Medallion ' establishes the link with Dillwyn. He received the medal on July 13th. So the pieces fall into place.

would in that case be merely Carlylean for 'left that Medal, which ultimately came into the said Miss Caroline's hands.' However that may be, what seems to be established is that Caroline was the means of conveying to Carlyle a Cromwell relic to which he attached great value. (The medal, I may add, is now, like the letters referring to it, in Mr Isaac Foot's possession in Cornwall.)

This letter reached Caroline at the beginning of March 1849. In May she once more made her biennial journey to London, Yearly Meeting and Cheyne Row. 'Steamed to Chelsea,' she writes on June 13th [Steamed from where? There is no means of knowing. Caroline never mentions where the family stayed when they came to London. It is no great matter, but it would have been interesting to know. However, steam to Chelsea she did on that particular June day], and 'paid Mrs Carlyle a humane little visit.' Mrs Carlyle, because this time Carlyle did not appear at all. Caroline does not say why. He spent most of that summer in Ireland, but he did not start on that adventure till the end of June. He may, of course, well enough have been out—perhaps at the London Library, which he played so large a part in founding a few years before. Anyhow, this visit was to Jane Carlyle only, and it was a humane little visit because 'I don't think she roasted a single soul, or even body.' She talked in rather a melancholy way of herself and of life in general, 'professing that it was only the Faith that all things are well put together—which all sensible people *must* believe—that prevents our sending to the nearest chemist's shop for sixpennyworth of arsenic; but now one just endures while it lasts, and that is all we can do.'

That was a subject which Jane Carlyle sometimes treated in lighter vein. 'We are in the gloomy month of November,' she had written eighteen months before to John Forster, 'when the people of England "commit suicide" under "attenuating circumstances." The expediency, nay necessity, of suiciding myself is no longer a question with me. I am only uncertain as to the manner.' But this time she seems to have been almost half serious. Caroline, not quite so seriously, 'said a few modest words in honour of existence,' which Jane answered by objecting that 'I can't enjoy Joy, as Henry Taylor (the author of *Philip van Artevelde*) says. He, however, cured this incapacity of his by taking to himself a bright little wife, who first came to him in the way of consolation but has now become real simple Joy.' Caroline makes no comment on this remark, and not too much must be read into it. But that Jane Carlyle was in her own mind contrasting Taylor's married happiness with the relationship at Cheyne Row cannot be doubted. There may or may not have been good reason for her feelings regarding Carlyle and Lady Ashburton, but their existence is not in question. Some four months after this conversation with Caroline, Mrs Carlyle was writing to her sister-in-law Jane Aitken, 'there is no change in me, so far as affection goes, depend upon that. But there are other changes, which give me the look of a very cold and hard woman generally. . . . I think it not likely, if I live, that I will be long of returning to Scotland. All that true, simple, pious kindness that I found stored up for me there ought to be turned to more account in my life. What have I more precious?' In later years she expressed herself more explicitly.

The Carlyles were both being painted. 'Carlyle,' Caroline mentions, 'is sitting now to a portrait-painter, and Samuel Laurence [who drew Caroline herself] has been drawing her; she bargained with him at starting not to treat the subject as an Italian artist had done, and make her a something between a St Cecilia and an improper female. She caught a glimpse of her own profile the other day, and it gave her a great start, it looked such a gloomy headachy creature. Laurence she likes vastly, thinking that he alone of artists has a fund of unrealised ideas; Richmond has produced his, but with Laurence there is more kept back than what is given. She talked with much affection and gratitude of W. E. Forster, and cannot understand his not marrying; remarking "I think he's the sort of person that would have suited me very well." ' Forster himself—author of the Education Bill of 1870—may have been rather of the same mind. The very next month, when Jane Carlyle was travelling from Rawdon, near Bradford, to Kirkcaldy, he insisted on going all the way to Morpeth with her, staying there the night and seeing her safe into the Kirkcaldy train. However, a year later he married a daughter of Arnold of Rugby.

About the last subject discussed before Caroline left there is a good deal to be said. Jane Carlyle, says Caroline, 'talked of the Sterling Memoir by Julius Hare, and of Captain Sterling's literary designs: in these her husband means to take no part; he would, by doing so, get into a controversy which he would sooner avoid: had he undertaken the matter at the beginning he would have been very short and avoided religious questions altogether.' This, be it noted, was in June 1849. Sterling, who had died in September 1844, had made Archdeacon Hare, his old Cambridge tutor, with whom he had worked as a curate at Hurstmonceux, in Sussex, and Carlyle his literary executors. They, as Carlyle subsequently explained, had agreed that the preparation of the writings Sterling had left, and the writing of a Memoir to be prefixed to them, should be left to one pair of hands, and that those hands should be Hare's. He accordingly published, at the beginning of 1848, two volumes of Sterling's *Essays and Tales*, with a biography running to 230 pages.[1] Now it was pretty obvious, certainly very obvious to Caroline Fox, that a Life of Sterling by Hare would not please Carlyle and a Life by Carlyle would not please Hare. The Life by Hare did not, in fact, please Sterling's family. In January 1848 Mrs Carlyle, writing to Carlyle at Alverstoke (the home of the Ashburtons, then still Barings), says, 'here is Hare's Sterling book come for you, and "with the publisher's compliments."

[1] Caroline occupied a June day in 1847 in putting her recollections of Sterling on paper for Hare.

No copy had been sent to Anthony when I saw him; he had bought it, and said if you did not feel yourself bound to place his brother in a true light, he must attempt it himself.' That, no doubt, explains Jane Carlyle's remark to Caroline that Carlyle means to take no part in Captain Sterling's [this was Sterling's father] literary designs, which were clearly what Sterling's brother Anthony had foreshadowed when the Hare Memoir came out—the publication of another Life of Sterling either by Carlyle or, failing that, by the family themselves.

Into that controversy we need not enter except in so far as it affects Caroline or is illuminated by her Journal. There is no doubt where her sympathies lay—not unnaturally. What Carlyle objected to in Hare's work was the emphasis laid on Sterling's religious life and its difficulties, Carlyle himself preferring to depict his friend as emancipated from bondage to religious orthodoxy. Caroline supported Hare from first to last, and on one point she provides a useful piece of evidence. Hare represents Sterling as having given up his curacy for reasons of health, Carlyle attributes it to reasons of belief—or difficulties about belief. Caroline, recording in 1840 a conversation with Sterling, says explicitly that his work as Hare's curate 'continued but seven months, when his health drove him from the active duties of life.' In December 1847 she received a 'long letter from Julius Hare detailing difficulties in the Sterling Memoir, which we had foreseen and could well enter into. He seems almost forced to publish more than he would wish in order to leave Mill and Carlyle no pretext for an opposition portrait.' Seven or eight weeks later the book itself arrived, and she gave it unqualified approval. 'The portrait,' she wrote, 'is very unsatisfactory, the volumes full of exquisite interest, though of a very mixed kind. Julius Hare has, I believe, done his part admirably well.' But had he succeeded in disarming Mill and Carlyle? A month after getting Hare's book she hears from Mill's sister Clara 'in answer to my cautious entreaties' [on her brother's then intention of writing a Life of John Sterling]. The entreaties are intelligible enough, for Caroline had long since lost sympathy with Mill's mechanical mind. How far the entreaties weighed with him is unknown, but he did not write a Life of Sterling. Carlyle, as all the world knows, did—in 1851—saying perfectly plainly that his motive was to give a different picture from Hare's. Carlyle's Life is a classic, Hare's is all but forgotten. To discuss their respective merits here would be completely irrelevant. All that is necessary is to record Caroline's verdict on Carlyle's work—a verdict which in one respect, the suggestion that the book would injure Carlyle's reputation, was far wide of the mark.

'Anna Maria,' she writes to her aunt, Mrs Charles Fox, on July 19th, 1851, 'says you wish to see this book (Carlyle's Life of Sterling), so here it is. That it is calculated to draw fresh obloquy on the subject of it is a very secondary consideration to the fact that it is a book likely to do much harm to Carlyle's wide enthusiastic public. It is painful enough to see the memorial of his friend made the text for utterances and innuendoes from which one *knows* that he would now shrink even more than ever, and God alone can limit the mischief. But He can. That the book is often brilliant and beautiful, and more human-hearted than most of Carlyle's, will make it but the more read, however little the world may care for the subject of the memoir. The graphic parts and the portraiture are generally admirable, but not by any means always so; however, you will judge for yourselves.'

What influence the publication of *The Life of John Sterling* had on Caroline's relations with Cheyne Row can only be conjectured, but there is no record of her ever turning her steps thither again. That means almost certainly that she never did turn them thither, for she would not have failed to chronicle a visit, or her editor to include it in the Journal as published. In 1851 she went to London as usual, and stayed there rather longer than usual. The Carlyles were not away.

Mrs Carlyle certainly was not, for Caroline, attending Thackeray's lecture on 'The English Humorists' at Willis's Rooms, mentions Jane and Dickens as among the audience. But there is no record of any talk with her, and no reference during the whole stay in London to Cheyne Row. Was it that Caroline knew that the Sterling Life was impending and, guessing what its character would be, had no desire for contact with its author? Once more that can only be conjectured, but it supplies a better explanation than any other that readily offers.

Jane Carlyle Caroline seems never to have seen again. Carlyle himself she heard of once and saw once. In 1858 George Cook (the author; a Chelsea neighbour) 'had much to tell of the Carlyles. He has just finished two volumes of *Frederick the Great*, which has been a weary work. He seems to grow drearier and drearier; his wife still full of life and power and sympathy, spite of the heavy weight of domestic dyspepsia. Kingsley pays him long visits, and comes away talking just like him: "Why, if a man will give himself over to serve the devil, God will just give him over to his choice to see how he likes it," etc.' The suggestion of Carlyle's influence over Kingsley was not new. In 1850 Jane Carlyle had written to her husband in Scotland: 'There is also come a novel, called *Alton Locke*, which I flung aside in my worry as not readable; but now I hear from Geraldine [Jewsbury], whom the *Athenaeum* has invited to review it, that it is the novel of young Kingsley; and though "too like Carlyle" a production of astounding merit.'

From the day in 1847 when Caroline Fox, not yet quite twenty-eight, had talked to Carlyle for the last time at Cheyne Row about George Fox and he had driven with her, talking all the time, to Sloane Square, to March of 1867, when as a woman of forty-seven she called on the old man of seventy-one at Mentone, a long span of life had passed for both of them. Caroline was in the south of France seeking health, Carlyle seeking escape from misery, for Jane Carlyle had died in the previous year. And the misery, as his own *Reminiscences* show, was not unmixed with remorse. He was staying in the second Lady Ashburton's villa. His old friend, Lord Ashburton's first wife, had died in 1857, and Lord Ashburton himself in 1864, having married a Miss Louisa Caroline Mackenzie in 1858. It was with her that Carlyle was staying. Caroline called on him 'by appointment,' and describes him as she saw him for the first time after twenty years. 'He has a sort of pavilion separate yet attached to the villa, where he may feel independent.[1] Found him alone reading Shakespeare, in a long dressing-gown, a drab comforter wrapped round and round his neck, and a dark blue cap on, for he had a cold. He received us very kindly, but would untwist his comforter, and take off his cap, and comb his shaggy mane in honour of the occasion. He looks thin and aged and sad as Jeremiah, though the red is still bright in his cheek and the blue in his eye, which seems to be set more deeply than ever; there is a grim expression in his face, which looks solemn enough.'

The conversation was, as usual, mainly denunciation. It began with the horrors of the journey from England. 'I should never have come but for Tyndall, who dragged me off by the hair of my head, so to speak, and flung me down here and then went his way. He had better have left me alone with my misery. Pleasures of travelling! In that accursed train, with its devilish howls and yells driving one distracted!' But couldn't he read in the train? Caroline asked mildly. 'Read? No; it's enough for me to reflect on my own misery; they ought to give you chloroform as you are a living creature.' So much on private martyrdoms for a start. Then came public discontents—the condition of England generally and the Reform Bill of that year in particular. 'Oh! this cry for Liberty! Liberty! which is just liberty to do the

[1] In a letter to a friend Caroline is more explicit : ' He has a pavilion quite apart from the house, where he can see his friends and be alone and sulk.'

The Carlyles

Devil's work, instead of binding him with ten thousand bands, just going the way of France and America and those sort of places. Why, it is all going downhill as fast as it can go, and of no significance to me; I have done with it. I can take no interest in it at all, nor feel any sort of hope for the country. It is not the Liberty to keep the Ten Commandments that they are crying out for—that used to be enough for the genuine man—but Liberty to carry on their own prosperity, as they call it, and so there is no longer anything genuine to be found; it is all shoddy. Go into any shop you will and ask for any article, and ye'll find it all one enormous lie. The country is going to perdition at a frightful pace. I give it about fifty years yet to accomplish its fall.'

Anxious to point to one gleam, however fitful, in the prevailing darkness, Caroline mentioned Gladstone. Wasn't he a man of principle? She might have known better than to try. 'Oh! Gladstone! I did hope well of him once, and so did John Sterling, though I heard he was a Puseyite and so forth; still, it seemed the right thing for a State to feel itself bound to God, and to lean on Him, and so I hoped something might come of him; but now he has been declaiming that England is in such a wonderfully prosperous state, meaning that it has plenty of money in its breeches-pockets and plenty of beef in its great ugly belly. But that's not the prosperity we want. And so I say to him "You are not the Life-giver to England; I go my way, you go yours, good morning" (with a most dramatic and final bow).' Caroline tried again. Which times were the most genuine in England? Cromwell's? Henry VIII's? If she thought that opened the door to a touch of cheerfulness she was wrong. 'Why, in each time it seems to me there was something genuine, some endeavour to keep God's commandments. Cromwell's time was only a revival of it. But now [here came the inevitable] things have been going down further and further since George III.'

There was a short interruption through someone coming in.

Then he harked back less gloomily to old days, talking of the
Sterlings and the time when that household was so closely
associated with the Foxes in Cornwall. 'I have always,' he
said, 'a sort of pious feeling about Falmouth and about you
all, and so had she who has gone away from me, for all your
kindness to John Welsh; you couldn't do a greater kindness
than all you did for him and his mother.' After a tribute to
John Welsh's qualities he went on: 'I was once in Falmouth
harbour for two hours in an Irish steamer, and I gave my card
to a respectable-looking seafaring sort of man, who promised
to take it to your late brother. I remember taking a leaf out
of my pocket-book and writing on it my regrets at not being
able to land.' With something almost approaching cheerfulness he spoke of the beauty of the Riviera country and contrasted
its warmth and sunshine and blue sky with the cold and mud
of London.

Caroline and her sister left him, after a word with his hostess
Lady Ashburton. The latter welcomed the Foxes' visit and
expressed satisfaction that he had spoken of anything with
pleasure, for (she added) 'I'm very fond of the old man, and
I did what I thought was for the best, and I really hope he is
the better for it in spite of himself, though sometimes it seems
as if it was altogether a failure.' That was almost the end.
Caroline saw him once more at Mentone, when the talk evidently turned once more on the Falmouth circle. Caroline
thus described it in a letter (dated March 17th, 1867) to
Sterling's daughter Julia, who had settled at Falmouth: 'Mr
Carlyle is gone; we only saw him once more, and then I
thought his "Goodbye" so impressive that it felt like parting,
and when we called again he was gone. I was so interested
to see how the true man came out when he talked of you—
he had been grim in his views on England and things in general,
but then the sympathy and tenderness shone out of him, and
he dwelt on kindred themes in his own noblest spirit. I am
very glad to have seen him again after an interval of many,

many years, though it makes one sad to think of him—his look and most of his talk were so dreary.'

Caroline might well feel that the goodbye betokened a final parting, for Carlyle was seventy-one, and he was alone in the world with no feeling of anything left to live for. It was, it is true, a final parting, but not for the reason that seemed most natural. The woman of forty-seven was dead four years later; the old man lived to finish all six volumes of his *Frederick the Great* and write *Shooting Niagara*—a dirge on the Reform Bill of 1867—and other things in various magazines. It was not till 1881 that, at the age of eighty-five, he passed out of a life which had brought him more of turmoil and conflict than of rest or content.

Chapter VIII
The Case of Michael Verran

Readers of Carlyle's *John Sterling* may perhaps remember a couple of pages devoted to an act of philanthropy directed, or at any rate initiated, from Chelsea, and executed mainly by the agency of Caroline Fox and her sister Anna Maria. Carlyle on the subject is succinct and characteristic, and his summary of the transaction is worth transcribing, as framework for the more detailed account contributed by Caroline:

'One other little event dwells with me, out of those Falmouth times, exact date now forgotten; a pleasant little matter, in which Sterling, and principally the Miss Foxes, bright, cheery young creatures, were concerned; which, for the sake of its human interest, is worth mention. In a certain Cornish mine, said the Newspapers duly specifying it, two miners deep down in the shaft were engaged in putting in a shot for blasting: they had completed their affair, and were about to give the signal for being hoisted up,—one at a time was all their coadjutor at the top could manage, and the second was to kindle the match and then mount with all speed. Now it chanced while they were both still below, one of them thought the match too long; tried to break it shorter, took a couple of stones, a flat and a sharp, to cut it shorter; did cut it of the due length, but, horrible to relate, kindled it at the same time, and both were still below! Both shouted vehemently to the coadjutor at the windlass, both sprang at the basket; the windlass man could not move it with them both. Here was a moment for poor miner Jack and miner Will! Instant horrible death hangs over both—when

Will generously resigns himself: "Go aloft, Jack" and sits
down; "Away; in one minute I shall be in Heaven." Jack
bounds aloft, the explosion instantly follows, bruises his face as
he looks over; he is safe above ground: and poor Will?
Descending eagerly, they find Will too, as if by miracle, buried
under rocks which had arched themselves over him, and little
injured: he too is brought up safe, and all ends joyfully, say
the Newspapers.

'Such a piece of manful promptitude, and salutary human
heroism, was worth investigating. It was investigated; found
to be accurate to the letter,—with this addition and explanation, that Will, an honest, ignorant, good man, entirely given
up to Methodism, had been perfect in the "faith of assurance,"
certain that *he* should get to Heaven if he died, certain that Jack
would not, which had been the ground of his decision in that
great moment;—for the rest, that he much wished to learn
reading and writing, and find some way of life above ground
instead of below. By the aid of the Misses Fox and the rest
of that family, a subscription (modest *Anti*-Hudson testimonial [1])
was raised to this Methodist hero: he emerged into daylight
with fifty pounds in his pocket; did strenuously try, for certain
months, to learn reading and writing; found he could not learn
those arts or either of them; took his money and bought cows
with it, wedding at the same time some religious likely milkmaid; and is, last time I heard of him, a prosperous modest
dairyman, thankful for the upper light and safety from the
wrath to come. Sterling had some hand in this affair: but,
as I said, it was the two young ladies of the family that mainly
did it.'

So, concisely and not quite accurately, Carlyle. Whether
miner Jack was so called by his friends or not, miner Will's
Christian name was Michael, and his surname Verran. The

---

[1] George Hudson (1800-1871), the railway-promoter, was presented with
£20,000 by his admirers, and trenchantly attacked by Carlyle in one of his *Latter-
Day Pamphlets*, entitled ' Hudson's Statue.'

The Case of Michael Verran

mine involved was Caradon, near the Cheesewring, about five miles from Liskeard. As it was, at the same time, fully thirty miles in a straight line from Falmouth, almoning for Carlyle was not quite as simple as it sounded, or as he perhaps imagined. However, let Caroline add a little precision to the record. In view of Carlyle's 'exact date now forgotten' it is useful to have her Journal entry on November 14th, 1842: 'Note from Carlyle begging Sterling to make enquiries about the miner at Caridon [Caroline always spells it thus], who so heroically devoted himself to the saving of his comrade, and suggesting whether anything, and what sort of thing, might be done for him. "At all events," he says, "let me know whether there is one other such brave true workman living and working with me at this time on this earth; there is help and profit in being sure of it."'

Someone, whether Sterling or Caroline herself, must have set enquiry effectively on foot, for only five days later she is able to note: 'Heard that the Caridon miner, Verran, is saving up his money till he has got £30 or £40, in order to leave off work and get six months' learning—a good fact.' A month later, on December 17th (Verran, it may be hoped, having employed the interval in continued saving for learning), another communication from Carlyle arrived. 'John Sterling,' Caroline wrote, 'brought a letter from Carlyle, written in the spirit of his *Essay on Burns*, together with the following petition

"To Michael Verran, seemingly a right brave man, and highly worthy of being educated, these small gifts of money, if they can assist him therein, are, with all hopefulness and good regard, presented by certain undersigned fellow-wayfarers and warfarers of his."'

Verran, 'this same most meritorious Verran,' has already put us in his debt as the *causa causans* of a flow of characteristically Carlylean English. And there is more to come, more than need be reproduced textually here. Caroline, to her gratification, got two letters from Chelsea in quick succession. The first, after a little heavy by-play about the use of 'thou,' goes on in regard to Verran: 'We are not to neglect such when they offer themselves among the half or wholly useless things so enormously copious among us.' Three days later there reached Rosehill this:

'DEAR CAROLINE,—Thanks for your excellent news. We will not scold the poor fellow much, at least not till he get fully well again.[1] As to the Hero Verran, I wish you to understand that, at such a distance, and with such friends' eyes close on the very scene, I cannot presume to form any farther judgement of his interests, but will leave them altogether to the heads and hearts of said friends. Do, therefore, what seems to *you* wisest. Perhaps if there be, as it seems there is, in Verran's personal neighbourhood a good discerning man who will take charge of this £20, to do his best therewith for the poor miner's behoof, it will be wiser in many ways to give it up to that man at once and for altogether; saying merely, "Do thy best with it for him." Verran may thus gain another friend and occasional guide and patron, which may be worth more to him than several guineas. "Twenty," I think, is no bad result. To find twenty persons in any locality, who reverence worth to the extent of paying one pound sterling for it, is verily something in these days. Days (as I sometimes feel, when I reflect sorrowfully on them) altogether unexampled since the creation of the world in that respect! Even the fickle Athenians did at least put Socrates to death, had at least the grace to hate him, did not merely seek to amuse themselves with him! It is unutterable, and will lead to conclusions by and by.

Meanwhile, what the good Caroline has to do is happily utterable enough; not abstruse or fearful at all! What I have to do is also alas! too plain: namely to go about my business, and, with many wishes and salutations, vanish, as one in haste

[1] This clearly refers to Sterling.

and double haste,—subscribing myself cordially once more, Caroline's friend,   T. CARLYLE.'

Here, then, was responsibility for Verran well settled on Caroline's youthful shoulders,—unless indeed she could discover 'a good discerning man' better placed geographically to take it over. The pious miner's financial resources, meanwhile, are not exactly assessable, Carlyle's various figures not all quite tallying. That, however, is of little consequence. What was of consequence was that the good discerning man—one, moreover, with a capable and co-operative daughter—had been opportunely discovered, and from the latter Caroline gets a report on January 21st. 'Fanny Allen,' she writes, 'sends a very interesting account of a visit she and her father [the Allens were Liskcard Friends, and therefore within easy distance of Caradon mine] paid to Michael Verran. He is a thorough Methodist, who sometimes feels so full of joy that his skin seems too small for him, and he is obliged to lie down and pray that he may be enlarged, to make room for his bursting happiness. He gave a simple, quiet account of the Caridon affair, during which, it seems, his mind was so full of the prospect of being so soon with his Saviour that the idea of death and its suffering hardly occurred to him; and on coming to the surface he fell down on his knees in the shed and "gave glory." He is not getting on very brilliantly at school, but is steady and persevering, and means to be a dairyman or an ore-dresser.'

Three weeks later, on February 11th, comes still more authentic information, the testimony of the beneficiary himself. 'Strong Methodist letter from Michael Verran,' Caroline writes, 'very grateful to God and man. Three years ago he found peace, a month later he received the second blessing, and the day following the third; his path is now like that of the Just, shining brighter and brighter to the perfect day. He finds spelling "asier than at first, and has got to the Rule of Three in refimatic." ' This was indeed progress, and through that year the miner-agriculturist apparently prospered, for on January 9th, 1844, after eleven months' silence, Fanny Allen forwards (presumably from Liskeard) 'a glorious letter from Verran. He says, "I have three cows, three slip pigs; I've plenty of grass, and a good sale for butter and cream. I've the pleasure to tell you that I've also got a wife, and my wedding-day was yesterday."'

Three cows, three pigs and a wife—this was not news to keep to Falmouth, and Caroline must have hastened to transmit the intelligence to Cheyne Row, for after the remarkably short interval of a week (if the dates are right; I find it hard to believe that Caroline could be in a position to enter in her Journal on January 16th a letter dated Chelsea January 15th) a reply reaches Rosehill.

'DEAR MISS CAROLINE,' it runs, 'Your message is far from an intrusion; such a musical little voice coming out of the remote West, in these dull days, is not unwelcome to me, is rather apt to be too welcome! For undue praise is the poison of human souls: he that would live healthily, let him learn to go along entirely without praise. Sincere praises, coming in a musical voice in dull times, how is one to guard against them?

I like Verran's picture of himself somewhat better this time. It is good that he has got a wife: his manner of announcing that great fact, too, is very original! "Four cows, with plenty of grass, three slip pigs." What are slip pigs? Pigs that have slipt or left their dam, and now feed on spoon-meat?[1] All these things are good. On the whole it was a benefit to lift this poor man out of the dark subterranean regions into the upper daylight, to the sight of the sky and green world. But it was not I mainly; no, it was another than I. The poor man, if well let alone, will, I think, now do well. Well let alone;

---

[1] Carlyle was not far wrong. Slip pigs in Cornwall today are young pigs from the age of ten to twelve weeks, until they weigh about 1 cwt.

The Case of Michael Verran

it is an invaluable rule in many things—apt to be miserably forgotten in the case of Grace Darlings and suchlike!

By the by, ought not you, with your swift, neat pen, to draw up, on half a sheet of paper, an exact narrative of this man's act of heroism—authentic, exact in every detail of it—and reposit it in some safe place for a memorial of the same? There is no more geniune use that the art of writing can be turned to than the like of this. Think of it.'

Caroline may have thought of it, but there is no indication that she did it,—unless indeed Carlyle's own subsequent account of the matter in his *John Sterling* had a half-sheet by Caroline as basis. And of that there is no evidence. There is, indeed, a slightly different version to record. John Allen, who published a history of Liskeard in 1856, and was a relative, I fancy a brother, of the Fanny Allen who had been keeping Caroline informed regarding Verran, remarks in that work a little severely that the story has been incorrectly related by Carlyle, but the details he himself gives leave the facts much as they were. Those concerned about sectarian distinctions may be glad to know that Verran was not merely a Methodist—a generic term in those days—but a Bryanite, or follower of William O'Bryan, founder of the Bible Christians, who flourished mainly in Devon and Cornwall; while any who set store by financial accuracy will note that according to John Allen the thrifty miner had £50 laid by, and was presented with a like sum by his well-wishers. 'Marrying respectably, he opened a dairy at Callington, which he still continues, and is much esteemed.' That was in 1856.

Thus in the moment of prosperity—for what more is necessary to human happiness than three cows, three pigs and 'a religious likely milkmaid to wife'?—Michael Verran vanishes from history. It would be pleasant to believe that his flocks and his herds multiplied and that his milkmaid wife was to him as a fruitful vine. And there is no reason why that should not be believed, even if there is no reason why it should.[1]   At any rate, Verran served his turn in prompting the first letter Caroline ever received from Carlyle, and beginning the conversion of her acquaintance with him into firm friendship.

[1] Verran apparently lived at Callington for some nineteen years, for he was buried there in June 1862.   His wife, whose Christian name the gravestone shows to have been Ann, survived him by fifteen years.

Chapter IX
John Stuart Mill

Through her acquaintance with Carlyle and John Sterling Caroline would have been certain to meet John Stuart Mill sooner or later, for Sterling, Mill and Carlyle were all closely associated. Mill, as he told Caroline in 1840, first came in contact with Sterling in the course of 'a hard fight at the Debating Society at Cambridge,' when Mill appeared as a Benthamite and Sterling as a Mystic —a statement which seems to need some explanation, for Mill was never a member of the University; it may be that he had been invited to take part in a debate at the Union or some other society; he had certainly visited Cambridge in 1822 as guest of Charles Austin (younger brother of the jurist), whom Mill describes as 'the really influential mind among the intellectual gladiators' at the Union. At any rate, Mill and Sterling did get to know one another, and some years later, in 1831, Mill first spoke of Sterling to Carlyle, to whom a couple of years later he sent a copy of Sterling's novel *Arthur Coningsby*, finally introducing novelist and sage to each other in the flesh at the India House in 1835. The beginning of the Mill-Carlyle friendship is described by Mill in his *Autobiography*. Early in 1831, he mentions, he was contributing to the *Examiner* a series of articles on 'The Spirit of the Age,' of which he observes: 'The only effect which I know to have been produced by them was that Carlyle, then living in a secluded part of Scotland, read them in his solitude, and saying to himself (as he afterwards told me) "Here is a new Mystic," enquired, on coming to London that autumn, concerning their authorship, an enquiry which was the immediate cause of our becoming personally acquainted.' In the Cambridge debate, it will be noted, it was Sterling who had figured as the Mystic; now, in Carlyle's view, Mill is the same—which goes some way towards confirming Mill's statement to Caroline that since their first meeting he and Sterling 'have more and more approximated.'

Actually it was through no offices of a common friend that Caroline first met John Mill. His younger brother Henry, who was dying of consumption, had gone to Falmouth, like so many invalids before and since, in the hope of postponing for a little the inevitable end. His sister Clara was nursing him, and it was characteristic that the Fox family should offer sympathy and help. In March 1840, when Henry Mill was obviously sinking, John came to Falmouth, and on the 16th of that month Clara took him to see the Foxes. He was then thirty-three, and Caroline, who was twenty, was at once impressed by him. 'He is a very uncommon-looking person,' she wrote in her Journal for that day, '—much acuteness and sensibility marked in his exquisitely-chiselled countenance, more resembling a portrait of Lavater than any other that I remember. His voice is refinement itself, and his mode of expressing himself tallies with voice and countenance.'

Mill at this time held a considerable position (with a salary of £1200 a year) at the India House, with which his father, James Mill, had long been associated. He was prominent as an exponent of the Benthamite philosophy, and though none of his more important works had yet been published he was a voluminous contributor on philosophic and political subjects to the reviews, particularly the *Westminster*. When the *London Review* amalgamated with the *Westminster*, under the title *The London and Westminster Review*, in 1836 Mill became its editor, but abandoned the position in 1840. He was in that year still unmarried, but his close friendship with Mrs Taylor, who became his wife in 1851, was already of ten years' standing.

There is no indication in the Journal that he spoke of it to Caroline. Her own relationship with Mill was curious. Meeting him for the first time in March 1840, she devotes more pages to him in the ten weeks between that date and the end of May than during all the rest of their acquaintance, which in fact seems to have ended in 1846 so far as personal contact was concerned, though there are references to Mill in the Journal down to 1859. A warm friendship seems gradually, for whatever reasons, to have cooled. Whether Caroline or Mill was chiefly responsible for that can hardly be decided, but it may be noted that much the same thing happened to the relationship between Mill and Carlyle. Mill, Carlyle wrote in an introduction to Jane Carlyle's Letters, 'had taken a great attachment to me, which lasted about ten years and then suddenly ended, I never knew how.' In the first instance there was a good deal to draw Caroline and Mill together— their common friendship with Sterling, the interest which Mill already took in the Society of Friends, Caroline's natural sympathy with him in his anxiety about his brother's condition and his no less natural gratitude to Caroline and her family for their thoughtful kindness to the invalid. And since Mill was a good talker and Caroline a good chronicler, and Sterling was also at Falmouth, those ten spring weeks of 1840 added substantially to the Journal's volume.

Mill and Caroline established an easy and natural friendship from the first, and the young Quakeress clearly awakened the economist-philosopher's interest. On the second day of their acquaintance he told her to let him know of any autographs she wanted, as he had great facilities for getting them. 'Today,' Caroline adds, in recording this agreeable offer, 'he was to have met Guizot at the Grotes',' the implication no doubt being that here were two trophies readily available if desired. A fortnight later Caroline makes an entry which serves to recall Mill's wide knowledge of botany: 'John Mill is going to concoct for me an almanack of the odours that scent the air, to be arranged chronologically according to the months, beginning with the laurel and ending with the lime.' This token of friendship seems to have taken a week or two to compile, which is not surprising, since Mill had been preoccupied with his brother's death and funeral, but on April 10th Caroline is able to mention the arrival of the Calendar 'which he has written for the first time.' Since it stands as well for today as for a century ago, and the little episode adds something to the data for any estimate of Mill's character, the document deserves to be perpetuated. As given by Caroline it runs thus:

A CALENDAR OF ODOURS, BEING IN IMITATION OF
   THE VARIOUS CALENDARS OF FLORA BY LINNAEUS
   AND OTHERS

The brilliant colouring of Nature is prolonged, with incessant changes, from March till October; but the fragrance of her breath is spent before the summer is half ended. From March to July an uninterrupted succession of sweet odours fills the air by day and still more by night, but the gentler perfumes of autumn, like many of the earlier ones here for that reason omitted, must be sought ere they can be found. The Calendar of Odours, therefore, begins with the laurel, and ends with the lime.

March. Common laurel.

April. Violets, furze, wall-flower, common broad-leaved willow, apple-blossom.

May. Lilac, night-flowering stocks and rockets, laburnum, hawthorn, seringa, sweet-briar.

June. Mignonette, bean-fields, the whole tribe of summer roses, hay, Portugal laurel, various species of pinks.

July. Common acacia, meadow-sweet, honeysuckle, sweetgale or double myrtle, Spanish broom, lime.

In latest autumn, one stray odour, forgotten by its companions, follows at a modest distance—the creeping clematis—which adorns cottage walls; but the thread of continuity being broken, this solitary straggler is not included in the Calendar of Odours.

To Miss Caroline Fox, from her grateful friend,
J. S. MILL.

[In the original at Penjerrick, in Mill's handwriting, the Latin name of each flower is given in brackets.]

On Mill's unique education and his almost incredible precocity Caroline has something, though not a great deal, to say. Mill's own references to the subject are almost classic; one passage from his *Autobiography* will serve sufficiently as example. 'I have no remembrance,' he wrote, 'of the time when I began to learn Greek. I have been told that it was when I was three years old. . . . I learnt no Latin till my eighth year. At that time I had read, under my father's tuition, a number of Greek prose authors, among whom I remember the whole of Herodotus, and of Xenophon's Cyropaedia and Memorials of Socrates; some of the lives of the philosophers by Diogenes Laertius; part of Lucian, and Isocrates ad Demonicum and Ad Nicoclem. I also read, in 1813 [he was seven this year], the first six dialogues of Plato, from the Euthyphron to the Theoctetus inclusive.' The postponement of Latin till the boy was eight, and had thoroughly mastered Greek, was no doubt an application of the educational principle which Mill expounded to Caroline during the few weeks of their first friendship at Falmouth. His father's idea, he told her, was to make children understand one thing thoroughly, this not only forming a good exercise for the mind but creating in them a standard by which to judge of their knowledge of other subjects, whether it was superficial or otherwise.

On the soundness of this principle Mill himself began to entertain some doubts. His father, he told Caroline, made him study Ecclesiastical History before he was ten; that method of early intense application he would not recommend to others. He added rather pathetically: 'I never was a boy, never played at cricket; it is better to let Nature have her own way.' That general picture of a lost childhood, in fact, needs a little modification. When Mill was staying with Sir Samuel Bentham and his family in France (where he spent the whole of his fifteenth year) he learned dancing, to which he showed considerable addiction, fencing and riding—none of them precisely athletic sports, but as a whole inconsistent with the idea that only the mental side of his personality was ever cultivated, and that cultivated to excess.

During these few weeks of 1840, the only period in which Caroline was in constant contact with Mill, he discoursed at large on a wide variety of topics, and his young auditor, striving, with the alertness of her twenty years, to keep pace with that swift mind, set down in paraphrase or direct quotation all she had been able to understand and remember; when in doubt she must have omitted, for all the entries are marked by perfect clarity. One subject recurred to more than once was the Society of Friends, in which Mill had long been interested. Two of the volumes which the phenomenal child consumed before the age of ten were Sewell's and Rutty's histories of Quakerism, and at a more mature age he was associated, like his father, with the well-known Friend William Allen, founder of the British and Foreign Schools Society. But he probably knew less of Friends' practice than of their principles, and it was no doubt with a genuine and characteristic desire for knowledge that at Falmouth he 'wanted to know all about the constitution of our Society (apropos of a Quarterly Meeting which was taking place here), then dilated on the different Friends' books he was reading; on John Woolman [1] he

---

[1] 1720-1772. Devoted his life in New Jersey to work for the negroes and Red Indians. His *Journal* is a Quaker classic. All readers of the *Essays of Elia* know of Lamb's injunction, 'Get the Writings of John Woolman by heart.'

philosophised on the principle that was active in him—that dependence on the immediate teaching of the Supreme Being which gave him clear views of what was essentially consistent or inconsistent with Christianity, independent of and often opposed to all recorded or common opinion, all self-interest.' That Mill should have singled out for special appreciation one Quaker principle—'He much admires the part Friends have taken about tithes and values that testimony against a priesthood as at present organised'—may seem a little surprising, but the question was of some importance at the moment and Mill's views on the 'priesthood' were strong.

There was more on Quakerism from Mill six weeks later, when Caroline was in London (for 'Yearly Meeting') and dined with the Mills at Kensington Square. After dinner, for some reason not explained, perhaps simply from admiration for the writing, 'He read us that striking passage in *Sartor Resartus* on George Fox making to himself a suit of leather. How his voice trembled with excitement as he read "stitch away thou noble Fox" etc.' It was natural enough that as they walked home across the Park, Mill, accompanying them part of the way and talking of the spirit of Sect as opposed to that of Christianity and subversive of it, should have added that 'Friends in their essential character must have less of it than any others; though of course in theirs as in all sects the *esprits bornés* will exalt the peculiarities and differences above the agreements—the very spirit of sect.' All of which suggests that if Mill had ever been inclined to associate himself with any body of professed Christians it would have been with the Society of Friends. But the marked absence of the inclination deprives the speculation of most of its interest.

The various conversations at Falmouth and in London which Caroline reports between March and July of 1840 cover a wide field, but there is a tendency to recur to certain subjects and concentrate on them, in particular on the social and political life of other countries. It is natural enough that India should be among the first of these, for Mill was in a high position at the India House and had been responsible there for relations with the Indian States, which were more numerous and more important a century ago than they are today. In regard to that he 'gave a very interesting sketch of the political history of India, the advantages derived by its princes from our supremacy there; preventing intestine wars, dethroning and pensioning sovereigns and princes, and thus preventing their extinction by rival powers. There is very little if any nationality in India, which must ever impede civilisation; the provinces, states and kingdoms are not clearly defined; the languor of the people hinders every species of improvement; but it is a curious fact that their effeminacy of constitution and habit is accompanied by a quickness and delicacy of perception generally known only among women. The difficulty of doing justice in India is great, in consequence of the involved terms of our alliances with the princes, and the pledges we make to all parties which it seems all but impossible to redeem. The progress of Christianity in those parts is slow, from the natural want of energy in the character of the people, as well as from their first samples of Europeans being those connected with politics, instead of, as in other parts of the world, men who gave the whole energy of their characters to the work of promoting Christianity and civilisation, as the missionaries in the Pacific Islands.'

There are references here, it may be observed, to the languor and effeminacy of the Indian people closely similar to judgements expressed by Miss Mayo (who had been to India, as Mill had not) in her *Mother India* nearly ninety years later. The comments on Christian missions in India are no doubt just, though by the date when Mill was speaking Henry Martyn and William Carey and their successors were providing notable examples of men who 'gave the whole energy of their characters to promoting Christianity and civilisation.'

On the republican form of government in France and the United States Mill made some interesting comments, which events signally failed to justify. France was, of course, at the time (1840) still a monarchy. 'In his essays on French affairs,' Caroline considers, 'he has infused more of himself than into any of his other writings—the whole subject of that country so deeply interests him. The present tone of feeling there indicates a great progressive change, not only among the thinking men, but the most influential, the middle class. They have reached the point of earnest seeking after what is good and true and immutable. Their first opinions—those which they have simply imbibed from tradition and prejudice—they have forsaken, and their minds are anxiously open to truth. A Republic, even if right on the abstract principle of men being trustworthy of the charge of self-government, would never suit them; they must follow a leader, so an Elective Monarchy will be their probable form of government in after-years.'

We look back on that prediction today after seventy years' experience of France as a republic and assess it accordingly, but other and later authorities than Mill—some of them, moreover, writing after, not before, the event—have used language curiously like his regarding an elective monarchy. Bainville, for example, in his history of the Third Republic heads his chapter on the election of Marshal MacMahon as first constitutional President 'Constitutional Monarchy under another Name,' and another historian has actually followed Mill in speaking of 'the elective monarchy.'

From one republic the discourser-at-large passed to another, the American. In this field, too, his reputation as reader of the future suffers. 'He is thankful that the experiment of a republic has been tried there; it had failed, and ever must fail, for want of the two contending powers which are always requisite to keep things in proper order—Government and Public Opinion. America subjects herself to the latter only, and public opinion there having decided in favour of one particular type of character all aim at a resemblance to it, and a great sameness is the result. There is as much of tyranny in this process as in that more commonly so called.' There is a good deal to challenge in this interpretation of American history of the moment. When Mill was talking, not to say dogmatising, on these lines, the United States had had eight years of Andrew Jackson, under whom public opinion was certainly not the supreme factor, and was working to the end of Van Buren's single term, which was substantially of the same order as his predecessor's. But Mill (who had read and reviewed De Tocqueville) held decided views on this subject. 'He thinks,' Caroline had written a fortnight earlier, 'in time the republican government in the country will be changed—perhaps for a monarchy. What especially fosters the spirit of Toryism there is the feeling of the richer class that there is not the same deference shown them that there would be in other countries; also the hunger for a literature, a history and a romance which other lands can produce, but not America.' That judgement might be discussed at some length, but it will suffice to relate to it a few lines from a passage bearing on this precise point in the article on the United States in the fourteenth edition of the *Encyclopaedia Britannica*. 'Between 1830 and 1840,' says the writer, 'Whittier, Longfellow, Holmes, Poe, Hawthorne, Emerson, Bancroft and Prescott joined the advance-guard of American writers—Bryant, Dana, Halleck, Drake, Irving and Cooper; and even those writers who had already made their place in literature showed the influence of new conditions by their growing tendency to look less to foreign models and methods.' Such was the trend of the decade which ended in 1840, the year in which Mill was deploring America's poverty in a literature, a history and a romance.

A century old though they are, Mill's views on such countries as Germany and Italy are still pertinent, the more so since they were concerned not with the political situation of the moment but with the more enduring qualities of the two nations (neither of which at the time had attained political unity). In regard to the Germans, the question arose of the reason for the contemplative character of its inhabitants. Mill 'lays great stress on the influence of the domestic affections, which are so strong there and so much called out by circumstances; then they are not continually striving either to become rich or to appear so, as the English are, but settle down into quiet, contemplative habits, without an idea of happiness but what is subjective to themselves; this constant habit of carrying in themselves the elements of their happiness increases and gives a tranquil tone to it; and then at the universities the studious men give the tone of feeling and superinduce a love of knowledge for its own sake; and Schelling being the president has its influence. He therefore likes the plan, now so much followed, of sending young men to German universities.' This, it is all too superfluous to remark, is not the Germany *de nos jours*. But in fact the difference between the Germany of 1840 and the Germany of 1940 was fundamental. The Germany Mill knew was the Germany of Goethe and Schiller, of Hegel and Fichte (on the aggressive side of whose philosophy little stress had then been laid), the Germany whose thinkers Carlyle was systematically introducing to English readers, the Germany which twenty-seven years before had thrown off the yoke of Napoleon at Leipsic and thereafter settled down to the pursuits of peace, a Germany in which the young Bismarck was as yet concerned with nothing more militant than the management of his family's estates in Pomerania.

Though Mill knew Italy much better than he knew Germany —he had visited the former country twice, the latter never—he said a good deal less about it, or else, which seems more probable, Caroline recorded less. What he did say was: 'The Italians carry with and in them such a sense of native dignity, the result of associating themselves with remembrances of Rome in its glory. They are exactly the figures that Raphael, Titian and others delineated, and serve in great measure to account for the cultivation of the Arts being so successful there. Their great sensibility and emotion he ascribes to the general prevalence of music, and to the magnificence of their ceremonies.' It was only in the cultural field that Mill or anyone else could generalise about Italy in 1840, for at that time there was no political Italy, —only Piedmont and Naples and Romagna, with the Austrians holding Lombardy and Venezia, and the achievements of Cavour and Mazzini and Garibaldi still to come.

Some more general comparisons in national characteristics on the whole deserve the adjective Caroline applies to them— 'luminous.' The conversation, or monologue, had its setting not, like those just reported, at Falmouth, but in London, a few weeks later—to be precise, on May 28th, 1840. It took place while Caroline and Mill were on their way from India House to visit the Pantheon, Mill, as has been said, 'very luminous all the way, spite of the noise. He considers the differences in national character one of the most interesting subjects for science and research. Thus the French are discovered to possess so much nationality; every great man amongst them is, in the first place, essentially a Frenchman, whatever he may have appended to that character. The individuality of the English, on the other hand, makes them little marked by qualities in common; each takes his own road and succeeds by his own merits. The French are peculiarly swayed by a leader, and so he be a man of talent, he can do anything with them. Custom and public opinion are the rulers in England. Any man of any pretension is sure to gather some disciples around him in this country, but can never inspire a universal enthusiasm. The French take in all that is new and original sooner than others, but rarely originate anything themselves; and when they have sufficiently diluted it, they re-introduce it to Europe. Thus almost all new doctrines come from France, in consequence of their being such clear statists; but if they find a subject too deep for them, they entirely give it the go-by. To the Germans a new idea is but an addition to their list of speculative truths, which at most it modifies, but creates little disturbance, so essentially are they a speculative people. The English, on the other hand, being equally in their essence practical, and whose speculative opinions generally bear reference to the conduct of life and moral duty, are very shy of new truths, lest they should force them to admit that they had hitherto lived in vain; few have courage to begin life *de novo*, but those who have do not lose their reward.' On this again the passage of a hundred years has provided an instructive commentary, but such judgements furnish profitable matter for reflection, whether events bear them out or not.

One or two sidelights on Mill as a humanitarian have their interest. He is quoted on capital punishment, 'to which he distinctly objects, and thinks with Carlyle that the worst thing you can do with a man is to hang him.' (This was a matter on which Caroline herself held strong views, and it was evidently a disappointment to her that Mill in course of time modified his. When she saw him in London two years later, in May 1842, 'He is inclined to agree with Wordsworth in the defence of capital punishments, but I am glad to say has not quite made up his mind.') 'John Mill has a peculiar antipathy to hunting the hare; it is such a striking subversion of this fine Christian innovation [protection of the weak] of which we had been speaking; he has never attended races either.' And, of a rather different order, 'Today he spoke of teetotalism: on first thoughts it seems a ridiculous idea that people should associate and pledge themselves *not* to do a thing, but the *rationale* of the experiment develops itself afterwards.'

Caroline's record of Mill's short stay at Falmouth in 1840 illuminates in many ways a side of his personality which rarely found expression (but see in this connexion the third of his posthumously published *Essays on Religion*). What he said on various occasions in those few weeks was no doubt evoked partly by his brother's illness and death, partly by the quiet but pervasive influences which emanated from the different Quaker households with which he became familiar—in particular that of which Caroline was a member.   One incident is impressive.   'Dr Calvert, in speaking of the great humility compatible with high metaphysical research, spoke of John Mill standing on one side, and himself on the other, of his brother's deathbed.   Dr Calvert remarked "This sort of scene puts an end to Reason, and Faith begins"; the other emphatically answered "Yes," the conversation which followed displaying such humility and deep feeling, and as coming from the first metaphysician of his age, was most edifying.'

That did not stand altogether alone—though insistence on principle is something of a different texture from confession of faith.   A fortnight or more earlier, Mill had been talking of Luther, and the great Reformer's dismay at some of the consequences of the liberation of thought for which his teaching had been responsible.   'No one,' he said with deep feeling, 'should attempt anything intended to benefit his age without at first making a stern resolution to take up his cross and bear it.   If he does not begin by counting the cost, all his schemes must end in disappointment; either he will sink under it like Chatterton, or yield to the counter-current like Erasmus, or pass his life in disappointment and vexation as Luther did.'   On which Caroline comments: 'This was evidently a process through which he [Mill] had passed, as is sufficiently attested by his careworn and anxious, though most beautiful and refined, countenance.'   The next day Caroline, Mill and Sterling were discussing that 'guiding principle' the idea of which, as Caroline observed, 'has been held by the best minds of all ages, alike by Socrates and St Augustine, though under different names.' We are not told what Sterling had to say on this; still less what, if anything, Caroline had to say herself.   Mill's contribution alone survives.

'Avoid all that you prove by experience or intuition to be wrong,' was his counsel, 'and you are safe; especially avoid the servile imitation of any other, be true to yourselves, find out your individuality, and live and act in the circle around it. Follow with earnestness the path into which it impels you, taking Reason for your Safety Lamp, and perpetually warring with inclination; then you will attain to that Freedom which results only from obedience to Right and Reason and that Happiness which proves to be such on retrospection. Everyone has a part to perform whilst stationed here, and he must strive with enthusiasm to perform it. Every advance brings its own particular snares, either exciting to ambition or display, but in the darkest passages of human existence a Pole Star may be discovered, if earnestly sought after, which will guide the wanderer into the effulgence of Light and Truth. What there is in us that appears evil is, if thoroughly examined, either disproportioned or misdirected good, for our Maker has stamped His own image on everything that lives.' That this is a little didactic and a little trite may be conceded. If it were characteristic Mill it would hardly be worth perpetuating, but it does, in fact, like a good deal that Caroline has recorded of him— more of the same nature could be quoted—show the metaphysician in a not completely familiar light.

Though they are given in quotation marks, these may not have been Mill's precise words, nor, probably, all his words, for there is no doubt substance in Caroline's closing comment: 'Oh! how much there was this evening of Poetry, of Truth, of Beauty; but I have given no idea of it on paper, though it has left its own idea engraven on my memory.' Caroline probably had in fact given a very good idea of it on paper, but her report could naturally not claim the same authority as Mill's own written word. With an example of that written word the brief account of these months of fresh and unclouded friendship may fitly be rounded off. After he left Falmouth Mill wrote to Barclay, Caroline's brother, a letter which was in reality addressed to the whole family, to express something of what their support and sympathy had meant through the weeks of anxiety and sorrow which ended in his brother's death. Caroline, with a sound sense of values, incorporated it in her Journal, and apart from one or two passages of purely ephemeral interest it deserves quotation in full.

'INDIA HOUSE,
16th April, 1840.

MY DEAR FRIEND (if you will allow me to adopt this "friendly" mode of address),—Your kind and sympathising letter has given us great pleasure. There is no use my saying more than has been said already about him who has gone before us, where we must so soon follow; the thought of him is here, and will remain here, and seldom has the memory of one who died so young been such as to leave a deeper or a more beneficial impression on the survivors. Among the many serious feelings which such an event calls forth, there is always some one which impresses us most, some moral which each person extracts from it for his own more especial guidance; with me that moral is "Work while it is called today; the night cometh in which no man can work." One never seems to have adequately *felt* the truth and meaning of life, till one loses some one whom one had hoped not only to carry with one as a companion through life, but to leave as a successor after it. Why he who had all his work to do has been taken, and I left who had done part of mine, and in some measure, as Carlyle would express it, "delivered my message," passes our wisdom to surmise. But if there be a purpose in this, that purpose, it would seem, can only be fulfilled in so far as the remainder of my life can be made even more useful than the remainder of his would have been if it had been spared. At least we know this, that on the day when we shall be as he is, the whole of life will appear but as a day, and the only question of any moment to us then will be, Has that day been wasted? Wasted it has not been by those who have been for however short a time a source of happiness and of moral good, even to the narrowest circle. But there is only one plain rule of life eternally binding, and independent of all variations in creeds, and in the interpretations of creeds, embracing equally the greatest moralities and the smallest; it is this—try thyself unweariedly till thou findest the highest thing thou art capable of doing, faculties and outward circumstances being both duly considered, and then DO IT.'

Then comes a sharp transition. Mill in the Falmouth days had sent the Foxes a complete set of the *London and Westminster Review*, with the names of the writers of unsigned articles appended, and in replying here to a letter of thanks from Barclay he digresses into a general discussion of his writings. A statement that such of his past articles as seemed of value 'will, I hope, during the time you are in London, be made into two little volumes' seems to foreshadow the publication of *Dissertations and Discussions*, which did not, in the event, appear till 1859, and ended by being four volumes, not two. Then comes what may almost be called a life's balance-sheet. (Rather surprisingly Mill says in his *Autobiography*: 'From this time [1840] what is worth relating of my life will come into a very small compass'—though he had yet to publish his *System of Logic*, *On Liberty* and *Representative Government* and marry Mrs Taylor.) In the Barclay Fox letter his literary work till 1840 is thus assessed:

'. . . Among a multitude of failures, I had only one instance of brilliant success. It is some satisfaction to me to know that, as far as such things can ever be said, I saved Lord Durham,— as he himself, with much feeling, acknowledged to me, saying that he knew not to what to ascribe the reception he met with on his return from Canada, except to an article of mine, which came out immediately before. If you were to read that article now, you would wonder what there was in it to bear out such a statement; but the *time* at which it appeared was everything; every one's hand seemed to be against him, no one dared speak

John Stuart Mill

a word for him; the very men who had been paying court and offering incense to him for years before (I never had) shrunk away or ventured only on a few tame and qualified phrases of excuse—not, I verily believe, from cowardice so much as because, not being accustomed to think about *principles* of politics, they were taken by surprise in a contingency which they had not looked for, and feared committing themselves to something they could not maintain; and if this had gone on, opinion would have decided against him so strongly, that even that admirable Report of his and Buller's[1] could hardly have turned the tide; and unless some one who could give evidence of thought and knowledge of the subject had thrown down the gauntlet at that critical moment, and determinedly claimed honour and glory for him instead of mere acquittal, and in doing this made a diversion in his favour, and kept people's minds *suspended* on the subject, he was in all probability a lost man; and if I had not been the man to do this, nobody else would. And three or four months later the Report came out, and then everybody said I had been right, and now it is being acted upon.

'This is one of only three things, among all I attempted in my reviewing life, which I can be said to have succeeded in. The second was to have greatly accelerated the success of Carlyle's *French Revolution*, a book so strange and incomprehensible to the greater part of the public that whether it should succeed or fail seemed to depend on the turn of a die; but I got the first word, blew the trumpet before it at its first coming out, and by claiming for it the honours of the highest genius, frightened the small fry of critics from pronouncing a hasty condemnation, got fair-play for it, and then its success was sure.

'My third success is that I have dinned into people's ears that Guizot is a great thinker and writer, till they are, though

[1] The famous Report was, of course, technically Durham's only, but his secretary, Charles Buller, has always been regarded as its principal author.

slowly, beginning to read him, which I do not believe they would be doing even yet, in this country, but for me.

'This, I think, is a full account of all the world has got by my editing and reviews.'

And there—in 1840, the year in which it began—anything like intimate friendship between Caroline and Mill seems to have ended. The reason is not entirely clear. Mill certainly had two sides. Dr Bowring, talking of him to Caroline in August 1840, referred to him contemptuously as a renegade from philosophy ('Anglicé, a renouncer of Bentham's creed and an expounder of Coleridge's,' observes Caroline parenthetically). 'Mill's newly-developed "Imagination" puzzles him [Bowring] not a little; he was most emphatically not a philosopher, but then he read Wordsworth and that muddled him, and he has been in a strange confusion ever since, endeavouring to unite poetry and philosophy.' No doubt there was something in this. No doubt, too, it was the Coleridge-Wordsworth-poetry side, or phase, that appealed to Caroline, and she seems to have seen much more of it during Mill's Falmouth visit than in later talks with him. No doubt propinquity, and subsequent absence of it, is a partial explanation of the change in the relationship. Mill never came to Falmouth again, and Caroline only went to London on an average once in two years, if as often ('Dined at the Mills'—a biennial jubilee,' she writes in May 1842, having last seen the family in London in May 1840); after this 1842 visit contacts between her and Mill were rare and casual and few signs of the old intimacy were evident. It might have been kept alive by letters, but Caroline does not seem on the whole to have been a very active correspondent. If she was, she makes little reference to the fact in her Journal.

But the talk at Kensington Square at the end of May 1842 was much on the old lines. If there was nothing quite on the 1840 note—'John Mill was quite himself; he had in the middle of dinner to sit still for a little to try to take in that we were really here'—the note of 1842, 'John Mill in glorious spirits; too happy to enter much into deep things,' is no bad approximation to it. A general disquisition inspired by this mood centred mainly on Goethe. 'Talked of Life not being all fun, though there is a great deal of fun in it. His view of Goethe's character is a refined selfishness, but then he added, with a sincere modesty: "Sterling used to say the same sort of things of Goethe as I do now, and as he is always making progress, I fully believe that he is right in his enthusiasm, though I cannot now sympathise with it. He says that 'Hermann and Dorothea' make you *love* Goethe; I confess that I never met with anything yet which had that effect on me." He is greatly relieved at having finished his *Logic*, and is going to mark the best passages for me with notes of admiration. He said "My family have no idea how great a man I am!"'

The account of this particular talk ends with an interesting entry: 'John Mill had designed writing a work on the French Revolution, when he heard of Carlyle's purpose, and accordingly made over his books of reference to him; the world has also been deprived of a History of Greece from his pen, because Thirlwall was just beforehand with him.' It may be added that the world was further deprived of a third work by Mill, a Life of Sterling, which he had projected but never wrote, possibly because of the appearance of Archdeacon Hare's biography. It was just a week after writing of Mill's renunciation of his French Revolution intentions that Caroline, calling at Cheyne Row, was told by Mrs Carlyle how the only manuscript of Carlyle's first volume on the Revolution had been lent to Mill, passed on by him to Mrs Taylor and accidentally destroyed while in her custody.[1] (Jane Carlyle, however, mentioned no names.) As the year ended, 'Barclay had a letter from J. S. Mill; he speaks of his growing conviction that individual regeneration must precede social progress, and in the mean time

[1] See p. 113.

he feels that the best work he can do is to perfect his book on Logic, so as to aid in giving solidity and definiteness to the work of others.' Nine or ten weeks later *A System of Logic* arrived, and Caroline read the chapter on Liberty and Necessity; whether she ever read any other chapter she does not say.

There is little more to tell. In 1844 Caroline happened to meet Mill in the Strand, but they seem merely to have exchanged a few casual words about some pictures in the National Gallery. Two years later, being in London again, she called at the Mills', but nothing of much importance was said. Mill mentioned that 'he scarcely ever now goes into society, for he gets no good there, and does more by staying away.' Apart from one or two letters to Clara Mill in which her brother is mentioned, that is all till 1859, when Caroline (now a mature woman of forty), expresses almost violent hostility to Mill's *On Liberty*, which had just appeared. 'I am reading,' she writes, 'that terrible book of John Mill's on Liberty, so clear and calm and cold; he lays it on one as a tremendous duty to get oneself well contradicted, and admit always a devil's advocate into the presence of your dearest, most sacred Truths, as they are apt to grow windy and worthless without such tests, if indeed they can stand the shock of argument at all. He looks you through like a basilisk, relentless as Fate. We knew him well at one time, and owe him very much; I fear his remorseless logic has led him far since then. This book is dedicated to his wife's memory in a few most touching words. He is in many senses isolated, and must sometimes shiver with the cold.'

Elizabeth Carne, the recipient of this denunciation, evidently replied, and a month later Caroline rejoins: 'No, my dear, I don't agree with Mill, though I too should be very glad to have some of my "ugly opinions" corrected, however painful the process; but Mill makes me shiver, his blade is so keen and so unhesitating.' But she adds, with her habitual fairness: 'I think there is much force in his criticism on the mental training provided for the community; the battles are fought *for* us, the objections to received views and the refutations of the same all provided for us, instead of ourselves being strengthened and armed for the combat. Then he greatly complains of our all growing so much alike that individuality is dying out of the land; we are more afraid of singularity than of Falsehood or Compromise, and this he thinks a very dark symptom of a nation's decay. France, he says, is further gone than we are in this path.'

This cry of pain and protest—for it is no less than that—is understandable enough. Mill pursued a very deliberate method in *On Liberty*. The book (as Professor Bain said in his critical summary of it) 'works round a central idea—the necessity of taking account of the *negative* to every positive affirmation; of laying down, side by side with every proposition, the *counter-proposition*. . . . When he proceeds to illustrate the enlivening influence of negation by the case of ethical and religious doctrines, I think that he fails to make out his case.' It is easy to realise how Caroline (in spite perhaps of some haunting memory of the apostolic 'prove all things; hold fast that which is good') would react against the questioning of all that she held stable and fundamental—and that at the hands of the friend who had, by his brother's bedside, exalted Faith above Reason, and had manifested community of feeling with her on so many of the tenets of the Society of Friends. And when the writer of *On Liberty* went on to criticise the accepted morality of Christianity as incomplete and one-sided she could not but be deeply wounded. Caroline's reading was reasonably catholic, and she was freer from preconceptions than most women of her age and time, but life contained for her certain inviolable sanctities, and Mill's 'remorseless logic' did them deadly despite. If she had read the *System of Logic* through she would have found its author affirming that one of the essential conditions of stability in any society was that there be something that was settled *and not to be called in question.*

But *Logic* appeared in 1843, *On Liberty* in 1859. The human mind may travel far in such an interval.

It was nineteen years since Caroline and Mill first met at the bedside and the grave of Henry Mill. In those days the girl of twenty hung on every word that fell from the philosopher of thirty-three. How and why the fire of friendship died down Caroline never fully explains, but her 'we knew him well at one time' shows how far they had drifted apart. The fundamental truth, no doubt, was that they had developed on different lines. As Clough's

> *'ships becalmed at eve, that lay*
> *With drooping canvas side by side,*
> *Two towers of sail at break of day*
> *Are scarce, long leagues apart, descried,'*

they found widening seas dividing them. Yet it can hardly be doubted that his brief contact with the Fox circle at Falmouth left some real mark on Mill, or that Caroline derived something of lasting value from those comments on life which she recorded with diligent devotion in her Journal day by day. Though the friendship faded its first-fruits were safely garnered.[1]

---

[1] The importance of the contribution made by Caroline to the understanding of Mill's character is not to be underestimated. Julia Wedgwood, in her review of the Journal in the *Spectator*, dwells at length on that, and part of what she says deserves quotation :

'We shall be surprised if the sketch of John Mill is not felt to possess that high and rare kind of charm belonging to those revelations of character which, in their striking contrast to the aspect already familiar, revive in us the conviction that the capacities of the human spirit are indeed infinite. This charm, finely indicated by a poet still among us, in an expressed desire for a sight of the solitary picture painted by Dante and the solitary poem written by Raphael, though it may be appreciated most keenly by a poet, is felt by all human beings. We all care most for those glimpses which show us the man as he does not habitually reveal himself ; and in looking back on a finished intercourse, we shall generally find that, however sweet the melody, the sweetest part has been some unexpected modulation, quickly deserted for the original key. Such an interest we find in this presentation of John Mill. It is evident that in the atmosphere of the Quakers of Falmouth some dim aspirations, faintly discernible here and there in his writings, found their appropriate atmosphere, and blossomed into a fullness of beauty that made the landscape a different thing from what it was elsewhere. We have always thought that John Mill was only half understood if this part of his nature were not allowed for ; but we never suspected how completely it would be thus misunderstood till we read this volume.'

Chapter X
Lake Poets and Others

Caroline never saw Samuel Taylor Coleridge, who died when she was only fifteen, and in the closing years of his life never moved far from Highgate. She must have heard much of him from Sterling, who was the most devoted of his disciples and had been one of the small company of close friends who gathered round the poet's grave. To him she was indebted for a brief and characteristically melancholy letter from Coleridge (given her for her autograph collection), written in the year before his death. Caroline hesitated to accept it, feeling that it ought to remain in Sterling's hands, and accordingly sent it back to him—a piece of self-abnegation which she describes as 'a moral conquest.' Sterling, however, was determined, and the letter went to Rosehill once more—and stayed there. It ran:

'MY DEAR STERLING,—With grief I tell you that I have been, and now am, worse—far worse than when you left me. God have mercy on me, and not withdraw the influence of His Spirit from me! I can now only thank you for your kind attentions to your most sincere and afflicted friend,

S. T. COLERIDGE.

P.S.—Mr Green is persuaded that it is gout, which I have not strength enough to throw from the nerves of the trunk to the extremities.'

The date was March 1833.

Various anecdotes about Coleridge are recorded as Caroline heard them. Some, like the story of his escape from Italy in

1806 (Caroline unaccountably gives the date as 1815; Sir E. K. Chambers[1] describes the story as 'probably in part apocryphal'), when Bonaparte ordered the arrest of all Englishmen in Rome, are familiar enough; another such is Coleridge's eulogium of his own preaching in the course of a conversation with Lamb, ending with the question 'You have heard me preach, I think?' and the answer, 'I never heard you do anything else.' Sterling, of course, was an impassioned admirer of Coleridge, who, he said, was best described in his own words in the passage in *Kubla Khan* beginning 'his flashing eye, his floating hair.' We may be grateful, all the same, to Caroline for transmitting the appraisal of the poet which Dean Milman gave her in 1854. 'The Dean,' she says, 'used often to see and hear S. T. Coleridge, but his wonderful talk was far too unvaried from day to day; also there were some absolute deficiencies in it, such as the total absence of wit; still it was very remarkable. "But," he added, "I used to be wicked enough to divide it into three parts: one third was admirable, beautiful in language and exalted in thought; another third was sheer absolute nonsense; and of the remaining third I knew not whether it were sense or nonsense."' The Journal, it may be added, is quoted (by Sir Edmund Chambers in his monograph on the poet) as authority on the disputed question of the colour of Coleridge's eyes: a common friend of Caroline and Coleridge who used often to see him till within a month of his death was, says the diarist, an ardent admirer of 'his prominent blue eyes, reverend hair and rapt expression.'

It was with S. T. Coleridge's sons, Hartley and Derwent, that Caroline was familiar. Hartley, the elder, rarely stirred from his successive homes in the Lake District, at Ambleside and Grasmere. It was at Grasmere that Caroline first met him. She and her sister, Anna Maria, paid a visit to the Lakes in 1837 equipped with a letter of introduction to Hartley from

[1] *Coleridge*, by E. K. Chambers, p. 190.

'Aunt Charles,' who before her marriage had lived at Ulverston and knew the whole Greta Hall and Dove Cottage circle. The letter was despatched by messenger, with the result that the same day 'as we were sitting after tea in the twilight, a little being was observed at the door, standing hat in hand, bowing to the earth round and round and round again, with eyes intensely twinkling—it was Hartley Coleridge; so he sat down, and what with nervous tremors and other infirmities amongst us, nothing very remarkable was elicited.' However, he volunteered to show the visitors round the next day, and in due course did so. ('In person and dress he was much brushed up; his vivid face sparkled in the shadow of a large straw hat.') He showed them the cottage where Wordsworth and De Quincey had lived, mentioning that Wordsworth was a most unpleasant companion on a tour, from his constant fear of being cheated, and not much thought of as a neighbour. They went to Rydal Mount to look for the poet, all the same, but he was in Hertfordshire, which was disappointing. Mrs Wordsworth, however, did the honours, entertaining them with ginger-wine and gingerbread.

Hartley went back with the Foxes to Ambleside, read some *Elia* aloud to them, and at dinner fell into an embarrassing choking-fit. He discoursed philosophically on various subjects, walking round the dining-table the while. One of the sisters asked him whether Wordsworth's daughter had inherited any of her father's genius, and for answer got the sharp counter-question 'Would you have the disease of genius descend like the scrofula?'—for disease he maintained it was, and one which amazingly interfered with the enjoyment of things as they were, and unfitted the possessor for communion with common friends. Then he produced a poem about their meeting the previous evening and their imminent parting, pressed a hand of each and disappeared. Caroline tried a not unskilled hand at a pen-picture. 'Conjure up unto thyself, O Caroline,' she wrote, with an unusual relapse into self-invocation, 'a little round high-shouldered man, shrunk into a little black coat, the features of his face moulded by habit into an expression of pleasantry and an appreciation of the exquisitely ludicrous, such as one could fancy Charles Lamb's. Little black eyes twinkling intensely, as if every sense were called on to taste every idea. He is very anxious to establish an Ugly Club and to be its chairman; but really he is quite unworthy of the station, for odd enough he is, but never ugly, there is such a radiant light of genius over all.'

That, as has been said, was in 1837. It was seven years before Caroline was in the Lakes again and could renew the contact. Meanwhile, in 1842, she had met Wordsworth in London and heard from him a considered estimate of Hartley Coleridge, in whose verse the older poet saw much talent but no genius. 'Hartley,' he said, 'has no originality; whenever he attempts it it is altogether a mistake; he is so fond of quaint-ness and contrariety, which is quite out of keeping with a true poet; and then he is of that class of extreme Radicals who can never mention a bishop or a king, from King David downward, without some atrabilious prefix or other. Surely this is ex-cessively narrow and excessively vain, to put yourself in opposition to the opinions and institutions which have so long existed with such acknowledged benefit; there must be some-thing in them to have attracted the sympathies of ages and generations.' All of which may be entirely true, but the vanity Wordsworth in his maturity thus rebuked was such as he and Hartley's father had not only displayed but gloried in in their youth.

When the Foxes met Hartley again in 1844 at Windermere he on his side 'spoke of Wordsworth with high respect but no enthusiasm.' He came on the visitors when Anna Maria was sketching near Dr Arnold's old house Fox How, and the talk naturally turned on the famous headmaster, who had died two years before. Hartley had sometimes gone walks with him, but not often, because Arnold walked so fast and so far. He observed that when he was at Oxford Rugby boys were proverbially the worst, their moral training having been so neglected, but that since then Arnold's influence had not only changed all that but substantially raised the tone of the other public schools.

Hartley Coleridge had done a little schoolmastering himself in his time. He recalled his experiences while at dinner with the Fox sisters a day or two later. After a few words on the Arnold family, who, he said, were 'suckled on Latin and weaned on Greek,' he talked of his own trials as a teacher—which were what one might have expected them to be. 'He likes teaching, but keeping the boys in order passes his powers; his experience convinces him that the clever boys are generally the best, the stupid ones taking refuge in cunning.' (Actually, though he had been a failure in a school in which he had taught for a short time at Ambleside, he got on reasonably well at Sedbergh, where he held posts for two brief periods some years later.) One day the next week Caroline and her sister sheltered from a shower in Hartley's singularly-named cottage the Knbbe, which apparently consisted of a single room. Its owner made some apology for it, and Anna Maria remarked, 'One might be very happy here.' 'Or very miserable,' came the answer, with (as Caroline noted) 'such a sad and terrible emphasis.' On the whole, it was an unhappy and disillusioned life. At Oxford Hartley Coleridge had just missed the Newdigate (his father at Cambridge had just missed the Craven), and soon afterwards had to leave the university owing to his intemperate habits, two failures which overshadowed all his future. He died in 1849 at the Knbbe at the age of fifty-two, and Caroline, on the strength of letters from his brother Derwent, speaks of his 'humble and prayerful' death. He wrote little and never married. The fact of his having been an eight months' child may explain some of his eccentricities, the fact of being his father's son others.

Derwent Coleridge was a more normal person than his elder

brother, whose Life he wrote. At Cambridge he was (like Sterling and F. D. Maurice) a member of the brilliant circle which included Charles Buller and Charles Austin, and soon after coming down became headmaster of the grammar school at Helston, some thirteen miles from Falmouth, where Charles Kingsley was among his pupils. Another link with the Christian Socialists was his friendship with Maurice, who dedicated *The Kingdom of Christ* to him. The Fox family knew the Derwent Coleridges well, and one of the first entries in the Journal as published tells how Caroline and her father spent an evening at Helston, when Derwent read passages from *Christabel* and others of his father's poems aloud, and 'talked of architecture, with reference to George Wightwick's designs for the Falmouth Polytechnic, and mentioned a double cube as the handsomest of all forms for a room.' The next entry indicates how easily Caroline might have met Southey (Derwent's uncle), for he was staying with the Coleridges at Helston in 1836; but she clearly did not meet him, merely giving a short account of his visit at second-hand. The poet is dismissed as 'very tall, about sixty-five years old [he was in fact sixty-two], and likes mealy potatoes,' but a passable anecdote is appended. One day while at Helston Southey took a book from a shelf, 'when Derwent Coleridge, who must have been in a deliciously dreamy state, murmured apologetically "I got that book cheap; it's one of Southey's." It was quietly replaced by the poet; Mary Coleridge exclaimed "Derwent!" and all enjoyed the joke except the immediate sufferers.'

In July 1837 the Coleridges dined at Caroline's home, and Derwent delivered himself of some rather reactionary sentiments on the legitimacy of influencing votes at an election, 'maintaining that people of superior character and talent should feel the responsibility of these possessions as a call to direct the judgement of those less gifted.' On that point, Caroline adds not quite dispassionately, 'a bright argument ensued between the poet and the man of sense,' the latter being her father.

In October of the same year Derwent Coleridge, as Caroline records, in conversation with Barclay Fox made a contribution of some interest to the interpretation of one of his father's best-known poems. *Christabel*, he thought, hinged on the lines:

> '*And she in the midnight wood will pray*
> *For the weal of her lover that's far away,*'

'and that this is a Catholic idea of expiation, that the lover had fallen into some great sin, and Christabel was thus permitted to do penance for him by her own great suffering.' This would, of course, be valuable if there were reason to believe that Derwent Coleridge had derived his theory from the poet himself. In the absence of any evidence for this the conjecture is worth no more than anybody else's. It is by no means confirmed by Gillman's account (based almost certainly on Coleridge's own authority) of the course the poem, if concluded, would have followed.

It is not till 1839 that Derwent Coleridge is mentioned again. Caroline then went to see him at Helston, and from an arm-chair—or rather, in emergence from an arm-chair for greater impressiveness of utterance—he delivered himself of a variety of views, some reactionary, some enlightened, this time on the subject of education. 'He, no more than his father, admires the present system of mutual instruction and its accessories; the nearer you approach the old dame-school principle the better; from that system how many constellations arose, but what results have we yet had from those of Bell and Lancaster?' Whatever the results, they were certainly better on an average than the dame-school could show, but Coleridge had a violent prejudice against systematising—or, it would seem, organising—education. 'All mechanical systems he holds as bad; wherever they appear to act well it is from the influence of individual minds, which makes them succeed in spite of the system. To build up the intellectual man is the purpose of education, and this is not effected by giving him a knowledge of the way in which one mass of matter acts on another mass of matter,—though he hopes he can appreciate this branch of knowledge too—but first his memory is to be taxed and strengthened, even before his judgement; this is to be followed by the exercise of the will. For instance, let him, instead of being told the meaning of a word, search the lexicon and select from a number of synonyms the particular word which best suits his purpose; this induces a logical balancing of words.' There is some clear wisdom here, and some doubtful. What is doubtful is whether the memory can in fact be thus deliberately strengthened—a question on which psychologists differ. What is no doubt sound is the principle of making a boy search out words for himself without being told them. Whether the *will* is developed thereby is another question.

From education to one or two minor aspects of religion. 'Having thus built up our intellectual man,' observes Caroline, who clearly thought the phrase deserved a touch of satirical repetition, 'we looked at him in his waywardness and vagaries. The Plymouth Brethren came first on the field, amongst whom, to his great vexation and grief, are many of his friends. He imagines their spiritual views to resemble closely those of the early Friends; he greatly doubts the verity of their self-denial, particularly in separating themselves from the ordinary world around them and consorting only with congenial spirits. He spoke very civilly of modern Quakerdom, congratulating them on their preference for the cultivation of the intellect rather than the accomplishments of the person; also on having thrown aside the Puritanical spirit of their forefathers, and distinguishing themselves instead by their own individual excellences and by their peculiar appreciation of the good and beautiful in others.' All of which it must have been very gratifying for a good Friend like Caroline to write down. She might be pardoned for knowing little about Plymouth Brethren, for the movement (made familiar to a later generation by Edmund Gosse's *Father and Son*) was then less than ten years old. It is true that it in some respects resembles Quakerism, particularly in its assertion of the spiritual priesthood of all believers, but the differences are greater than any resemblance.

To wind up, Caroline gives a little vignette of her host in his native setting. 'He took us into his library, a most fascinating room, heated by a mild fire, just up to the temperature of our poet's imagination; coffee for one on a little table, a reading-desk for the lexicon to rest on, and near it a little table covered with classic lore; in the centre the easy-chair of our intellectual man'—the last words obviously repeated with intent.

Another visit exactly a year later, in August 1840, elicited some suggestive criticism of Carlyle, in whom Coleridge was much interested, 'though of course he does not sympathise with him in many things. He thinks his style has the faulti-ness peculiar to self-taught men—an inequality; sometimes uttering gorgeous pieces of eloquence and deep and everlasting truths, at others spending equal strength in announcing the merest trivialities. Then again, he thinks that he hardly ever modifies his manner to suit his matter,—an essential to ex-cellence in art.'

The next time Caroline and Derwent Coleridge met was after the latter had left Helston, in 1841, to become the first principal of St Mark's College, Chelsea, established by the National Society (the Church of England educational organisa-tion) as a training college for teachers. There Caroline found him when she was in London in 1842, full of zeal for his work, and showing her over the new buildings with unconcealed enthusiasm. As an educational experiment St Mark's had its interest. Its object, Caroline explained, 'is to train up a class of teachers intermediate between the present aristocratic con-stitution of the Church and the extremely ignorant set who have now to fulfil its inferior offices. This link is in the way to be supplied, as this is a sort of college where they not only study but practise teaching and reading subordinate parts of the service. He [Coleridge] sees that a similar plan has been of wonderful use among the Methodists and has long been a desideratum in the Church.' This clearly refers to the Methodist system of 'local preachers' and foreshadows the institution of lay readers in the Church of England; but the sanction of the bishops to this was not given till 1866.

Seven years later, when the visit was repeated, Coleridge, developing his views a little in the light of fuller experience, 'talked on the duty of dignifying the office of a schoolmaster, and giving him the hope of rising to preferment in the Church.' The conversation ranged widely, touching on Macaulay's brilliant talk; on Helen Faucit—'full of strength and grace, and though cold in surface there is a burning Etna underneath'; on S. T. Coleridge and Mrs Derwent Coleridge's earliest memories of him; they had, she said, tried hard to bring him to Cornwall (in which case Caroline would no doubt have met him), but the Gillmans, in whose household he was living at Highgate, were very much against it, though the old man wanted it so much, and the family were too grateful to the Gillmans for their care of the poet to insist. Though Caroline lived till 1871 and Derwent Coleridge till 1883 there is no evidence that their paths ever crossed again.

Meanwhile she had met a far greater man. In 1842 Wordsworth was at the height of his fame. All his greatest works had been written; he had just been offered a Civil List Pension by Peel, and within a few months he was to be appointed Poet Laureate in succession to his friend and neighbour Southey. As one of his biographers puts it, 'Between the years 1830 and 1840 Wordsworth passed from the apostle of a clique into the most illustrious man of letters in England.'[1] Before she saw the poet in the flesh Caroline was a worshipper at the shrine. She went, as has been said, to Rydal Mount in 1837 with Hartley Coleridge, but Wordsworth was away from home, and she had to be content with the last and best portrait of him

[1] *Wordsworth*, by F. W. H. Myers (' English Men of Letters '), p. 165.

taken in Italy, with 'a fine cast from Chantrey's bust'—and with Mrs Wordsworth. It was not till 1842 that she was compensated for the disappointment of five years earlier, and then, rather surprisingly, not at Grasmere but at Hampstead. 'Gurney Hoare,' she wrote on June 4th of that year (Yearly Meeting season again) 'brought us the good news that William Wordsworth was staying at old Mrs Hoare's, so thither he took us.' Mrs Hoare was a Gurney, a first cousin of Caroline's mother, and a great friend of all the Wordsworths.

The 'us' included Caroline's brother Barclay and, a little unusually, her mother. Little in the way of introduction was needed, for 'Aunt Charles,' Mrs Charles Fox of Trebah, had before her marriage known Wordsworth and all the Grasmere and Keswick circle well. The occasion seems to have challenged Caroline's descriptive faculties, and she depicts the poet thus: 'He is a man of middle height and not of very striking appearance, the lower part of the face retreating a little, his eye of a somewhat French diplomatic character, with heavy eyelids, and none of the flashing which one connects with poetic genius.[1] When speaking earnestly his manner and voice become extremely energetic; and the peculiar emphasis, and even accent, he throws into some of his words add considerably to their force. He evidently loves the monologue style of conversation, but shows great candour in giving due consideration to any remarks which others may make. His manner is simple, his general appearance that of the abstract thinker, whom his subject gradually warms into poetry.' He was then seventy-two.

The conversation, so far as Caroline reports it, began with a question from Mrs Fox about the beauty of Rydal. Did it not rather spoil the poet for common scenery?' 'Oh no,' he said. 'It rather opens my eyes to see the beauty there is in all; God is everywhere, and thus nothing is common or devoid of beauty. No, ma'am, it is the *feeling* that instructs the *seeing*. Wherever

[1] Barclay Fox mentions the detail that Wordsworth took off his spectacles so that his visitors might see him as he was.

there is a heart to feel there is also an eye to see; even in a city you have light and shade, reflections, probably views of the water and trees, and a blue sky above you, and can you want for beauty with all these? People often pity me while residing in a city, but they need not, for I can enjoy its characteristic beauties as well as any'—sentiments which will surprise no one who has ever read the sonnet on Westminster Bridge.

The talk then shifted, via a criticism of Hartley Coleridge and those extreme Radicals who invariably comment atra-biliously on kings and bishops, to a series of strictures on glorification of the past and discontents with the present. 'I hold,' Wordsworth declared, 'that the degree in which the Poets dwell in sympathy with the Past marks exactly the degree of their poetical faculty. Shelley, you see, was one of these, and what did his poetry come to?' Caroline (aged twenty-three) intervened. 'But,' she objected, 'some would not be true to themselves unless they gave a voice to their yearnings after the Ideal rather than the Actual.' 'Ah,' rejoined Wordsworth, 'but I object to the perpetual ill-humour with things round them, and ill-humour is no spiritual condition which can turn to poetry. Shakespeare never declaimed against kings or bishops, but took the world as he found it.' That may be true enough, but there are two sides to the invocation of Shakespeare. Browning had not yet written of Wordsworth:

'*Shakespeare was of us, Milton was for us,*
Burns, Shelley were with us, they watch from their graves!
He alone breaks from the van and the freemen,
He alone sinks to the rear and the slaves,'

but Wordsworth lived to read and reflect on the reproach.

They moved next ('I forget how,' says Caroline) to the eternal problem of the Divine toleration of evil, 'which, said Wordsworth, he had always felt the hardest problem of man's being'; when four years old he had quaked in sharp conflict of spirit on this subject. 'Nothing but Faith,' he continued, 'can keep you quiet and at peace with such awful problems pressing on you—Faith that what you know not now you will know in God's good time. It is curious, in that verse of St Paul's about Faith, Hope and Charity, or Love, that Charity should be placed the highest of the three; it must be because it is so universal and limitless in its operations; but Faith is the highest individual experience, because it conquers the pride of the understanding—man's greatest foe. Oh, how this mechanical age does battle against the Faith; it is altogether calculated to puff up the pride of the understanding, while it contains no counteracting principle which can regulate the feelings; the love of the beautiful is lost in notions of shallow utility, and men little think that the thoughts which are embodied in form around them, and on which peasants' shoon can trample, are worth more than all their steam-engines and railroads.' 'But this cannot last, there must be a reaction,' Caroline suggested with some optimism. 'No,' he said, 'it cannot last. God is merciful and loves His earth, and it cannot last. I have raised my voice loudly against it, particularly in the poem on the treaty of Cintra; and others have taken up the sound, and under many forms have given the world to know that there are thoughts in man by which he holds communion with his God, of far higher moment than any outward act or circumstance whatever.'

This first meeting had gone singularly well, and Caroline was entitled to be gratified. Their leave-taking she describes as 'truly affectionate,' adding: 'He held my hand in both of his for some time, which I consider a marked fact in my existence.' Finally, and a little summarily, 'Mrs Wordsworth was there, but we were too much absorbed for any collateral observations.'

The next year, 1843, there was news of Wordsworth, but no personal contact. Aunt Charles had been in the Lakes, and wrote home about Hartley Coleridge and Wordsworth.

The latter had just been given the Laureateship, and was 'very sensible and simple' about it. 'He speaks of it very kindly, but has quite declined doing any work connected with it on compulsion. [In fact he never did do any.] He says it is most gratifying to fill the same station that Dryden and Southey have done.'

But a rich harvest for the Journal was in prospect. In October 1844 Caroline and her sister Anna Maria were themselves in the Lakes, and in the first week of that month they paid a visit to the Wordsworths. 'He was in great force,' observed Caroline [this phrase, now obsolete, was then common] 'and evidently enjoyed a patient audience. He wanted to know how we came from Cornwall'——a piece of information in which readers of the Journal would be equally interested; unfortunately Caroline records the question but not the answer. That started the whole question of railroads, on which Wordsworth, as is well known, felt intensely, at any rate so far as the projected Kendal and Windermere Railway was concerned. His two famous letters on the subject were published during this year, 1844, but hope of frustrating the project had been abandoned, and the poet contented himself, in talk with Caroline, with 'a short lament' over the prospect. 'He grieves,' she writes, 'that the ravens and eagles should be disturbed in their meditations, and fears that their endeavours after lyric poetry will be checked. However, he admits that railroads and all the mechanical achievements of this day are doing wonders for the next generation; indeed it is the appropriate work of this age and country, and it is doing it gloriously. That anxious money-getting spirit which is a ruling principle in England, and a passion and a law in America, is doing much by exhausting itself; we may therefore look forward with hopeful trust.' From which it may be concluded that not much in the way of news about the railway-share speculation boom had yet reached Rydal Mount.

Then——why this particular theme, is not explained——some

rather odd remarks on health. 'He discoursed on the utter folly of sacrificing health to books. No book-knowledge in the world can compensate you for such a loss; nothing can excuse your trifling with health except duty to God and to your neighbour, and that you can learn from your Bible.' Admirable doctrine, but health and books in moderation are fortunately not incompatible. Wordsworth had not heard of Sterling's recent death (he had actually died less than three weeks before), and seemed genuinely affected by the news. 'Dead,' he exclaimed. 'That *is* a loss to his friends, his country and his age. A man of such learning and piety! So he is gone, and Bowles and Rogers[1] left, who are so much older,' and he added: 'I was just going to have sent him a message by you to say how much I admired his poetry.' On that Caroline read to him some lines in Sterling's last note to her:

> *'Regent of poetic mountains,*
> *Drawing from their deepest fountains*
> *Freshness pure and everlasting,*
> *Wordsworth, dear and honoured name,*
> *O'er thee pause the stars, forecasting*
> *Thine imperishable fame'*—

and he asked her to copy them out for him.

One thing led to another. Speaking still of Bowles, 'it was Amy Fisher,' he said, 'who encouraged him to write. Spoke of her with enthusiasm; after what she wrote as a child it was impossible she could go on progressing; her poetry was pure inspiration showered down direct from heaven, and did not admit of any further perfection. She is a very modest, womanly person, not allowing herself to come forward in society, nor abandoning herself to the eloquence of which he believes her very capable.' That is sufficiently lavish eulogy on a writer

---

[1] Rogers is, of course, Samuel Rogers, known equally for his poetry and his breakfast-parties ; Bowles is the Rev. William Lisle Bowles, ultimately prebendary and canon of Salisbury, whose sonnets, now completely forgotten, had on publication a remarkable vogue, arousing in particular Coleridge's youthful enthusiasm, and to a less degree Southey's.

for whose name the reference-books of today may be searched in vain.

This Amy Fisher I failed, after long endeavour, to identify,—as it turned out, for an obvious, if rather curious, reason. Research finally led to the conclusion that Caroline misheard Wordsworth by the length of a vowel. What he said was not 'Amy' but 'Emmie' Fisher. That once settled, all is clear. Emmie—more properly Emma—was the daughter of the Rev. William Fisher, Canon of Salisbury, whose wife was a first cousin of Wordsworth's. In the summer of 1841 the child went to stay at Rydal Mount, and Wordsworth commits himself to almost extravagant eulogies on her gifts. For example: 'Nothing can surpass her modest, her obedient, her affectionate and beautiful demeanour to everyone. . . . This inspired creature . . . We had some more of her smaller poems read, which are really wonderful, so that I will repeat what I said in your hearing, that this is the greatest Prodigy I ever read or heard.' The complete oblivion that has overtaken the works of this unparalleled infant suggests some deficiency either in Wordsworth's critical faculties or in the literary taste of the present generation.

A characterisation of Archdeacon Hare as 'very excellent and very learned,' but more distinguished for his classical than for his German attainments, led naturally to some observations on German literature. Wordsworth was doubtful as to its effect on the English mind. 'We must wait to find out what it is'; he said, 'my hope is that the good will assimilate itself with all the good in the English character, and the mischievous element will pass away like so much else.' His criticisms of the Germans are of some interest. 'They often sacrifice truth to originality, and in their hurry to produce new and startling ideas do not wait to weigh their worth. When they have exhausted themselves and are obliged to sit down and think they just go back to the former thinkers, and thus there is a constant revolution without their being quite conscious of it.

Kant, Schelling, Fichte; Fichte, Schelling, Kant; all this is dreary work and does not denote progress.'

On the French the poet was equally provocative, particularly regarding what he called their equalising methods of education. 'It is all formal, military, conventional, levelling,' he declared, 'encouraging in all a certain amount of talent, but cramping the finer natures, and obliging Guizot and the few other men of real genius whom God Almighty is too good to leave them entirely destitute of, to stoop to the common limits, and teach their mouths to flatter and conciliate the headstrong, ardent, unthinking multitude of ordinary men, who dictate to France through the journals which they edit. There is little of large stirring life in politics now, all is conducted for some small immediate ends; this is the case in Germany as well as France. Goethe was amusing himself with fine fancies when his country was invaded; how unlike Milton, who only asked himself whether he could best serve his country as a soldier or a statesman and decided that he could fight no better than others, but he might govern them better. Schiller had far more heart and ardour than Goethe, and would not, like him, have professed indifference to Theology and Politics, which are the two deepest things in man—indeed all a man is worth, involving duty to God and to man.'

To end what to the young visitor from Cornwall must have been a memorable day, and one which she rightly chronicled at length, Wordsworth took them on to his terrace, with its haunting view over lake and hills. Caroline describes what was in effect a valediction admirably. 'It had been a wet morning,' she says, 'but the landscape was then coming out with perfect clearness.' The poet's eye discerned it as an imagery. 'It is,' he said, 'like the human heart emerging from sorrow, shone on by the grace of God.' One of the company wondered whether the scenery had any effect on the minds of the work-people. Wordsworth thought it had; they did not learn to express it in neat phrases, but it dwelt silently within them.

That conviction he developed in a striking soliloquy on the mountains he loved. 'How constantly,' he recalled, 'mountains are mentioned in Scripture as the scene of extraordinary events; the Law was given on a mountain, Christ was transfigured on a mountain, on a mountain the great Act of our Redemption was accomplished, and I cannot but believe that when the poor read of these things in their Bibles, and the frequent mention of mountains in the Psalms, their minds glow at the thought of their own mountains, and they realise it all more clearly than others.' It is strange that the poet, who had so many opportunities of talking of such things with the dalesmen, should have had to remain so purely conjectural on a question on which he might have been expected to speak with authority.

The next day the Foxes looked in at Rydal Mount with a copy of the 'Beadroll of Scamps and Heroes' (this reference defeats me) which Wordsworth had asked for, but there was nothing but quite casual conversation, and Caroline took leave of the poet for, as it turned out, the last time. 'The old man,' she comments, 'looks much aged; his manner is emphatic, almost peremptory, and his whole deportment is virtuous and didactic.' As to looking aged, he was, after all, seventy-four, and that was a greater age a century ago than now.

Wordsworth died in April 1850. In the last week of the previous year Aunt Charles, writing on a visit to him at Rydal Mount, said: 'The gentle softened evening light of his spirit is very lovely, and there is a quiet sublimity about him as he waits on the shores of that Eternal World which seems already to cast over him some sense of its beauty and its peace.' To that may be added mention of one other last interview, between Anna Braithwaite, a Westmoreland Friend, and the aged poet. 'He spoke,' she told Caroline, 'of having long had a great desire for Fame, but that that had now all ceased, and his sole desire was to become one of "the poor in spirit" whom our Lord had declared to be blest.'

If Caroline never met Wordsworth's predecessor as Poet

Laureate she was more fortunate in the matter of his successor. Sterling had read Tennyson's poetry to a party of Foxes and others on a Falmouth beach in 1841, and in 1846 Caroline had seen his portrait, in common with Hare's, Carlyle's and others, in Samuel Laurence's studio in London. In 1849 (the year before *In Memoriam* was published) she met the two Hallams, father and son—the latter, of course, Henry, not Arthur, who had been dead seventeen years—at Sir Charles Lemon's house, Carclew. Among various other topics the historian told of an earlier journey he had made with Tennyson through Cornwall, and of the poet's delight with the scenery. 'At one point, Looe,' Hallam continued, according to Caroline, 'where he arrived in the evening, he cried "Where is the sea? show me the sea." So after the sea he went stumbling in the dark, and fell down and hurt his leg so much that he had to be nursed for six weeks by a surgeon there, who introduced some of his friends to him, and thus he got into a class of society totally new to him; and when he left, they gave him a series of introductions, so that instead of going to hotels he was passed on from town to town and abode with little grocers and shop-keepers along his line of travel. He says that he cannot have better got a true general impression of the class, and thinks the Cornish very superior to the generality. They all knew about Tennyson, and had heard his poems, and one miner hid behind a wall that he might see him. Tennyson hates being lionised and even assumes bad health to avoid it!'

This Cornish trip of Tennyson's is of some interest, because it helped to confirm his intention to write on the Arthurian legend, but either Hallam or Caroline was at fault on the facts. The misadventure which the Journal associates with Looe, on the south coast of Cornwall, actually took place at Bude, nearly forty miles away on the north. Tennyson himself handles it concisely in a diary entry some time in May 1848: 'Arrived at Bude in dark, askt girl way to sea, she opens the back door. . . . I go out, and in a moment go sheer down, upward of six feet, over wall on fanged cobbles. Up again and walked to sea over dark hill' [1]—which hardly lends colour to the six-weeks-surgical-treatment story. (Bude is substituted for Looe in the second edition of the Journal.)

In 1860, Caroline being then forty-one, Tennyson again toured Cornwall, this time with Francis Palgrave, Holman Hunt and Val Prinsep, and in September he and Palgrave found themselves at Falmouth. Their experiences there were chequered. On September 20th the poet wrote in his diary: 'Falmouth. Have not found it easy to write [he was composing *The Idylls of the King*] every day in the bustle and bother of travellers' inns. I am now writing on my knees in my bedroom at a fishmonger's, there being no room at the hotel, and the whole town mad with a bazaar for riflemen, who get drunk every night and squabble and fight and disgrace themselves and their corps.' [2]

So much for one diary. Turn now to another—Caroline's. She owed her contact with Tennyson to the existence at Grove Hill (which had belonged to her brother Barclay) of a Leonardo, supposed an original sketch for 'The Last Supper.' Tennyson and Palgrave had heard of this, and were invited to come and see it, which they accordingly did, spending two hours studying the Leonardo, a Cuyp, a Correggio and a Guido, and then walking and talking in the garden. Tennyson always professed an intense dislike to being lionised. (How he would have liked not being lionised can only be surmised.) Caroline mentions that on this occasion 'as Tennyson has a perfect horror of being lionised we left him very much to himself for a while, till he took the initiative and came forth'—signalising this emergence by 'groaning over the lionising to which he is subject and wondering how it came out at Falmouth that he was here.' Then he talked of his previous visit to Cornwall 'and his accident at Bude [not Looe this time, it will be noted] all owing to a

---

[1] *Tennyson, A Memoir*, by Hallam Lord Tennyson, p. 229.
[2] *Ibid.*, p. 389.

stupid servant-maid.' An ardent gardener himself at Farring-
ford, he was greatly interested in the Grove Hill garden, which
he found far ahead of his.

But the most interesting part of the conversation was about
Tennyson's own poems. 'By degrees,' says Caroline, 'we got
to Guinevere' and a picture of her at the Falmouth Polytechnic.
'This led to real talk of Arthur and the "Idylls," and his firm
belief in him as a historical personage, though old Speed's
narrative has much that can be only traditional. He found great
difficulty in reconstructing the character, in connecting modern
with ancient feeling in representing the Ideal King. I asked
whether Vivien might not be the old Brittany fairy who wiled
Merlin into her net, and not an actual woman. "But no," he
said, "it is full of distinct personality, though I never expect
women to like it." The River Camel he well believes in,
particularly as he slipped his foot and fell in the other day, but
found no Excalibur. Camel means simply winding, crooked,
like the Cam at Cambridge. The Welsh claim Arthur as
their own, but Tennyson gives all his votes to us. Some have
urged him to continue the "Idylls," but he does not feel it
expedient to take people's advice as an absolute law, but to wait
for the vision.'

Caroline ends with an attempt to depict Tennyson, as she
had Wordsworth, whom physically he so little resembled. She
sees him as 'a grand specimen of a man, with a magnificent
head set on his shoulders like the capital of a mighty pillar. His
hair is long and wavy, and covers a massive head. He wears
a beard and moustache, which one begrudges as hiding so much
of that firm, powerful but finely-chiselled mouth. His eyes
are large and grey, and open wide when a subject interests him;
they are well shaded by the noble brow, with its strong lines of
thought and suffering. I can quite understand Samuel Laurence
calling it the best balance of head he had ever seen.' So the
poet departed. 'We grieved,' says Caroline, 'not to take them
to Penjerrick, but they were engaged to the Truro river.'

Palgrave, who mentions the voyage to Truro, adds the distressing intelligence that on the steamer Tennyson was scandalously lionised—and bore it with conspicuous fortitude.

A transition from Wordsworth and Tennyson to any other poets of the day must be something of a descent; but the fact that John Moultrie's poems are rarely read, and his name hardly known today, does not mean that Caroline's sense of value is wrong when she devotes substantial space to her first (and apparently her only) meeting with him, in 1840. She was only twenty then, and Moultrie was sufficiently established to be looked on as a considerable personage. He wrote verse at Eton (under Keate), was a member of the same set as Macaulay, Charles Austin and Derwent Coleridge at Cambridge, and settled down a few years later as Rector of Rugby just when Arnold was beginning his headmastership there. Poems he wrote as early as 1820, when he was twenty-one, won the approval of Wordsworth, and he published a further collection in 1837. Whether Caroline had read these or not, she had probably seen a favourable notice of them in the *Edinburgh*, which the Foxes seem to have taken in regularly. In any case, Derwent Coleridge, who was Moultrie's closest friend, would certainly have talked to her about him.

It was in company with Coleridge that she met Moultrie, at the home of her uncle and aunt, Charles and Sarah Fox (who had not yet moved permanently to Trebah). 'Went to Perran to breakfast,' she writes, 'and found we had been preceded about five minutes by Derwent Coleridge and his friend John Moultrie. The first half-hour was spent in petting the cats; but I should begin by describing the Leo Novo.[1] Moultrie is not a prepossessing-looking personage—a large, broad-shouldered, athletic man, if he had but energy enough to develop his power—a sort of Athelstane of Coningsburgh—but his countenance grows on you amazingly; you discover in the

[1] There is a linguistic problem here ; *leo novus* is intelligible ; so is *leone novo* ; but *leo novo* is neither Latin nor Italian.

upper part a delicacy and refinement of feeling before un-
recognised, and in the whole a magnanimity which would
inspire confidence. But certainly his face is no directing-post
for wayfaring men and women: "Take notice, a Poet lives
here." He talks as if it were too much trouble to arrange
his words, but out they tumble, and you gladly pick them up
and pocket them for better or for worse; though, truth to
tell, his conversation would not suggest the author of "Three
Sons."'

Derwent Coleridge seems to have contributed more than
Moultrie to the morning's talk, but Moultrie did Caroline the
honour of writing a sonnet specially for her. (It does not
appear to be included in his published works.) 'J. Moultrie,'
she says, 'wrote a sonnet for me, illustrating the difference
between the sister arts of Poetry and Painting, and read it; his
voice and reading a painful contrast to the almost too dulcet
strains of his beloved friend. But there is such honesty in his
tones! He quarrelled with certain gilt scissors of Anna Maria's
because they were a deceit in wishing to appear gold, and an
unreasonable deceit, because gold is not the metal best adapted
for cutting, and doubly unsuitable for Anna Maria, considering
her religious principles, which bound her over to abhor alike
gilding and deceit. He very properly lectured her for saying
"thee" [i.e. for using it, as Friends regularly did, and to some
extent do, as a nominative: "Will thee take sugar in thy tea?"]
promised to *tutoyer* us as long as we liked, but not to answer to
thee. Coleridge had mentioned to him as one of the attractions
of the place that *thou* was spoken here.'

That is all, but it is enough to recall a forgotten poet, some
of whose verse is worth reading still. The *Dictionary of National
Biography*, by the way, raises doubts about Caroline's mention
of 'Three Sons,' by describing it as 'the best of his *later* poems.'
If it had been that, Caroline could clearly not have mentioned
it in 1840, for Moultrie was writing till not long before his
death, which took place in 1874. She was, however, perfectly

right. 'Three Sons' is to be found in the first volume he ever published, in 1837.

The chronicle of Caroline's encounter with poets still lacks full completeness. One portrait has yet to be added to the gallery. Visiting her mother's family, the Barclays, at Bury Hill, near Dorking, in 1856, she found there Martin Farquhar Tupper (he was living at Albury, half a dozen miles away), who wrote what passed for poetry contemporaneously with Tennyson, and, incredible though it may seem, established no less strong a hold on the public—though not necessarily the same public. We can have the full picture, for it demands little space. 'Met the author of *Proverbial Philosophy* [more properly, *Proverbial Philosophy*, *A Book of Thoughts and Arguments Originally Treated*], and heard him expatiate on the beautiful scene before him, and not in hexameters. He is a happy little blue-eyed man, who evidently enjoys talking, but does not approach the dignity of his didactic poem.' The reference to hexameters hardly seems apt. Tupper mainly favoured blank verse as the vehicle for his *Thoughts and Arguments*—much of it more blank than verse. But his vogue for a time was remarkable; and he could always boast that at Oxford he had won a prize (in theology, too) for which Mr Gladstone competed unsuccessfully.

Chapter XI
De Bunsens and their Circle

We may be grateful to Caroline for perpetuating the memory of Baron de Bunsen, Prussian Ambassador at the Court of St James's, and the cultured Anglo-Saxon circle he gathered round him, for both de Bunsen (why he was always known in England by *de*, not his rightful *von*, is unexplained) and the Germany he represented had something to contribute to civilisation of which their successors of today are lamentably devoid. De Bunsen's wife was English—or, to be strictly accurate, Welsh—and part of the family became Anglicised. His second son, Ernst, married Elizabeth Gurney (one of the large Earlham circle), Caroline's second cousin, which explains Caroline's association with the family. Ernst's son, Sir Maurice de Bunsen, was British Ambassador at Vienna at the outbreak of the last war.

Before Caroline first met him, Baron de Bunsen (to anticipate a title which was not conferred on him till 1857; he was known as 'Chevalier' when in England) had already been in London for five years, and among other activities had established the Prussian Embassy in Carlton House Terrace, then Carlton Terrace, where, as the German Embassy, it still remains. But something needs to be said of de Bunsen's earlier life. Born in 1791 at Korbach, in the little principality of Waldeck, in south-west Germany, he went in 1815 to Berlin to consult the historian Niebuhr on the plan of study he had mapped out for himself on the religion, laws and languages of the Teutonic races. The association developed, and when, two years later, Niebuhr went as envoy to the Papal Court he took young de Bunsen with him as secretary. When Niebuhr resigned in 1823 de Bunsen succeeded him, and remained at Rome till 1838 In 1842, after serving a short term at Berne, he came to London as Ambassador and remained there for twelve years. He was, as already stated, made a Baron in 1857, and died in 1860.

What made de Bunsen's mission in England both important and congenial was his personal relationship with the King of Prussia, Frederick William IV, who had succeeded to the throne in 1840. Both shared unusual religious views, strongly admiring the Anglican Church and endeavouring to achieve some association between it and the Lutheran,—an operation which took visible form in the establishment of that Prusso-Anglican bishopric of Jerusalem which so scandalised Newman and contributed materially to his decision to exchange the Church of England for the Church of Rome. This friendship, which smoothed de Bunsen's path in London for the first six years of his mission there, was considerably strained by the liberal movements of 1848, with which de Bunsen was much more in sympathy than the King. The Ambassador finally resigned when his insistent advice that Prussia should join Britain and France in what came to be called the Crimean War was rejected.

As has been said, Caroline's first acquaintance with the de Bunsens was the result of the marriage of her cousin Elizabeth Gurney to Chevalier de Bunsen's second son Ernst. That had taken place in August 1845, but Caroline was not in London that year, and did not meet Ernst de Bunsen till the August of 1846, when she was on her way home from a holiday in Switzerland. Then she went to breakfast with Ernst and Elizabeth, who were now well settled in the house they occupied for several years, Abbey Lodge, Regent's Park. Nothing of great interest appears to have been said, apart from a discussion about introducing Caroline to the Chevalier, whose reputation as a scholar evidently inspired her with some awe. But that satisfaction had to wait till Caroline was up for Yearly Meeting the next year. Caroline then met Ernst de Bunsen at Ham House (the home of Samuel Gurney, Elizabeth de Bunsen's father), and he took unconsciously the shortest of all paths to her approval by talking enthusiastically of the Maurices and Archdeacon Hare, who was then hard at work on his Life of Sterling. (She makes a note that she must read the Chevalier's *The Church of the Future*, which had been published a couple of years earlier.) Two days later Ernst de Bunsen—whose marriage to a Friend had not made a Friend of him—went to Meeting with Caroline's party. Afterwards he explained his views. His own instinct was for some compromise; in a Friends' Meeting he would have liked to read his New Testament; at Church he always contrived a little silent service for himself before the sermon by a not difficult effort of abstraction. Later Ernst, who had a fine voice, sang some old German hymns. 'The other day,' Caroline mentions, 'Sarah Gurney heard him sing, and Mendelssohn accompany him. Mendelssohn is beautiful, poetical and childlike, clinging to those he loves; his playing is like Ariel in *The Tempest*.'

Two days later Ernst de Bunsen took 'us,' which no doubt means, as usual, Caroline and Anna Maria, to Carlton Terrace to present them to his parents. The conversation on the way was discursive and interesting. 'His father and he find much good in coursing about to different places of worship, both because the novelty of form is striking and tends to bring home old truths with new force, and because you can thus get some test notion of what in you is spiritual, and what habitual and accidental.' Ernst talked of his father's early life and marriage. Bunsen the elder was at Rome with Niebuhr when a Mrs Waddington, an Englishwoman, was much struck by him and sought his acquaintance, with the result that in a surprisingly short space of time he married one of her daughters, an arrangement that brought both parties from the first unqualified happiness.

The De Bunsens and their Circle

At a late breakfast Caroline sat next to the Chevalier, F. D. Maurice and one or two of the Bunsen family being also present. They talked of the German Hospital at Dalston (still in existence), in which the Ambassador took a particular interest; of Fliedner's deaconess house and hospital at Kaiserswerth, from which Florence Nightingale derived many ideas; of Schleiermacher and his privations during 'the war,' i.e. the Napoleonic war; of the Irish, of whom Bunsen spoke with deep sympathy. 'Ernest tells us of his father's intimacy with our Queen [who was, of course, half German], whom he finds high-principled, religious and judicious.' The morning ended with a visit to George Richmond's studio, where the artist 'showed us his life-like portrait of Bunsen, and then exhibited one of an English judge as an extreme contrast: the one dreamy and beautiful, the other solid, self-satisfied and practical.' There is unfortunately no clue to the identity of this member of the judiciary.

The usual two years now intervened before Caroline was in London again, renewing old friendships. Then, in May 1849, she met the Chevalier at dinner at Samuel Gurney's (Mrs Ernst de Bunsen's father) in Lombard Street. 'His face,' says Caroline, 'and Samuel Gurney's were fine studies of genial humanity'—an impression which their respective portraits fully confirm. Bunsen talked a good deal about contemporary politics, both British and German, showing himself as well versed in the former as in the latter. The question of the Oregon boundary, in effect the frontier between the United States and Canada, had strained relations between the British and American Governments to the danger-point for a generation. Finally, in 1846, a reasonable compromise was agreed to by both countries. According to de Bunsen, a deputation of Friends whom Sir Robert Peel received had a good deal to do with the settlement. 'The earnestness of their appeal struck him deeply, and he asked why the American Friends did not in the same way memorialise their own Government. This he was told they had already done; some of the facts concerning America which J. J. Gurney was able to give from his own knowledge buttressed their arguments capitally, and that evening Bunsen was at Sir Robert Peel's when he and Lord Aberdeen talked over the matter in the most satisfactory manner, and the business was arranged very soon after.'

After dinner (which was taken in those days in the afternoon, not the evening) the whole party visited the German Hospital, where some of the sisters from Kaiserswerth, already mentioned, were now installed. Caroline was much impressed by them. 'One of them in particular might have sat to Fra Angelico, so seraphic was her face; it told of a heart perfectly devoted, and perfectly happy in its devotion.' On the way, or at the hospital, Caroline had 'much pleasant talk' with Bunsen, particularly on the theological controversy of the moment. 'He is not surprised at the outcry against Hare and Maurice, because he knows the depth of ignorance and malice in human nature to be absolutely unfathomable; they have many bad things in Germany, but are spared the sorrow and shame of having any newspaper which issues lies and malice in the name of the God of Truth, the Prince of Peace.' The reference is plainly to the evangelical *Record*,[1] which insistently and implacably assailed Maurice for his alleged heterodoxy on various cardinal points of Christian doctrine, and for the crime of stirring up the people to demand improvement in their social conditions.

After a little more of such themes Bunsen turned to the tangled politics of his own country, where the King, Frederick William IV, a close personal friend of the Ambassador's, was busy playing fast and loose with the popular forces which were insistently demanding a democratic constitution. After prolonged vicissitudes a situation had been reached which Caroline

---

[1] ' His [Maurice's] life was a long, fierce warfare against a collection of newspapers, notably *The Record*, which recognized that in fighting him they were fighting for their very existence, and which gave and took no quarter ' (C. F. G. Masterman, *Frederick Denison Maurice*, p. 43).

describes in Bunsen's words. 'Bunsen,' she writes, 'talked much of recent German politics; the distressing conflict of mind in which the King has recently been. Peel considered his conduct almost inconceivably unselfish in refusing the Governorship of the Four Kingdoms for so long, but the King thought he should assuredly involve Europe in war if he were to accept it before the other Powers had acceded; this they have now done, and today is arranged for his proclamation, the beginning of a great and perfectly new experiment. It is an American Federal Government adapted to Monarchical Institutions, and the extent of this hereditary protectorate is enormous.' Unfortunately the new experiment never materialised. The 'today' mentioned by Caroline was May 25th, 1849. On May 17th representatives of Austria, Bavaria, Hanover and Saxony did indeed meet in Berlin to achieve the unity of Germany, but they failed to achieve unity even among themselves, and whatever proclamation was contemplated for May 25th was certainly never issued.

During her next visit to London, in 1851, Caroline had long and interesting talks with the de Bunsens. One day in June she dined with the Ernst de Bunsens at their house, Abbey Lodge. Ernst's father, the Chevalier, was there. So was his brother George, Dr Pauli, the Chevalier's secretary, and others. The first of the company to attract Caroline's attention brought her suddenly and rather strangely in touch with one of Goethe's personal romances. Augustus Kestner was the son of one of the many women with whom the poet fell temporarily in love. That in itself would have amounted to little, but Frau Kestner had been before her marriage Charlotte Buff, and as the Lotte of *The Sorrows of Werther* she was immortalised by Goethe for all the world. Caroline describes the product of the Kestner-Charlotte marriage, and recalls accurately the story of his parents. 'A bright dinner at Abbey Lodge. Kestner was there; a dry, thin gentleman of the old school, who looks as if he had had his romance done for him long before his birth.

He has a most interesting correspondence between his mother and Goethe, who had greatly admired and loved her, but as she was betrothed to his friend he had the prudence to retire from the great peril he felt himself in; and even after her marriage he left Frankfort whenever they were coming there. These experiences, and the awful death of a friend who had not been so self-controlled, were combined into the Wertherian romance. But of all this Kestner said nothing. He is quite happy when talking of his six Giottos, the gems of his collection.'

But Bunsen (the father), not Kestner, was her neighbour at table (with Pauli on the other side), and to him she put a direct question on the controversy that was strangely agitating the whole of England at the moment, arising out of assumption by Roman Catholic bishops of English territorial titles. Ridiculously trivial as the affair seems in retrospect, and ridiculous as Lord John Russell's denunciation of 'papal aggression' incontestably was, that was not the view taken in 1851, and Caroline showed herself well alive to actualities in eliciting the views of a detached foreigner, incidentally a strong Protestant, on the subject. Bunsen's reply was more interesting than convincing. He said (Caroline reports him a little confusingly in a mixture of direct and indirect speech): 'That the Roman scheme is one that would not be submitted to for a moment in other countries, but simply on the ground of politics, not of religion; it is our lack of Faith which is inconveniently brought home to us by questions of this sort, and we rebel against the inference rather than the fact that systematising a black and white theology is a substitute for Faith, not an evidence of it. You are excellent people, but very material; you are afraid to give yourselves up to any teaching but what has existed on parchment for hundreds of years; if an angel brought you a new truth direct from Heaven you would not believe it till it was successfully copied on the parchment; no, you are excellent people, but you terribly want Faith. You are afraid of Reason and oppose it to Faith, and accordingly miss them both.' There is more than one point here that invites comment, but it is more important to report Bunsen's words than to controvert them; his strictures on the English devotion to those truths only that are recorded on parchment come addressed a little strangely to a citizen of a country without a written constitution and a member of a religious society bound by no formal articles of faith. A moment or two later the Chevalier made a better diagnosis. Caroline makes no comment on his suggestion that the Society of Friends is subject to grave peril of 'an idolatry of the form of formlessness,' but she was of far too sincere and self-searching a spirit to dismiss the criticism as groundless.

Of the remainder of the conversation on this June afternoon or evening the most interesting phase was devoted to what Caroline calls mesmerism, though the anecdotes quoted turn rather on clairvoyance or thought transference. The first story told, by George de Bunsen, falls a little flat. He learned, he said, when studying Greek history at College that a book of Aristotle's on contemporary Athenian politics (? the recently discovered *Constitution of the Athenians*) was lost. The sense of what the value of the work would be if it were available haunted him; his mind was perpetually on the subject. While all this was disturbing him 'he received a letter from a friend, telling that he had been consulting a clairvoyante about him, who had seen him groping among dusty parchments in the dark.' Unfortunately he had not been groping among dusty parchments in the dark, except mentally, and still more unfortunately the clairvoyante's power did not extend to identifying and locating the missing manuscript.

The second anecdote, about George's father, the Chevalier, was more impressive. 'When his father was with his King and our Queen at Stolzenfels [in the course of a short continental tour undertaken by the Queen and the Prince Consort in 1845] he (George) wanted to know something about him, and accordingly mesmerised a clairvoyante and sent her in spirit to the castle. "Do you see my father?" "No, he is not there." "Then go and look for him." At length she announced having found him sitting with an elderly lady. George de Bunsen could not conceive him anywhere but at Stolzenfels, till the thought struck him, he may have gone to Karlsruhe to see his sister; so he asked "It is a very neat regular-looking town, is it not, and the houses new?" and asked particulars of the room in which he thought his aunt likely to be found. "No, nothing of the sort; an old town, an old house and an old lady." She gave many details which he could make nothing of, and [he] gave up the geographical problem in despair. In a few days a letter from his father arrived, saying that the King had taken a fancy to go somewhere in a steamer and had asked Bunsen to accompany him. This brought him within moderate distance of another sister, so he was actually with her at the time of the clairvoyance.' This, unlike the Aristotle story, is a clear-cut and convincing example of straightforward clairvoyance. It is not mesmerism as commonly understood, but Caroline's misuse of that term matters little.

One of the features of this particular evening, as of another two days later at Carlton Terrace, was the playing of the aged Chevalier Neukomm, the celebrated organist and composer, who was related to, and had been trained by, the Haydns. Caroline had, so far as can be discovered, no special musical education—Friends of that day paid too little attention to music —and her delight at what she listened to at the de Bunsens' gains in interest on that account. After mentioning some casual talk about British universities, in the course of which Bunsen 'is much amused to think how little the English Universities educate for the times we live in,' she continues: 'but the spirit of the evening was Neukomm. The inventor of a silvery lute of some sort came to introduce his instrument, and its breathings were indeed exquisite; and very marvellous was it when the two musicians improvised together, just taking the

Ranz des Vaches as a motive, to hear how they blended their thoughts and feelings in true harmony. But I was glad when the flute was silent, and Neukomm poured out his own heart through the voice of the organ. He led one whither he would, through regions of beauty and magnificence, and then through quiet little valleys where nothing could be heard but the heart's whisper—so pure, so tender, you leant forward to catch what it said; and then you were carried onward into a spirit world, where all around were "such things as dreams are made of." And then such a swell of harmony, such exulting strains, would bespeak the presence and the triumph of some great Idea, revealing to man more of himself and of his Maker. Then again that trembling voice, "Can He love such an one as I?" And then the final magnificent swell of sound, triumphing over doubt and fear and weakness. I never heard music without words say half as much as I heard this evening; but very likely I quite misinterpret its real meaning, for each one must translate it for himself.'

Caroline met Neukomm again the next year at Dublin, where the British Association was meeting, and she notes some interesting facts about his connexion with Talleyrand. 'Neukomm's judgement of individuals,' she writes, 'is noble and generous, only to the masses everywhere he denies the guidance of any principle: self-interest and ambition he thinks the motive-power of every national movement to which we would give a higher origin, and he thinks he sees distinctly that a nation is always the worse for it. But then he lived for twenty years with Talleyrand—twenty years of the generous and hopeful believing part of his life. He speaks affectionately of the latter, he was so kind and considerate to his servants, so friendly to his friends, so devoted to France, though true to no Frenchman and no Dynasty. He cared not at all for music, but Neukomm gave some instruction to his niece. At Rome Neukomm became acquainted with the Bunsens, and what a change of intimates it was for him!'

The De Bunsens and their Circle

Baron de Bunsen died in December 1860. It must have been some time earlier in that year that Caroline saw him for the last time, in the South of France. She had gone out to bring home her late brother's children, their mother having died suddenly at Pau. In reference to that she writes (to Lucy Hodgkin) three years later, from the Hôtel du Pavillon, Cannes: 'When we were here before, Madame de Bunsen had a birthday. . . . We passed the house where we dined that bright day and listened to the loving speeches—the old Baron made one about G. Fox and liberty of conscience in drinking our healths—and that was the last time we saw him.'

Meanwhile Caroline had seen more of the Ernst de Bunsens, who had been at Falmouth twice in 1857, staying with the Foxes. In April she writes with enthusiasm: 'Ernest de Bunsen is with us. I wish I could chronicle a great deal of his talk; it is marvellously vivid, and he seems equally at home in all regions of human thought: deep metaphysics, devout theology, downright boyish merry-making, the most tangled complexities of court intrigues—and then his singing! He is truly a man of infinite aptitudes. Took him to Carclew where he was a perfect bottle of champagne to Sir Charles [Lemon]; and to Roscrow, where the boys were lost in admiration and delight. He has been translating William Penn's Life into German, and sent a copy to Humboldt,[1] from whom he has received two charming letters about it, in one saying that he has read every word, and that the contemplation of such a life has contributed to the peace of his old age. We had German hymns, original and of olden time, very full of devout thought as well as of feeling. Then he sang Handel's "Comfort Ye My People" and "Thou wilt not leave His Soul in Hell" and Haydn's "Creation of Eve"; the one so mighty and overwhelming in its grandeur and expressiveness, the other so varied, picturesque and exquisite. At Tregedna ["Uncle Joshua" Fox's] we had one deep-hearted Irish melody and one

[1] Alexander ; Wilhelm had died in 1835.

Sicilian, full of love and patriotism and triumphant hope. He is perfectly ingenuous about his voice. At Heidelberg three Bunsen brothers and a brother in law would sing quartettes. In the course of our talk he said "Forgive to the fullest extent and in the freest spirit, but never forget anything: it is all intended to be a lesson to profit our after life, for there is no such thing as chance." '

The October visit produces only one short entry, but it embodies memories of some interest. 'The Ernest de Bunsens are with us: he read us last night Mendelssohn's "Elijah," illustrating it whenever he could with such exquisite feeling, power and pathos. The last time he saw Mendelssohn they had played and sung several things together, when Mendelssohn asked for one more. He chose "Be thou faithful unto Death and I will give thee a Crown of Life." When he had ended, Mendelssohn slipped away from the room, overcome with emotion. Ernest de Bunsen followed him; he said "*Gott segne euch alle!*" and was gone.'

So the Journal, which about this time becomes very fragmentary (perhaps from its editor's hesitations about publishing references to persons still living), takes leave of a family which held a notable place in pre-Imperial Prussia, embodying many of the best of German qualities and few if any of the worst, and which, in the person of one of the Baron's grandsons, Sir Maurice de Bunsen, provided, strangely enough, the first British diplomatist abroad to sound a decisive warning of the imminence of German aggression in July 1914.[1]

[1] Gooch and Temperley, *Documents on the Origins of the War*, vol. xi. p. 123.

Chapter XII
Sir John Bowring

One of the most striking figures encountered in Caroline's Journal is Sir John Bowring, author of a number of hymns, including the well-known 'In the Cross of Christ I glory,' editor of the *Westminster Review*, executor of Jeremy Bentham, M.P., first for Kilmarnock and then for Bolton, Governor of Hong Kong, and towards the end of his life, singularly enough, Minister of Hawaii to various courts of Europe. Though he had achieved only a few of these distinctions at the time when Caroline first met him, in 1837, she had a sound enough sense of the interest of his personality to report his conversation both then and on later occasions at unusual length.

In 1837 Bowring was forty-five. Like Caroline, he was of West-country stock, having been born at Exeter in 1792 of Unitarian parents. He was sent to school at Moretonhampstead, on the edge of Dartmoor, at a time when there were no roads practicable for wheeled vehicles between there and Exeter, everything (as he explains) being conveyed on 'crooks'— bent branches of trees fastened to pack-saddles—seated on one of which the small Unitarian made his first departure from home for school. During four years in a merchant's office in Exeter he learned by one means and another an astonishing number of European languages,[1] and a little later, in the course of commercial journeys on the Continent, he met a number of well-known men, most or all of them Liberals, in different countries. Meanwhile he came considerably under the influence of Jeremy

[1] In later life he claimed to know two hundred languages, and to speak a hundred.

Bentham, of whose newly-founded *Westminster Review* he became editor in 1825. In 1829 an LL.D. degree was conferred on him by the University of Groningen in Holland; in 1830 he visited Sir Walter Scott at Abbotsford, and in 1835 Lafayette at Lagrange; in 1835 he was elected Liberal M.P. for Kilmarnock, after being defeated at Blackburn two years earlier. Through all his campaigns, and in the *Westminster Review*, he was advocating Free Trade before Bright and Cobden.

In November 1837 Bowring, having lost his seat at Kilmarnock at the General Election necessitated by the demise of King William IV, visited Egypt, for whose ruler Mehemet Ali he had a great admiration, returning by way of Syria and Constantinople. Whether or not he landed at Falmouth, as so many travellers from the East did in those days, he appeared there in December 1838. Information regarding his advent is best left to Caroline herself to impart. 'Whilst paying a visit at Carclew [Sir Charles Lemon's home],' she wrote, 'in came the butler, stifling a giggle and announcing "Dr Bowring and his foreign friend," who accordingly marched in. This egregious individual is Edhem Bey, Egyptian Minister of Instruction and Generalissimo of the Forces He was dressed in a large blue pelisse with loose sleeves, and full blue trousers, with scarlet gaiters and slippers, a gold waistband a foot and a half in width, and on his right breast his decoration of the crescent in uncommonly large diamonds, said to be worth £50,000! He is a tall man and very stout, with a rich complexion and black rolling eyes, aged about thirty-four. He is married to a beautiful Circassian, and only one, whom he bought at twelve years of age and married at fourteen. He is accompanied by Dr Bowring, late editor of the *Foreign Quarterly* [it looks as if Caroline meant the *Westminster Review*], and Mr Joyce, a civil engineer, who has just refused a professorship at King's College. So these good people are come into Cornwall to inspect the mines and acquire what information they can, for the Bey is a remarkably intelligent man, and bent on educating his countrymen. He talks French fluently.'

Bowring's own very fragmentary Memoirs devote considerable space to his visit to Egypt, but there is no mention of his bringing an Egyptian Minister home with him. He does, however, record that the Minister of Public Instruction of the day, presumably the same individual whose graces Caroline observed in the Carclew drawing-room, 'gave two thousand three hundred blows on the foot to one of his dependents, who died the next day, but he paid £45 and the affair was hushed up.'

It is perhaps a little uncharitable to recall that Greville wrote of Bowring: 'I have never been able to understand the enormous unpopularity of this man'; he added, however, that it was really due to Bowring's having made an early success in public life, on the basis possibly of rather superficial knowledge, so arousing the jealousy of the envious. Caroline had not read Greville, for he was then unpublished, and she formed her own opinion of the visitor (as she would have done in any case). Bowring, as she saw him, 'is a very striking-looking personage, with a most poetical, ardent, imaginative forehead, and a temperament all in keeping, as evidenced by his whole look and manner.' He was naturally full of travellers' tales of the countries from which he had recently come. For all that, the first note he sounded was one of scepticism. 'Dr Bowring,' says Caroline, 'has no opinion of the Egyptian miracles recorded by Lane; [1] but ascribes them to a practical knowledge of the language, leading questions and boundless credulity. He says they are now so much at a discount in their own neighbourhood that when he was there he had not moral courage to investigate for himself. He has, however, seen the power exercised over serpents precisely similar to that described in Exodus as exhibited by the magicians. In a party he was at a sorcerer declared "I can strike any of you dumb";

[1] E. W. Lane, translator of the *Arabian Nights*, had a year before this (in 1836) published *Manners and Customs of the Modern Egyptians*.

so one was selected who took his station in the centre of the group, when with a wave of his hand the magician proclaimed "In Allah's name be dumb," when the man writhed in apparent anguish, utterly unable to disobey the command. The effect he attributes (not to electro-biology) but to a feeling in the patient that it was the mandate of Allah, and that disobedience would be equally criminal and impossible.'

Then the Bey took a hand in the conversation—we are not told in what language. He spoke of Queen Victoria, 'whom he thinks a very interesting and dignified girl [the Queen was then nineteen],' but not being familiar with the idea of constitutional monarchy 'he laughs at her title, as belonging far more properly to her Ministers.' A slightly un-Quakerly interlude followed. 'His long pipe was brought into the library by his servant Hassan, and we had a puff all round; it has an amber mouthpiece set with diamonds. Opium and aromatic herbs,' adds Caroline, 'are his tobacco, wine and lemonade his little byplay.' Bowring, who seemed a little hurt that Caroline was not familiar with his *Matins and Vespers*, referred in a critical vein to Joseph Wolff;[1] the ex-Jewish Christian missionary, confessed his own failure to secure an interview with Lady Hester Stanhope in the Lebanon, and then went on to talk of Shelley and Byron. Here either he or Caroline is at fault on fact. Bowring, according to the Journal, possessed an unpublished manuscript by Shelley, of which he repeated a good deal. Caroline quotes (inaccurately) one couplet, the famous

> '*I met Murder on the way,*
> *He had a mask like Castlereagh,*'

and that was not at this time unpublished; it had appeared in 1832 in a volume edited by Leigh Hunt. 'In company,' Caroline reports the visitor as saying, 'Shelley was a diffident, retiring creature, but most beautiful, with an interpenetrating

[1] See p. 336.

eye of intense feeling; he had a fascinating influence over those who were much with him, over Byron especially. His unhappy views on religion were much strengthened, if not originated, by the constant persecution he endured, but these views had very little effect on his conduct.' Caroline may or may not have been sufficiently versed in particulars of Shelley's conduct to accept the last assertion with reservations. On Mary Howitt, to whom Bowring referred with some appreciation, she would be in a better position to form a judgement. Her family would naturally be familiar with the Howitts, for these prolific writers (they were responsible for about a hundred and fifty books between them, including translations) were still members of the Society of Friends, as they had been from birth. Later they left Quakerism for spiritualism, and from that Mary Howitt's evolving views took her ultimately into the Roman Catholic Church.

Finally, so far as this particular conversation was concerned, an experience or two of Bowring the hymn-writer. 'On going to the Holy Land the first voices Dr Bowring heard were engaged in singing his hymn "Watchman, watchman, what of the night?", which had been imported and translated by the American missionaries. His "Matins and Vespers" were the means of converting a poor Syrian, who on being shipwrecked possessed that and that only, which copy is now in the possession of the Bishop of Stockholm. He spoke of the striking effect in Mahometan countries of the sudden suspension of business and everything else at the hour of prayer; this induced an animated discussion on the advantages and disadvantages of these positive signs of devotion—whether they did not rather satisfy the devotees with signs independent of the thing signified, or even familiarise the habit when the mind is not in a prepared state. The name "Allah" is perpetually introduced in Oriental conversation, but still with a solemnity of intention and manner very different to our "God knows."'

Just a year later, on December 13th, 1839, Dr Bowring

unexpectedly appeared again. 'Papa and I were busy writing, when, to our surprise, in walked Dr Bowring. He is come to stand for this place, an enterprise in which Papa said what he could to discourage him. He promises to incur no illegitimate expenses, and therefore has not the least chance of success. He has just returned from a diplomatic visit to Berlin.' The diplomatic visit was made (as Bowring explains in his own memoirs) at the instance of the British Government in connexion with the *Zollverein* of the German States at Berlin, with a view to discovering how far British commercial relations with Germany could be extended, but—adds the emissary in language which the passage of time has done little to stale—'the German delegates appeared to me for the most part very narrow in their views, opposed to Free Trade and afraid of competition, most of them indeed being manufacturers or the representatives of manufacturing interests.' There is more of this moralising, but, uncompromising Free Trader as he was, Bowring was constrained to admit that the British example in the matter of tariffs—he was writing seven years before the repeal of the Corn Laws—gave the Germans no great encouragement. His other experiences during his Berlin visit, including a dinner with King Frederick William III, while of interest in themselves, have no relevance to his subsequent visit to Falmouth.

This visit too, as already seen, had its purpose. Dr Bowring, rejected at Kilmarnock, was looking for another seat. He wanted to be back in the House again, mainly in order to agitate there against the Corn Laws, and the Penryn constituency for some reason attracted him. (Penryn and Falmouth are virtually one town.) His solicitation of the Penryn electors made so little impression on him that in a chapter of reminiscence written twenty years later he referred to his chances of return for 'Penzance'; the fact that an old man approached him on behalf of the Wesleyans, with the intimation that since it was reported that he did not believe in the Trinity he must pay double for their votes, casts an instructive light on Caroline's summary estimate of the chances of a candidate who refused to incur any illegitimate expenses.

To return to the Journal, Caroline records, on the day after Bowring's first appearance, that 'Dr Bowring dined with us after addressing the Penryn constituency and being rather disgusted by their appearance. The only thing in his speech that at all touched them was his declaration that he was half a Cornishman, his mother being the daughter of a clergyman and schoolmaster of St Ives, Mr Lane, whose memory, he understood, is still held in the odour of sanctity.' There followed various reminiscences of no special interest today, primarily regarding contemporary Popes. Bowring had visited Gregory XVI in 1836 and told the Foxes something about it. He had, inevitably, sounded His Holiness on Free Trade and elicited the diplomatic answer 'It's all very good, but I think my Monopoly is a better thing.'

At this point there is a certain conflict between memories. According to Caroline, 'Dr Bowring had also formerly had an audience of Napoleon's Pope, a very pleasant man; they talked on poetry, each repeating passages from Dante, who His Holiness informed the Doctor had lived in the very same cell which he once inhabited in a Carthusian monastery.' Dr Bowring's own version, in his Memoirs, is different. He associated the conversation regarding Dante not with 'Napoleon's Pope' but with Gregory XVI, who mentioned that 'one of Dante's verses was addressed to a room in a convent in which he had been a monk.' The discrepancy is obviously of literary interest rather than material importance. Caroline in this case is pretty clearly wrong. There is no reason to believe that Bowring ever met Napoleon's Pope, Pius VII, who died in 1823.

Bowring knew the Buxtons and Gurneys well, which no doubt stimulated his interest in the Foxes after he had first met them at Carclew. Mention of these Norfolk relatives in the course of conversation started a new series of anecdotes. Bowring had lately had an interesting letter from Sarah Buxton (sister of Sir Thomas Fowell Buxton) acknowledging a gift of some flowers gathered at Bethlehem and Nazareth. 'When in the Holy Land,' Caroline reports, 'he felt himself completely thrown back into gospel history and gospel times, so stationary are the customs of the people. Often were passages of Scripture recalled to his mind by events passing around him, as when on the shore of the Lake of Tiberias one of those sudden storms arose so beautifully described in the Bible. He was once at Sychar in Samaria, just at the foot of Mount Gerizim, and had been recommended to the High Priest, with injunctions to show him everything in his church. Amongst other treasures he showed him the oldest MS. extant, namely the Samaritan version of the Bible, 3500 years of age. In this the High Priest pointed out to him a text, "On Mount Gerizim is the place where men ought to worship," which he said the Jews had purposely omitted in their version; he inveighed against them in the very same spirit described 1800 years ago. In accordance with this text all the Samaritans assemble annually on Mount Gerizim and perform their worship there.'

It is worth while interpolating here a not irrelevant reminiscence. Forty years and more before Bowring's visit to Mount Gerizim, as a small boy in George's Meeting House at Exeter he had been called on by the Minister on one occasion to record in his own words the Scripture story of Christ's talk with the woman of Samaria. 'At the point,' he recalls, a little ungrammatically, 'where availing herself of the presence of so high an authority for the solution of a question fiercely disputed between Jews and Samaritans, I inserted the phrase "impelled by a natural curiosity," I was reproved for the introduction of a something not to be found in the gospel narrative.' Did— one cannot but wonder—the traveller standing on the green slopes of Gerizim with the son of the High Priest in 1839 see suddenly before his eyes the austere interior of a plain Devonshire bethel in one of the closing years of the previous century, and the figure of a nervous little boy standing up to receive an unjust reprimand for lending a touch of reality to his story of what happened on Gerizim before the first generation of the Christian era had lived its life? If it was so, Bowring says nothing of it.

Other features of note in Syria were Damascus and Lady Hester Stanhope—the one more accessible than the other. The former, Bowring said, 'is an extremely interesting city, everything kept as of yore—the street called Straight, the house of Ananias, the prison in the wall, through whose window Paul escaped in a basket; every cherished event has here "a local habitation and a name" handed down by tradition.' As for Lady Hester, he was very anxious to see her, and wrote to her physician [Dr Meryan, who was also her secretary] for permission to pay her a visit. 'Her reply was, "No, I won't receive any of those rascally English." She had a notion that the Scotch and Albanians were the only honest people to be found anywhere. She greatly blamed Joseph Wolff [1] for apostatising from so old and respectable a religion as Judaism, and in a celebrated letter to him she says, "Can you for an instant think anything of Christianity if it requires the aid of such a vagabond adventurer as yourself to make it known?"' So much for the fantastic Englishwoman of Djoun. Brief observations on various topics followed, the only one worth recalling being the statement that 'in Phoenicia the people eat cream just like the Cornish folk,' a fact, says Caroline, 'which raised the question whether it was imported from Cornwall with the tin.' 'It' manifestly means the process, not the commodity itself, as Caroline's rather ambiguous entry would imply.

On the fourth day Dr Bowring's visit ended abruptly. Caroline relates the frustration of his hopes. 'A Government messenger has persuaded Dr Bowring to resign his Parliamentary views in favour of another who has a long purse and is willing to use it. He was low and vexed about the business,

[1] See p. 337.

having had the trouble and expense of coming here to no purpose; however, he does not wish to split the Falmouth Reformers, and accordingly published his farewell address and retired.' In other words, and more briefly, he came on the 13th, spoke on the 14th, left on the 16th.

In 1840 Bowring was at Falmouth again, for the third year in succession. He was this time more in a philosophical than a political mood. It was, in fact, the Benthamite editor of the *Westminster Review* rather than the Oriental traveller who provided Caroline with material for another page or two of her Journal. He talked first of the National Convention—a body representing the Chartist movement (which Caroline, incidentally, strongly disapproved), which sat from February to July 1839 to promote the Chartist petition to Parliament and advance Chartism generally by all available means. 'He has been much blamed,' says Caroline, 'for countenancing such a political union, but he thinks the enthusiasm manifested therein not only excusable but necessary, as it rouses the quiet philosophical thinkers to do well what they see would otherwise be done in a very unsystematic fashion, and so the work makes progress.' Then follow comments, quoted elsewhere in this volume, on John Stuart Mill and Coleridge,[1] and the record closes with some reference to Bowring's literary tasks. They run thus: 'Dr Bowring has lately had to look over multitudes of James Mill's, Bentham's and Romilly's letters, in which there are many illusions to the young prodigy who read Plato at five years old. The elder Mill was stern, harsh and sceptical. Bentham said of him "He rather hated the ruling few than loved the suffering many." He was formerly a Scotch farmer, patronised for his mental power by Sir John Stuart, who had the credit of directing his education. For Carlyle Dr Bowring professes a respect, in so far as he calls people's attention with some power to the sufferings of the many, and points out where sympathy is wanted; but he regards him as ignorant of himself,

[1] See p. 161.

and sometimes of his meaning, for his writings are full of odd, unintelligible entanglements, and all truth is simple. "The further men wander from simplicity, the further are they from Truth." ' [1]

This, says Caroline, 'is the last of Dr Bowring's recorded axioms. He is Bentham's executor, and is bringing out a new edition of his works. He lives in the Queen's Square [on the site of the present Queen Anne's Gate; not to be confused with the existing Queen's Square in Bloomsbury], where Milton's house still stands, and the garden in which he mused still flourishes, as much as London smoke will let it.' Both house and garden have now gone.

To the rest of Bowring's varied activities—as an ardent advocate of the decimal system he claimed to have been responsible for the introduction of the florin as a first instalment of that reform; he went out to Canton in 1849 as British consul, and being appointed Governor of Hong Kong in 1854, as Sir John Bowring, he got Britain into the Second Chinese War, over the lorcha *Arrow*; he published many books on many subjects, and died in 1872 at Exeter, where he had been born eighty years earlier—Caroline makes no reference. It is a pity, for she might have been able to throw more light on an interesting and versatile personality.

[1] With Bowring on Carlyle may be compared Carlyle on Bowring :
' Aug. 15th, 1831. Next morning I went to Bowring's. Figure to yourself a thin man about my height and bent at the *middle* into an angle of 150°, the *back* quite straight, with large grey eyes, a huge turn-up nose with straight nostrils to the very point, and large projecting close-shut mouth ; figure such a one walking restlessly about the room (for he had been thrown out of a gig and was in pain), frank of speech, vivid, emphatic and *verständig*. Such is the Radical doctor, he talked copiously, he utterly utilitarian and Radical, I utterly mystical and Radical ; and parted about noon with a standing invitation on his part to come again ' (Froude's *Thomas Carlyle*, 1795-1835, vol. ii. p. 172).

Chapter XIII
Sovereigns and Statesmen

Living in a remote corner of England as she did, there was no reason why Caroline should see much, or anything, of any of the Royal Family, even at a distance, and in any case there was little in her temperament or her associations to inspire her with more than the average citizen's interest in the Kings and Queen under whom she lived. There are signs, indeed, that they interested her very little. In 1846, for example, the Queen and Prince Albert visited Falmouth, and were received by Caroline's uncle, Alfred Fox, who was then Mayor. (As a Friend he would have scruples about uncovering to any human dignitary, and those of his family who, like Caroline, were not present asked him afterwards with some curiosity what he had done about his hat. 'It was so hot,' he replied, disingenuously apologetic, 'that I simply could not keep it on my head.') Of this royal visit Caroline does not say a word. She is equally silent about a visit by the Prince and Princess of Wales in the 'sixties, when Their Royal Highnesses were taken round the Castle Drive in the Penjerrick carriage (said to have been the only private carriage and pair in the neighbourhood at that time). Regarding hats and royalty she tells a story which has appeared elsewhere since, and possibly before. She got it from Sterling; according to his version, 'When a certain conceited peer, who professed the right of appearing before Royalty with his hat on, actually took advantage of it and appeared hatted at a Drawing-room, George III said "It is true, my lord, that you may wear your hat in the presence of the King, but it is not usual to wear it in the presence of ladies," at which he appeared much confounded.'

Though her own memory did not go back to George III, who had vanished from the public scene years before she was born, Caroline heard, and recounts, one or two anecdotes about his consort Queen Charlotte. The first of them came from '"Mrs Corgie," the rightful Lady George Murray,' who visited Rosehill in September 1836. Why 'Mrs Corgie' and why 'the rightful' I have failed to discover; the lady was a sister of the Marquis of Anglesey and widow of Sir James Erskine, and married Sir George Murray in 1826; Caroline should properly have spoken of her as Lady Louisa Murray. However that may be, she was, says Caroline, 'a delightful woman, and told us many anecdotes of the late Queen Charlotte, whom she knew intimately. Many of the autograph letters of the Royal Family she gave me are addressed to herself. The Queen (Charlotte) japanned three little tables; one she gave to the King, another to the Prince of Wales, and the third to Lady George, which she has filled with the letters she has received from the Royal Family. She told us that about four years ago the Princess Victoria was made acquainted with her probable dignity by her mother's desiring that when in reading the history of England she came to the death of the Princess Charlotte,[1] she should bring the book and read to her, and on coming to that period she made a dead halt, and asked the Duchess if it were possible she would ever be queen. Her mother replied, "As this is a very possible circumstance, I am anxious to bring you up as a good woman, then you will be a good queen also." The care observed in the Princess's education is exemplary, and everything is indeed done to bring about this result. She is a good linguist, an acute foreign politician, and possesses very sound common sense.'

[1] Princess Charlotte, who married Prince Leopold of Saxe-Coburg, the future King of the Belgians, and died in 1817 after the birth of a still-born child, was the only child of the Prince Regent, and therefore stood next to him in succession to the throne.

That, and the hat incident just mentioned, are Caroline's only references to George III and his household, and George IV appears in the Journal only through Davies Gilbert's interesting account [1] of his conversation with the King about the Royal Society. William IV makes no appearance at all, except for a brief reference to the absence of any reason for grief at his death, but at one time Caroline heard something of Queen Adelaide from Courtney Boyle, who had been Maid of Honour to the Queen for twenty years, and who came to call at Rosehill in 1853 with the Enyses of Enys. In Queen Victoria, as I have suggested, Caroline might have been expected to feel some special interest as being her exact contemporary, but there is not much to indicate that she did. She quotes Lady Dunstanville (Sir Charles Lemon's sister), who had been in the House of Lords when the young Queen made her first appearance there, to the effect that 'it was a most imposing sight. Her voice was full, clear and sweet and distinctly heard'; and being in London at the time of the Coronation in 1838, she walked across the Park with Sir Henry de la Beche to look at the carriages drawn up ('ranged,' Caroline says, the verb 'parked' being happily not in common usage then) outside the Abbey. In 1840 she notes briefly the Queen's wedding-day ('Neck ribands arrived, with Victoria and Albert and loves and doves daintily woven in. Falmouth very gay with flags'), an entry which perhaps she remembered when twenty-one years later she recorded the end of that ideal partnership. 'This,' she wrote on December 23rd, 1861, 'has been a sad day with its tolling bells, its minute-guns, the band parading the streets playing the "Dead March in Saul"; but also a day on which many and fervent prayers have arisen from loving hearts, which we will hope have been felt as a sort of warm atmosphere round the poor stricken heart, which we hear is firmly resolved not to forget its high duties in the midst of its great desolation. The Union prayer-meeting was held today that there might be a concentration of spiritual

[1] See p. 256.

force in this direction, and very true I thought the prayers were for the Queen, and for her son and for all the mourners. It made one almost feel as if fresh blessings would be granted her, deeper perhaps than she has yet known. Is not this the experience of many a bereaved heart?' And in a letter to a friend on Caroline's own birthday and the Queen's in the following May occur the sentences: 'What the post has brought me today of palpable and impalpable! How can I ever be grateful enough to Him who has put such loving thoughts and feelings into the hearts of those I love so dearly. I trust that our poor Queen has had the same atmosphere of loving kindness spread around her to help her through her first solitary birthday.'

Caroline, so far as can be discovered, never saw the Queen, but she had seen Prince Albert, who was just three months younger than the Queen, and consequently than Caroline herself, presiding at the anti-slavery meeting at Exeter Hall in 1840, and 'Cousin Elizabeth Fry' had sent to Falmouth a brief account of a most interesting talk she had had with the young Prince on a variety of subjects in 1842.[1] Barclay Fox refers with horror in his Journal to the attempts on the Queen's life. Caroline does not refer to them at all. She was a perfectly loyal subject, but Royalty interested her much less than Sterling or Mill or Wordsworth or Carlyle. Who shall say that she was wrong?

Politicians were more to her taste, though she was not a politician herself. In spite of her association with Philosophic Radicals like Sterling and Mill and Bowring, it would be hard to tell from her Journal whether she reckoned herself a Whig or a Tory. (Her father tended to be Conservative, her brother Liberal.) Probably she never thought of affixing a party label to herself at all. In the politics of the day she displayed interest only in so far as they were concerned with some humanitarian end like prison reform or the abolition of slavery. The names of the political leaders of the day—Wellington, Melbourne, Peel,

[1] See p. 330.

Brougham—crop up here and there in her pages, but they become living figures only when Peel is receiving a deputation of Friends on the Oregon boundary dispute or Brougham presiding at an anti-slavery demonstration at Exeter Hall. Being, as a Friend, opposed to all war, she argued good-humouredly with her friend Elizabeth Carne over the Crimean campaign, and she held and expressed decided views on the methods employed by Governor Eyre in the suppression of negro disturbances in Jamaica in 1865. A few lines of her letter on that subject are worth quoting as providing one of the few indications to be found in the Journal that the London daily papers penetrated to Penjerrick. 'Where art thou in that strife? Not with the *Times*, I trust? Hast thou seen any of the documents in the *Daily News* of the 20th or 23rd? But the governor's despatch is enough to make one sick without note or comment.' For the rest, Caroline meets Bright, hears Cobden, both hears and meets Fowell Buxton, regards W. E. Forster as a family friend and is the interested witness of a lively platform scene in which Brougham figures conspicuously. Her own friends and neighbours, Sir Charles Lemon and Davies Gilbert, were Members of Parliament, but her contacts with them were personal rather than political. Gladstone she only mentions once, and Disraeli not at all.

John Bright was, of course, a Friend, and a 'well-concerned' Friend, all his life, but he lived in Lancashire and Caroline in Cornwall. She was therefore unlikely to meet him except in London during Yearly Meeting, and that does not seem to have happened till 1851, when Caroline was thirty-two, and Bright, just under forty, had been an M.P. for seven years. With Cobden he had founded the Anti-Corn Law League in 1838, and with him was to dissolve it in 1846 because its work was done. He had gained notoriety by his opposition to capital punishment, church rates and the Established Church in Ireland. Caroline's first reference to him is at first sight a little perplexing. 'Dined with the Priestmans,' she writes on

May 30th, 1851. 'John Bright was there, fighting his Parliamentary battles over again like a bull-dog. It was quite curious to watch his talk with his quiet father-in-law.' Who is this quiet father-in-law? Bright at this time was married to Elizabeth Leatham, of Wakefield. His father-in-law was therefore her father, William Leatham. But it was clearly not to him that Caroline was referring, but to Jonathan Priestman, the father of Bright's first wife, who had died ten years before. The description is defensible, but a little ambiguous.

During another Yearly Meeting season in 1861, ten years later, Caroline found herself in much closer contact with the Birmingham orator, for both he and she were staying at the house of one of the Barclays at Leyton. She has, however, disappointingly little to say about him. Only this: 'The Brights are here, so we consider ourselves a very pleasant party. John Bright is great fun, always ready for a chat and a fulmination, and filling up the intervals of business with "Paradise Regained." . . . One likes to have his opinion on men and things, as it is strong, clear and honest, however one-sided. But he flies off provokingly into pounds, shillings and pence when one wants him to abide for a little amongst deeper and less tangible motives, powers and arguments.' Brief as this entry is, it casts an interesting light on one side of Bright's personality; not even his warmest admirers were accustomed to describe him as 'great fun.' His preoccupation with pounds, shillings and pence was no doubt due to his concern about the battle Gladstone was waging with the House of Lords at that moment over the repeal of the paper duty—a reform which he carried into law a few weeks later by 'tacking' it on to a money-bill, which the Lords had no power to reject. This was the last of a series of measures which secured to the country a cheap Press. That affected Bright directly owing to his interest in the *Morning Star*, which was edited by his brother-in-law, but his real concern, no doubt, was with the principle.

Seven years later again Caroline saw Bright at closer quarters still, for he was the guest of the Foxes at Penjerrick. Once more Caroline is disinclined to spend much space on him, but what she does say is warmly appreciative. At this time, October 1868, it may be recalled, Bright was deeply concerned about the Bill for disestablishing the Irish Church, a subject on which he had made an important speech at Limerick some three months earlier. It is to an Irish friend that Caroline writes about him: 'We have just had the John Brights staying with us, and enjoyed it very much; his conversation is so varied, he is so simple and unreserved in telling one all manner of things one wishes to hear about, and then there is such downright manliness in the whole nature of the man, which is refreshing in this rather feeble age. How did you like him in your part of Ireland? Here he had nothing for the public, though they wanted to present an address, but would talk and read poetry till ten o'clock with us.'

Bright in 1868 was a man of fifty-seven. He lived till 1889, and was buried in the Friends' Burial Ground at Rochdale. Caroline by then had been lying for eighteen years in the Friends' Burial Ground at Budock.

Cobden was seven years older than Bright. Caroline does not seem to have known him personally, though her brother Barclay clearly did. That at least is the natural inference to draw from an entry in the Journal of April 1853 to the effect that 'Cobden is so delighted with Barclay's tract "My Friend Mr B." that he requests it may be printed on good paper and sent to every member of both Houses, which is to be done.' Barclay Fox had, in fact, spoken with Cobden at a Peace Conference at Manchester a few weeks earlier. During the conference Cobden had appealed for 'an army of lecturers and a deluge of tracts to counteract the poison that is being infused into the minds of the people'; [1] Barclay Fox's effort may have been part of the response. But this is, chronologically, Caroline's last reference to Cobden. The first is in 1848, when she

[1] Morley's *Cobden*, p. 604.

'read and was thankful for Cobden's speech declaring this was not the time to lose faith in principles so boldly asserted and toiled for; now we must prove that we believe them, and not shriek at the French as a nation of pirates. He read extracts from French speeches just delivered, one by a member of the Chamber, in the best tone of an English Peace Advocate.'

The entry is of interest as another evidence of the limitations of Caroline's concern with politics. It was less than two years since the Corn Laws had been repealed, but of the Anti-Corn Law League and the greatest achievement of Cobden's life there is not a word in the Journal. It is Cobden the peace advocate who alone engages its author's attention. An entry in 1849 emphasises that still further. 'Went to the House of Commons,' Caroline wrote on June 12th, 'and heard Cobden bring on his Arbitration Motion to produce Universal Peace. He has a good face, and is a clear, manly speaker. . . . We were much pleased with the debate; it showed that there was much more willingness to listen to moral argument, and much less disposition to snub and ridicule such a proposal than we had expected. Lord Palmerston's was a very manly speech.' Cobden's motion took the form of an Address to Her Majesty praying that foreign Powers might be invited to concur in treaties binding the parties to refer matters in dispute to arbitration. Palmerston moved the previous question, and carried it by 176 votes to 79, but Cobden described the Foreign Minister's speech as 'full of admissions' and preferred the previous question to a direct negative.[1]

W. E. Forster, notable subsequently for his Education Bill of 1870 and his Chief Secretaryship of Ireland ten years later, was like John Bright a Friend, and a close friend of Barclay Fox; Caroline speaks in 1843 of 'Barclay and his beloved W. E. Forster.' He had wooed, untiringly but in vain, first Jane Backhouse, whom Barclay subsequently married, and then Uncle Charles' daughter, Juliet. (Forster was

[1] Morley's *Cobden*, p. 509.

a few months older than Caroline and two years younger than Barclay.) The first mention of him comes early in the Journal, in October 1837, but it conveys no more information than that 'W. E. Forster has come to stay a little, and looks taller than ever.' The next encounter, in London in 1838, has its entertaining aspect. Caroline describes it thus: 'A breakfast party of the Backhouses and William Edward Forster [this is during one of Caroline's spring visits to London], after which we sallied forth to Deville's (the phrenologist). A gentleman and lady were there when we entered, and he was explaining several of the casts with which his room was lined, notably a very interesting series of American boys; another of a man who put himself under Deville's care for reformation, who told him that there was a lady whose development he had taken, and it would precisely suit him, so he married her! Upon which one of our gentlemen said "Oh, that's what makes your science so popular." Inquiries were made about large heads, and they proved to be generally lymphatic, small heads more energetic. W. E. Forster asked for the casts of Richard Carlisle [*sic*], having seen them there on a former occasion, but Deville said they had departed, which W. E. Forster believed to be a mistake. He asked twice for them, and communicated his suspicions to us. At last, the gentleman and lady leaving the room, Deville said, "That was Mr and Mrs Carlisle"—a singularly awkward coincidence. He is now, Deville says, going mad on religion; the lady he has married, a very lovely one, having had a wonderful effect on him, and he is preparing a new version of the Bible.' Carlyle, a few years later, said something rather similar to Caroline about Carlile.[1]

Two years later, almost to a day, Forster breakfasted with the Foxes in London again. But this time the Mills were of the party, and either John Mill talked the rest down or else Caroline thought his contribution alone worth recording, for of

[1] See p. 109.

what Forster said we are told nothing. Still another two years and the contact is renewed—at Falmouth, where Sterling was then staying. He and Forster, for some reason, discussed the purity of motive in martyrdom, 'whether any would yield his life for the sake of an abstract moral truth, if there were no prospect of reward or punishment in the background. Sterling said Life would not be worth living without such a faith in the entire devotion to Truth being experienced by some high minds. Both parties argued well, and it was continued for the evening, William admitting that all actual martyrs were probably actuated by both motives, and that in this, as in most cases, a mixed theory was the true one.' One remark was added by Sterling which, though it forms no part of the argument, is worth recording for its own sake: Sterling was pointing out many things that were to be remembered when in St Peter's. 'What is to be forgotten?' Caroline put in a little provocatively. 'Nothing but yourself,' he answered.

Forster is only mentioned twice more—once when a letter comes from him from Daniel O'Connell's house, where he is staying, and once when (in 1849) Caroline is reading his 'manly, spirited answer to Macaulay's libels on William Penn; he has most satisfactory contemporary evidence to adduce in favour of the fine old moral Hero.' The first two volumes of Macaulay's *History* containing the charges against Penn, most of them relating to very secondary matters, had appeared in 1848. Forster refuted them in a preface to a new edition of Clarkson's *Life of Penn*. A further refutation, by Hepworth Dixon, followed in 1851. Caroline lived just long enough to see the great achievement of Forster's career, the passage of the Education Act of 1870.

Sir Thomas Fowell Buxton, who had married Hannah Gurney of Earlham, and was therefore related to Caroline, deserves more recognition than modern historians have always given him. Intensely philanthropic, he was no mere idealist, but an essentially practical politician, and he lived to see the greatest reform he ever worked for, the abolition of slavery in British colonies, finally carried into law. Wilberforce was, of course, the pioneer in the great campaign. He and Clarkson had been the leaders in the long crusade which ended in the abolition of the slave *trade* so far as British citizens were concerned, culminating in the Act of 1807, which stamped the traffic out for ever. But Wilberforce was ageing, and in 1821 he resigned the leadership of the anti-slavery movement to Buxton, who in the three years he had sat in the House of Commons had made a marked impression there by his ability and moral earnestness. He had already proved his capacity in business as a member of the brewing firm of Truman, Hanbury and Co., which, after he became a partner in 1811, took the name by which it has been famous ever since—Truman, Hanbury and Buxton. For twelve years Buxton worked ceaselessly inside the House and out of it, with Brougham among his supporters in the Lords and on public platforms, and in 1833, while Wilberforce lay dying, the Bill passed which ended the institution of slavery in every British colony for ever.

That was four years before Caroline's first meeting with Buxton, and it might have been supposed that his mission was accomplished, the more so since in 1837 he lost the seat at Weymouth which he had held since 1818. That misfortune was one of the subjects of conversation at a dinner at the Frys' (Joseph and Elizabeth Fry) in 1838, at which Caroline 'had the pleasure of meeting the Buxton family.' Buxton had then been out of the House for nearly a year, the election at which he was defeated being in July 1837. 'Fowell Buxton,' Caroline writes, 'described his non-election at Weymouth as a most pathetic time. When he made his parting speech he began in a jocose fashion, but soon saw that that would not do, as one old man after another turned aside to cry. On the Sunday [evidently the Sunday *before* the election] he went to church and listened to a most violent sermon against himself, person and principle. He spoke afterwards to one of his party on the bad taste and impropriety of introducing politics into the pulpit; in this he quite agreed, but added, "You had better say nothing on the subject, as at all the Dissenting chapels they are telling the people that they are sure to go to a very uncomfortable place if they don't vote for you."'

Exclusion from the House of Commons—for he did not try to enter it again—meant no diminution of Buxton's zeal for the improvement of the lot of the ex-slaves or of his concern for the suppression of the slave trade outside British territory. In an attempt, moreover, to introduce civilisation into the regions of Africa whence the slaves had been drawn he initiated a new enterprise, secured for it the support of Macaulay among others (his father, Zachary Macaulay, had been one of Wilberforce's closest associates) and enlisted influential sympathy, notably that of Lord John Russell, inside the Cabinet. This explains an entry in Caroline's Journal for May 24th, 1840 (incidentally, though she does not refer to the fact, her twenty-first birthday). She is writing at Upton, in Essex—no doubt at Ham House, the home of Samuel Gurney. 'The Buxtons,' she says, 'dined here today, and after dinner Thomas Fowell Buxton addressed the assembly on the subject of the Anti-Slavery Meeting next month, which he thinks it is the duty of Friends to attend. Prince Albert has become President, the first society which he has patronised. Afterwards, walking in the garden with Barclay and me, he talked much more about it, regretting the scruples of many as to the armed vessels which are to accompany the Niger expedition; he thinks their arguments apply equally to mail-coach travelling'—for the coaches, of course, carried armed guards.

The expedition itself was by this time a matter of general discussion, but doubts about the practicability of the scheme were entertained by some even of those who had most warmly applauded Buxton's zeal for the abolition of the slave trade. Sterling, for example, talking to Caroline on the subject in

May 1841, just after the ships had set sail, was mildly satirical. 'He [Sterling] has little faith that the savages of Africa will perceive the principles of political economy, when we remember the fact that the highly educated classes of England oppose the alteration of the Corn Laws. What he would recommend is the establishment of British Empire in Africa, to be accomplished by alliances with the natives in their different international wars, though he does not expect us to agree with him here.' But this is to anticipate by a year or more. The meeting about which Buxton discoursed at Upton is still in the future, and before Caroline comes to that she provides an agreeable interlude in the shape of a pleasant glimpse of the Buxton family life. 'This afternoon,' says the Journal on May 25th, 'the young Buxton party returned from Rome; their advent was performed in characteristic fashion. Fowell Buxton was sauntering in the park when a bruit reached him that they were approaching; so he flung his ill-hung legs across the back of a coach-horse which crossed his path, with blinkers and harness on but no saddle, and thus mounted flew to the house shouting "They are come!" So the family were fairly aroused to give such a welcome as Gurneys well know how to give.' A journey to Rome and back, after all, was rather more of an undertaking in 1840 than a century later, and a generation accustomed to hearing by telegram precisely when its friends will arrive, and seeing them arrive precisely then, can only inadequately appreciate the excitement with which travellers vaguely heralded if heralded at all (for wind and weather could be counted on to derange the best-laid plans) would be greeted by the household at home.

The meeting discussed so earnestly on May 24th took place —in Exeter Hall—on June 13th. Caroline, as she made her way along the Strand to it, must have recalled the lively scene of which she had been a witness on a similar occasion in the same setting two years before. On that occasion Brougham, who was in the chair, was unexpectedly assailed by a Lincolnshire M.P. called Eardley [1] for having referred in unfriendly terms to Lord John Russell, 'a really upright man who had fallen under the Brougham-stick' (Brougham's name was pronounced Broom). It was not in Brougham's character to let a challenge lie dormant, and the meeting was considerably roused before the incident closed. Nothing of that kind could happen at the 1840 meeting, for the chairman this time was the second personage in the land. It was a notable assembly, and Caroline's description of it must be given as she wrote it.

'Went with the Mills to the Anti-Slavery Meeting at Exeter Hall, and had capital places assigned us. It was soon immediately crowded, and at eleven we were all ordered to take off our hats, as Prince Albert and an illustrious train appeared on the platform. The acclamations attending his entry were perfectly deafening, and he bore them all with calm, modest dignity, repeatedly bowing with considerable grace. He certainly is a very beautiful young man [the Prince at this time was not quite twenty-one], a thorough German, and a fine poetical specimen of the race. He uttered his speech in a rather low tone and with the prettiest foreign accent. As the history of the meeting is in print, I need not go into details of the brilliant set of speakers to whom we listened. Fowell Buxton's was a very fine, manly speech; and the style in which he managed the public feeling on O'Connell's entrance greatly raised my notion of his talent and address. Samuel Wilberforce's [2] was a torrent of eloquence, seeking and finding a fitting vent. The Prince's eyes were riveted upon him. Sir Robert Peel's demeanour was calm, dignified and statesmanlike; the expression of his face I did not like, it was so very supercilious. He was received with shouts of applause, and truly it is a fine thing to have him enlisted in the enterprise. Lord Northampton was very agreeable, speaking as the representative of British science, which he

---

[1] Greville, who is more likely to be right on such a point, gives the name as Handley; Caroline's editor may have misread her handwriting.

[2] At this time Archdeacon of Surrey; he did not become Bishop of Oxford till 1844.

hoped might have a new field opened in Africa. Sir Thomas Acland was manly and energetic, and would make himself heard and felt. Lord Ashley,[1] a very handsome young noble, spoke well and worthily. Guizot was on the platform. O'Connell seemed heartily to enjoy the triumph of his own presence: though not permitted to speak, a large minority of the audience would hardly allow any one else to address them whilst he was silent. The meeting was altogether considered a most triumphant one; the Prince's appearance, the very first as patron of any benevolent enterprise, is likely to tell well on other countries; and the unanimity of so many parties in resolving to try this great commercial experiment in Africa was most encouraging.'

Buxton's, as Caroline's account indicates, was the first speech after the chairman's and ended with a resolution pledging support to the African Civilisation Society, and in particular to the Niger expedition on which such hopes were set. Soon after the date of the meeting Buxton accepted the baronetcy which the Government desired to confer on him. But a heavy blow was in store. The Niger expedition rapidly took shape, and three iron steamers (then something of an innovation) were fitted out. Two of them were named appropriately the *Albert* and the *Wilberforce*, the third being called the *Soudan*. Scientists in different fields, and other pioneers of civilisation, were engaged. Setting sail in April 1841, the ships duly reached the African coast, and in August the commander wrote home that the health of the whole company was good; but within fifteen days a malignant fever had broken out, first in the *Albert* and then in the other two vessels. The *Albert* did indeed get more than three hundred miles up the river, but it was impossible to go further under such conditions. With 41 out of 193 of the ships' companies dead the expedition was abandoned and the vessels headed for home. Public reactions were hostile, the African Civilisation Society was disbanded, and the blow un-

---

[1] Better known by his later title of Earl of Shaftesbury.

doubtedly hastened Fowell Buxton's death. Caroline got a glimpse of the effect the disaster had on him when she went to stay at his Norfolk home, Northrepps Hall, in 1843. 'Our first visit at Northrepps Hall,' she wrote, 'a droll, irregular, unconventional-looking place, which must have had some share in shaping the character of its inhabitants. . . . A wild horse-back party of eleven, with Sir Fowell Buxton at our head, scampering over everything in tremendous rain, which only increased the animation of our party. Then dined with the Buxtons. Sir Fowell is capital now and then, but not at all to be depended upon as a man of society. Most pleasant inter-course with the family, individually and collectively, but there is little of steady conversation to record. Sir Fowell Buxton has never recovered his old tone of joyous mental energy since the failure of the Niger Expedition, and looked sometimes very sadly.' Buxton, indeed, was more deeply wounded than Caroline realised. He died less than eighteen months later at the age of 58.

Yet more had been achieved than the depressed and dis-illusioned organisers of the Niger Expedition realised. Twelve years after Buxton's death, Caroline heard Dr Livingstone speak at the British Association at Dublin. Much of the account he gave of progress registered in Africa she found 'very, very cheering. And almost even more so than that was his assurance that the Niger Expedition had not been made in vain; that frequently in the interior, and more and more as he approached the coasts, he found there had been tidings of a white nation who loved black people; and he reaped abundant benefit from this prestige. Oh, if Sir Fowell Buxton might have known it! But doubtless *he does*, and gives glory where alone it is due.' Regarding that, Caroline is no better an authority than anyone else, and no worse. But this, at least, will be agreed, that Livingstone's testimony must carry sub-stantial weight in any assessment of a venture which seemed to have ended in nothing but disaster.

But the greatest statesman, as it happened, with whom Caroline came into personal contact figured on the stage not of British but of French political life. At one moment she seemed, and indeed was, much more interested in French politics than in British. That was in 1848. It was the year of the Chartist Petition, about which she says nothing, in London, and the year of revolution, about which she says much, in Paris. It was the year which, among the other events it gave birth to, brought to London and safety one great Frenchman, Guizot, for whom Caroline entertained an unqualified admiration. She never actually met him till he came to this country as a refugee in 1848, but she had heard enough about him before that to excite the keenest expectations. Down to 1830 Guizot had been primarily a historian, and a historian of the first distinction, but having supported the July revolution of that year he entered Louis Philippe's first Government, and remained a member of successive Ministries till 1840, when he came to London for a brief term as Ambassador. He was soon recalled to office at home and filled the post of Foreign Minister till the revolution of 1848, which compelled him, as Caroline relates in some detail, to seek asylum in England. Whether she knew anything of Guizot before he came to represent his country in London may be doubted, but during his period of office here she saw him on the platform of an anti-slavery meeting at Exeter Hall, and thus described her impressions: 'Guizot was on the platform; his face is very interesting, illustrating what John Mill said the other day about every great Frenchman being first essentially French, whatever else might be superadded. Guizot's head and face are indisputably French, but "de première qualité." He entered with much animation into the spirit of the occasion, nodding and gesticulating in unison with the speakers.' A month or so later, when she was at Sterling's house at Clifton, he produced from his portfolio a portrait of Guizot, and recalled an anecdote about him. 'The other day,' so Caroline retails it,

'Guizot was sitting at dinner next a Madame M——, who has just written a novel, on which she imagines herself to have founded a literary reputation. She wished to extend a little patronage to her next neighbour, so began, "Et vous, Monsieur, est-ce que vous avez écrit quelque chose?" "Oui, Madame, quelques brochures," was the cool reply.'

Immediately after that Guizot went back to France, but Caroline had her interest in him further stimulated by a declaration of Sterling's that Guizot's *History of Civilisation* was 'the highest history that has appeared in modern times; a thorough acquaintance with that work alone would constitute an educated and civilised man.' Silence regarding Guizot for seven years now ensues. Then comes the year of revolution, and in February 1848 the Journal knows him once more. On the 23rd, Clara Mill 'is frightened at the prospect of the Paris Reform Banquet, lest it should not go off quietly.' On the 24th, 'her doubt is soon answered—the Banquet was forbidden by Government,' and in the rioting that ensued 'the Chamber of Deputies and Guizot's house are the chief points of attack.' (Guizot was at this time Prime Minister as well as Foreign Minister.) On the 26th, 'Louis Philippe and Guizot have both abdicated, and the Royal Family have quitted Paris.' On the 29th, 'Duc de Nemours and his sister Clementine have arrived in London without even a change of raiment. No news of the King, Guizot or the others.' Five days later news came, and on March 4th Caroline writes: 'Poor Louis Philippe and his Queen arrived at Newhaven; they have been skulking in various farms near Eu in strange disguises. Guizot too is come; he crossed from Ostend to Folkestone. His safety is a great comfort.'

Anxiety thus assuaged, Caroline turned to other topics till March 21st, when we find her 'deep in French Politics for the evening: most of Europe has caught the infection; Metternich resigns at Vienna, the King of Prussia calming his people with noble and honest-seeming protestations, Mitchel haranguing and printing in Dublin, in Paris the National Guard and the mob at daggers-drawn. It is a wild world, and nothing need surprise us.' Nothing indeed, though considerable strains have been laid on humanity's capacity for astonishment since then.

Though Guizot was in England, Caroline for some time got nothing better than second-hand news of him. At the beginning of June 'Barclay dined at the Buxtons' and met M. Guizot, his daughter, Arthur Stanley and others. He had much chat with Guizot on French matters, who expects sharper work in France, and a collision between the National Guards and the National Workmen.' It was not till the June of 1849 that the great occasion of a personal meeting arrived. On the 7th of that month 'the Buxtons, the Guizot party and their friend, Mademoiselle Chabot Latour, came here, and we went together to the Joseph Frys at Plasket Cottage—a long and interesting drive.' (This is corrected in the second edition of the Journal to 'Mademoiselle de Latour Chabaud' and 'Plashet Cottage.') Mademoiselle Latour, Caroline explains, was born in prison during the former Revolution just after her father had been beheaded. 'Old Madame Guizot, who was in attendance on her imprisoned husband, looked after the poor lying-in lady and finally adopted the child, who has turned out admirably, addicting herself to all sorts of philanthropies, schools etc. in Paris, and renouncing them all to share and soothe her friends' exile now. She spoke with warm affection of the old Madame Guizot; it was beautifully ordered that she should believe a report true that her son had reached England four days before he actually arrived. Mademoiselle Chabot Latour knew that it was false, but did not think it necessary to undeceive the dear old lady—the days were then like months. Pauline Guizot gave very interesting accounts of their and their father's escape. They left their house at the beginning of the Revolution and took refuge at the houses of their friends, and the girls were very soon able to come over to England with no great difficulty. Their brother came as an American gentleman, and began by remembering he must always *tutoyer*, which he felt very awkward. "How d'ye do?" was his entire stock of English, and for a whole hour he had the fright of totally forgetting his assumed name.'

It was no doubt easier for Guizot's son to escape than for Guizot, who was likely to be so much better known by sight, and his adventures, as Caroline relates them, were distinctly more arduous. She tells how he 'escaped in a woman's dress, into which he had a good deal of difficulty in insinuating himself; and when he arrived at his friend's house the portress looked into his face and said "You are M. Guizot." "Yes," he said, "but you'll do me no injury?" "Certainly not," said she, "for you have always protected honest men." So she took him upstairs and hid him, and for the rest of the day entertained him with an account of the difficulties she and her husband had in bringing up their four children. Then he was arrayed as a livery servant and attached to a gentleman who was in anguish at his carrying his carpet-bag. They had to wait two terrible hours at the railway station before they could get off. On arriving in England, a railway director gave him instantly the blessed news that his daughters and all his dear belongings were safe. They none of them have any patience with Lamartine, thinking him an altogether would-be great man, attempting impossibilities and failing utterly, yet still considering himself the greatest of his age.'

But there was better than this to come, a direct conversation with Guizot himself—or what would have been a conversation if it had ever occurred to Caroline to interrupt so impressive a monologue. She drove home with him, his eldest daughter and Mlle Chabot, and she must have rejoiced that the journey, sometimes tedious, was so long. What did Guizot talk of? Well, to begin with, he talked of Michelet, whom he considered rather mad (if not, he must be rather bad), but he soon passed from that topic to the state of the poor in England and France. The French 'have nothing like Poor-laws, but the poor are supported by private charity, which is found amply sufficient. Then the multitude of small allotments encourage industry and increase property, as well as giving their owners a happy sense of independence. In regard to food and houses they live much less expensively than the English, but their clothing costs more; there is none of the accumulation of poverty which there is with us, owing to the proportion of agriculturists to manufacturers being exactly the converse of ours, and manufacturing property being so precarious.

'As for the Free Trade question,' Caroline continues, 'he thinks it an experiment which it must take ten years to determine upon [the Corn Laws had at this time been abolished for just three years], but he inclines to think that the Farmers must suffer when they would compete with Russia, Denmark and Holland. As for Ireland and its woful problems, he can only shrug his shoulders, and has no political panacea to offer. The happy state of the French peasants, he fears, is all over for the present; they have accounts of grievous distress from the over-turn of so many regular sources of income. He spoke of London as the first commercial city in the world, Liverpool the second, New York the third and Marseilles the fourth. Gazing at the endless multitude of shops, he remarked, "It looks as if there were people who had nothing to do but to buy."'

It was nine years since Caroline had seen Guizot—on the Exeter Hall platform—and she noted the changes time had wrought. He was shorter than he had seemed then; now 'he looks about sixty [he was not quite sixty-two], a face of many furrows, quiet, deep-set, grey eyes, a thin expressive face, full of quiet sagacity, though very animated in conversation, hands and all taking their share. His little bit of red ribbon seems the only relic of official greatness left.'

The next day she found him in company that provided an interesting comparison. 'We met Bunsen and Guizot,' she says, 'at an out-of-doors party at the Frys'. The two politicians walked up and down the lawn in earnest discourse; the character of their faces as unlike as that of two men whose objects in life have been in many respects so similar can well be. The Frenchman sagacious, circumspect and lean; the German's ample, genial countenance spoke of trust in God, trust in man, and trust in himself.'

That was the last time Caroline saw Guizot, for the turmoil in his native country subsided, and he was able to return to it, though not to active politics. A few months later, in September, she got news of him from Henry Hallam. 'Guizot,' he reported, 'is going on quietly and happily in Normandy, waiting till his country wants him, and meanwhile continuing his English history from Cromwell—a work likely to be extremely valuable.' He does not appear to have come to England again.

Chapter XIV
Divers Divines

As a convinced and unquestioning Friend, Caroline moved to only a limited extent in Anglican circles. But there was nothing narrow in her Quakerism, and her alert and catholic mind was always ready to descry new facets of truth. Moreover, most of her Gurney relatives at Earlham (Elizabeth Fry was an exception) had 'married out of the Society,' and become, as Barclays or Buxtons or Hoares, Evangelical Anglicans. John Sterling, too, however he might describe himself during the years when Caroline knew him, still remained an ordained deacon in the Church of England. Sterling, incidentally, could not have failed to arouse her interest in one of the foremost figures in the Church of England in her younger days, F. D. Maurice,—'the greatest mind since Plato,' as Julius Hare challengingly, if hyperbolically, declared. Sterling and Maurice had been contemporaries and friends at Cambridge, for a short time edited the *Athenaeum* together, and subsequently became brothers-in-law. Another close friend of Maurice's was Derwent Coleridge, also a Cambridge contemporary, and from him Caroline must certainly have heard from time to time of the Christian Socialist theologian.

When Caroline first saw Maurice, in May 1842, he was already prominent in the religious life of London and of England, having since 1840 held the Chair of English History and Literature in King's College, in conjunction with the chaplaincy of Guy's Hospital, to which he had been appointed in 1836 and which he retained for ten years. What is more important, this year, 1842, saw the publication of what was in many respects his most notable book, *The Kingdom of Christ*. Caroline, on this her first visit to them, reached the Maurices' by water, steaming (as she says) from Chelsea, where she had been seeing the Derwent Coleridges, to London Bridge. (Maurice appears at this time to have been living in Guy's.) Her first impressions were markedly favourable. 'He is not at all dogmatic in his manner,' she wrote, 'but kind and conciliating. He thinks that Carlyle had much more real sympathy with moral excellence than with intellectual force, thus that he raves a great deal,[1] but never really sympathises with Goethe as he does with Dante.' If that is all that Caroline could find worth recording, at any rate the ice had been broken and the acquaintanceship struck, with the result that when the Foxes were in London in 1846 Maurice in his turn called on them. (It was in this year that he resigned his Guy's chaplaincy to become chaplain at Lincoln's Inn, and was also appointed to the Chair of Divinity, in addition to that of English History and Literature, at King's College.) They had, in fact, been talking about him only the day before with Derwent Coleridge, who declared that 'whatever country clergymen may think of him, he is appreciated in London and recognised as a Leader in the exposition of fundamental, eternal Truth.' Maurice spent two or three hours with the Foxes in what Caroline describes as 'varied conversation.' It turned primarily on the Newmans, and not unnaturally, for it was only in the previous autumn that John Henry Newman had been received into the Roman Catholic Church at Littlemore. Maurice thought John Henry had far more imagination than his brother Frank (whose spiritual haven was far other than Roman Catholicism). 'He' [Maurice], Caroline mentions, 'was so little prepared for John's last change that he hardly feels sure it will now be a final one.'

---

[1] With this may profitably be compared Carlyle's opinion of Maurice : 'One of the most entirely uninteresting men of genius that I can meet is poor Maurice to me ; all twisted, crude, wire-drawn, with such restless sensitiveness and the utmost inability to let Nature have fair play with him' (Froude, *Carlyle's Life in London*, vol. i. p. 126).

Then they talked of the Chevalier de Bunsen, whom Caroline was not to meet for the first time till the following year. Maurice and the de Bunsen family were on intimate terms, and Caroline mentions them together more than once. Maurice spoke of de Bunsen's book *The Church of the Future*, which had just been published in German, saying that 'it was in part a defence against the German charge that he was in favour of introducing episcopacy into his Fatherland; by this book he proved himself a German Lutheran in the ordinary sense, valuing episcopacy, but not deeming it essential, and, in the Arnold spirit, recognising the spiritual priesthood of every man.' Not much else is recorded of this particular meeting, but when Caroline was back in London in August she saw the Maurices again. Maurice had just taken up the Lincoln's Inn chaplaincy, and he showed his visitors over the Chapel and Hall, noting (or else Caroline noted on her own account), in regard to Hogarth's window in the Hall representing Paul before Felix, 'the quiet irony of the Apostle evidently talking down the Orator Tertullus, very funny in a picture painted for the lawyers.' Of the books of the now almost forgotten Frederika Bremer (Mrs Howitt, however, thought it worth while to fill two volumes with reminiscences of her) Maurice spoke with marked appreciation.

Henceforward Maurice tends to figure in the Journal at two-yearly intervals. In 1847 he spent an evening with the Foxes in London, and talked mainly of the sufferings of Ireland after the potato famine. In 1849 they had another evening together. This time the first topic of conversation was Edward Irving (who had died fifteen years earlier). Maurice spoke of Irving 'and the blessing he proved in spite of all his vagaries. He awakened people from their tacit idolatry of systems to the sense of a living Power amidst as well as above them; John the Baptist's mission was to bid people to repent because the Kingdom of Heaven is at hand—not near in point of time so much as now present, now around your whole being.' Shelley somehow came up. Maurice 'said he was victim of the want of sympathy; someone had remarked, he disbelieved in the Devil, not in God. The God of Love had never been revealed to him, and the powers that were had done everything to veil Him from that glowing heart, so that in his despair he had conjured up a power of evil, an almighty malignity, and supposed that he it was that men worshipped.' Ten days later the Foxes went to two of Maurice's lectures at Queen's College, Harley Street, the Church of England College for women which he had taken so large a part in founding.

In 1851 they were introduced to another, and one of the most characteristic, of his activities when they attended an Associated Trades Tea at St Martin's Hall. ('Our chairman, F. D. Maurice, is at his place behind the urn, but he springs up to welcome his friends.') Here Caroline saw at close quarters one aspect of that practical Christian Socialism to which Maurice devoted so much of his time and strength. What precisely the term 'Associated Trades' denotes is not clear; Caroline may not have got it quite right. Maurice's friend J. M. Ludlow had come back from Paris—the Paris of the short-lived Second Republic—full of enthusiasm for the *Associations Ouvrières* which had been formed there, and largely as a consequence of that a Society for Promoting Working Men's Associations had been formed in London. Maurice made a beginning in one particular trade with a Tailors' Association, and another like it for needlewomen followed. Whether the function Caroline attended was concerned with one trade or more is unimportant. At any rate, it represented applied Christian Socialism, and as such it made a good impression on her. 'In listening to the workmen's speeches,' she affirms in a passage which comes rather dangerously near the pietistic, 'we could not help feeling very thankful that such fiery spirits had been brought under such high and holy influences, leading them to apprehend self-sacrifice as the vital principle on which all successful co-operation must be founded.

One hopeful feature in this associative experiment is that they are prepared and expect to make mistakes in application, but the principles of sympathy and self-sacrifice they hold by for ever. Archdeacon Hare was delighted at the spirit and genius of some of the speakers; there was so much of calm practical wisdom, so much of applied Christianity, humbly acknowledging its origin, as made it altogether a deeply interesting and thankworthy occasion.' The first adjective was no doubt justified, and so on the whole was the second, for though Christian Socialism did not change the face of England, nor perhaps make any profound mark on it, it did affect the thought and attitude of thousands who never formally associated themselves with it in regard to the dignity of labour and the economic rights of the worker.

Caroline does not seem to have seen Maurice again, but the vicissitudes of his career interested her considerably, and there are several later references to him in her letters. In 1852, for example, writing to Elizabeth Carne, she contrasts with those zealous missionaries who feel it necessary to destroy the existing faith of their protégés the service Maurice renders in helping everyone 'to feel how momentous and how fruitful is the Truth—it may be hidden, yet still living—in that form of religion which you profess,' and she adds the pertinent query, 'Was our Lord's teaching destructive or creative in tone?' To the same friend in 1853 she reveals a little perplexity and some reservations about Maurice's controversial *Theological Essays*, whose publication brought to a head his differences with the King's College authorities and involved the loss of his Chair there. The book was rather strong meat in parts even for Caroline, who was not narrow-minded. What she says of it is: 'Maurice's new book, *Theological Essays*, is a great event to me. . . . It fills one with pondering on large subjects, and I trust he helps one to ponder them in a large and trustful spirit, or at least to desire to do so. In his special results there is plenty of matter for difference as well as agreement, but for the spirit in which he seeks them——thank God.'

Whatever matter for difference there may have been, Caroline, with her liberal and tolerant spirit, could have nothing but condemnation for heresy-hunting. In a letter a month later to her cousin J. M. Backhouse, after the blow at King's College had fallen, she writes: 'Tell her [Aunt Charles] that the King's College Council has decided *against* F. D. Maurice, proclaiming him (as Socrates before him) a dangerous teacher for youth! This may probably be but the beginning of ordeals for the brave and faithful soul. He has expected it for months, but it comes at last as a very painful blow. His beautiful book *The Kings and Prophets of the Old Testament*, dedicated to your friend Thomas Erskine in such a lovely letter, seems to me an admirable preparation for his present discipline. But I imagine him in deep anxiety lest party spirit and revenge should be awakened in the hearts of those who feel how much they owe him.' But loss of the King's College Chair only released Maurice's energy for other activities. Chief of them in his later life was the foundation of the Working Men's College, then in Great Ormond Street, now in Crowndale Road, St Pancras. Caroline refers to this in another letter to Elizabeth Carne in November 1854 (the College having actually opened its doors in the previous month). 'F. Maurice,' she mentions, 'was much cheered by the good beginning of his People's College, and especially by the unexpectedly large attendance at his own Bible Class on Sunday evening; his inaugural lecture, I hear, was very fine and telling.' Where Caroline got her information she does not say. The last ten words make it clear that it was not from Maurice himself.

There is one other reference only to this intense and courageous personality. It is retrospective, and the conversation it records cannot be dated. But it is worth quoting, both for the force and pertinence of Maurice's last remark and as evidence of the character of Caroline's relationship with so prominent an Anglican. 'My silence on the subject of War,' she writes to E. Carne (who differs from her on that question) in 1855 during the Crimean campaign, 'has, like thine, reached the third page, so I will *break* it by a winding-up remark of my dear friend F. D. Maurice after a chat we had had on this same topic.

I. Won't the world come to see with us some day ?

F. D. M. They will be brought to think *rightly* on the subject, though it may be very differently from either you or me.'

It would have been difficult for Caroline to know much of Maurice without knowing something of Charles Kingsley, but in fact her acquaintance with him was slight, and only calls for mention here as supplement to what has been said of her friendship with Maurice. When once Kingsley had become famous she would no doubt recall that when she was in the schoolroom at Rosehill, Kingsley, almost exactly the same age as herself, had been a pupil at Derwent Coleridge's school at Helston a few miles away. But it is not till 1853, when she is thirty-four, and Kingsley consequently the same, that she first mentions him—in a letter to E. Carne which indicates that she has read *Alton Locke* (which had been published in 1849). The next year she met him in the flesh. Both the Kingsleys and the Foxes were staying at Torquay, and Kingsley—at the instance, it is reasonable to assume, of Maurice—called, but found the Foxes out. Three days later the call was returned. 'A very happy call,' Caroline said of it, 'he fraternising at once, and stuttering pleasant and discriminating things concerning F. D. Maurice, Coleridge and others. He looks sunburnt with dredging all the morning, has a piercing eye under an overhanging brow, and his voice is most melodious and his pronunciation exquisite. He is strangely attractive.' What Kingsley stuttered about Coleridge must pretty clearly have been based on hearsay, for he was only a boy of fifteen, still at school at Helston, when the poet died at Highgate. But he might well have heard a good deal that was worth repeating from his headmaster, Derwent Coleridge.

To those scanty details a little more is added in a letter, again to Miss Carne, who had already displayed a lively curiosity on the subject. But the questionnaire she had evidently put met with only a limited response. 'As for C. Kingsley,' Caroline wrote to her, 'I can't half answer thy questions: we saw much more of his wife than himself, and of her rather intimately. He has rather the look which thou suggests *a priori*, but his wife's stories of him are delightful: the solemn sense of duty under which he writes, the confirming letters he has received from ardent young spirits, who thank him for having rescued them from infidelity. Such things console him greatly for being ranked among his country's plagues. *Yeast* was the book which was written with his heart's blood; it was the outcome of circumstances, and cost him an illness. Thou knows that Anthony Froude, the author of the burnt "Nemesis," has become his brother-in-law.' That is all, except for a mention of having read *Westward Ho!* in the year of its publication (1855), and a report which someone brought to Falmouth in 1858 about Carlyle, saying that 'Kingsley pays him long visits and comes away talking just like him.' In 1864 Caroline spent some days in Cambridge, where Kingsley had been made Professor of History four years earlier, but there is nothing to indicate that she renewed acquaintance with him there, or indeed, what is more surprising, with Maurice, who held the Chair of Philosophy. The explanation may be that the Long Vacation had begun, and Cambridge dons were already scattered.

Other Anglicans of some note among Caroline's acquaintance included two Deans of Westminster, Buckland and Stanley, a Dean of St Paul's, Milman, and Archdeacon Hare. Except in the case of Buckland, her references to them are brief, and Buckland would perhaps be more properly treated as a scientist than as a divine. He made his reputation at Oxford as a geologist, becoming Reader there in that science. He was later an F.R.S., and in 1832 presided over the annual meeting of the British Association, held that year at Oxford. It was at another British Association meeting, at Bristol in 1836, that Caroline, who went there with her father at the age of seventeen, first met him. He was at this time a Doctor of Divinity and a Canon of Christ Church. Returning from the Bristol meeting, Dr Buckland travelled outside on the coach in which the Foxes were inside passengers, and at stopping-places he usually came and chatted with them. He was going to Falmouth to lecture at the Polytechnic, and the Foxes were to be his hosts. To the public lecture Caroline makes no reference, summarising instead a drawing-room talk with which Buckland, like two other members of the Rosehill party, helped to while away a wet afternoon. 'We listened,' she says, 'with great and growing interest to a description of his geological map, the frontispiece to his forthcoming Bridgewater treatise. [The will of the eighth Earl of Bridgewater provided for the publication of a series of works by different authors, designed to exhibit "the power, wisdom and goodness of God as manifested in the Creation"; Dr Buckland's volume was on "Geology and Mineralogy."] He gave very clear details of the gradual formation of our earth, which, he is thoroughly convinced, took its rise ages before the Mosaic record. He says that Luther must have taken a similar view, as in his translation of the Bible he puts "1st" at the third verse of the first chapter of Genesis ["God said, Let there be light and there was light"], which showed his belief that the two first verses refer to something anterior.' This is not perfectly lucid, but it is clear that Buckland took a reasonably advanced and enlightened view at a date when anything in the nature of Higher Criticism was regarded as heterodox—and when *The Origin of Species* was still twenty-three years, and *The Descent of Man* thirty-five, in the future. Buckland sprained his leg while at Falmouth, was nursed by the Foxes, and on getting home sent them two pieces of good news, one of the birth of a daughter, the other of a print-order for 5000 more copies of his book (the Bridgewater Treatise already mentioned).

Three years later Dr Buckland was again at Falmouth, and again lecturing at the Polytechnic, this time bringing Mrs Buckland with him. Caroline specially mentions this fact to give point to an anecdote for which Davies Gilbert (M.P. successively for Helston and Bodmin and President of the Royal Society) was responsible. Buckland, it seems, was once travelling somewhere in Dorsetshire and reading a new book by Cuvier which he had just received from the publisher, when he observed that a lady in the coach had this identical work (it had just been presented to her by the author himself). They got into conversation and found so much in common that Buckland soon exclaimed, 'You must be Miss ———, to whom I have a letter of introduction.' It was so, and the lady after no long interval became Mrs Buckland. Why Caroline left the lady's name blank is not clear; perhaps Davies Gilbert had forgotten it. She was, in fact, Miss Mary Morland, of Sheepstead, near Abingdon. Caroline summarises the Polytechnic lecture, in which there was nothing that today would be considered very striking; one paragraph, none the less, on the relations of religion and science, has its interest as coming from one who was at the same time an F.R.S. and a D.D. 'Shall we,' the lecturer asked, 'who are endowed by a gracious Creator with power and intelligence and a capacity to use them—shall we sit lazily down and say "Our God has indeed given us eyes, but we will not see with them; reason and intelligence, but we will exert neither"? Is this our gratitude to our Maker for some of His choicest gifts, and not rather a stupid indifference most displeasing in His sight?' Again an enlightened view for the fourth decade of the nineteenth century.

An interval of nearly eight years separates this meeting from the next between Caroline and Buckland. In 1847, when the

Foxes were in London in May, they called on the Dean of Westminster, as he had now been for two years, in what Caroline terms 'his solemn habitation.' Their visit was agreeable rather than momentous. The Dean 'took us through the old Abbey, so full of death and of life. There was solemn music going on in keeping with the serious Gothic architecture and the quiet memory of the great dead. The Dean was full of anecdote—historical, architectural, artistic and scientific. The new-found planet is now recognised as a joint discovery [by Adams and Leverrier], and is to be called Neptune. On Prince Albert condoling with Professor Adams on the vexatious incidents of the affair he answered "Oh! I hope we shall find another planet during your Royal Highness's Chancellorship."' Buckland lived till 1856, but there is nothing to indicate that Caroline ever saw him again.

Dean Stanley, who succeeded Buckland's successor, Trench, must have been known to Caroline indirectly, for he was a friend of Sterling's, as Catherine Stanley, his sister, reminded Caroline when she was visiting Bishop Stanley (Arthur Stanley's father) at his Palace at Norwich in 1843. She speaks in 1856 of having read the Dean's *Palestine* with peculiar pleasure: 'He writes charmingly, seeing things so clearly and seeing them in their bearings, geographical and otherwise, like a true pupil of Dr Arnold's; and there is such a high and thoughtful tone over it all.' Finally, in 1864, she met the Dean for the first, and it would seem the only, time, not at Westminster but at Trinity, during her visit to Cambridge. She had 'a pleasant talk' with him, and no more.

Milman, Dean of St Paul's, and chiefly remembered today for his *History of the Jews*, Caroline met, or at any rate saw, twice. The first time was in 1846, when the entry is simply 'To the Coleridges' examination by Milman; he is a man with great black eyebrows and a strongly expressive countenance, displaying more of strength than sensibility, more of the critic than the poet.' What the examination was is unexplained; it could not have been connected with Derwent Coleridge's candidature for the principalship of St Mark's College, for he had already taken up that post. As to Milman being more of the critic than the poet, he was in fact both, if 'critic' be read in the sense of Higher Critic. The 'rationalisation' of some of the Old Testament stories in his *History of the Jews* had brought him under heavy attack.

Whether or not Caroline actually made Milman's acquaintance on that occasion, she had an opportunity of talking to him at some length when he was staying with Sir Charles Lemon at Carclew in 1854, and both host and guest came over to see the Foxes. Of the Dean, as he then was, Caroline writes: 'He is bowed down more with study than age, for his eyes are bright and keen, and have a depth of geniality and poetic feeling lying in them, overshadowed as they are by black, shaggy eyebrows; the features are all good, and the mouth very mobile in form and expression. . . . They are going to explore our coast, winding up with Tintagel, whither as a boy he was poetically attracted, and wrote a poem called *The City of Light*, made up of King Arthur, the Anglo-Saxons and all sorts of things which he was utterly incompetent to put together. "And when is Arthur coming again?" said I, with a laudable desire for information. "He has come," was the reply; "we have had our second Arthur: can he be better represented than in the Duke of Wellington?"' It was during this visit that Milman delivered himself of the judgement on Coleridge already quoted.[1]

No Church dignitary could be more familiar to Caroline by repute than Julius Hare, whose curate John Sterling had been at Hurstmonceux, for he constantly came up in Sterling's conversation. He was also Sterling's first biographer, his book appearing three years before Carlyle's; Caroline had given him some assistance in the preparation of it by sending him a note on her recollections of their common friend. Yet, so far as

[1] See p. 167.

can be discovered from the Journal, she actually met Hare only once (apart from a casual contact at Maurice's Associated Trades Tea). That was in 1847, three years after Sterling's death. Caroline was in London that spring, and her entry for May 17th opens with the words 'Archdeacon Hare joined us' —which suggests that her editor must have omitted some immediately preceding passage indicating where the meeting took place; Caroline is always specific on such matters. There was not really much more to record than the bare fact. All that is added is a description of the Archdeacon: 'as nervous, dragged-looking [? draggled] a man as in his portrait, but far more genial and approachable than that would lead you to expect. Plenty of pleasant talk, but nothing extremely marked. We were presently [1] on the footing of old friends'—which was natural enough with John Sterling's memory to draw them together. The pleasant talk seems to have consisted largely of quotations by Hare from a conversation he had been having that morning with Walter Savage Landor. At the end of December 1847, Hare wrote to Caroline detailing difficulties he was having with the Sterling Memoir, but in the following month the book itself reached her. On the whole, Caroline approved it. 'The portrait,' she decided, 'is very unsatisfactory, the volumes full of exquisite interest, though of a very mixed kind. Julius Hare has, I believe, done his part admirably well, but F. D. Maurice has (by his letters) quite spoiled us for any other handling of such a subject.' It is noteworthy that Caroline, knowing Sterling as intimately as she did, should have rated Hare's biography of him so much higher than Carlyle's.

One notable character about whom we should have been glad to hear more is the pugnacious Bishop Phillpotts—Henry of Exeter, as he was familiarly called—famous historically for his fight over the notorious Gorham case. Falmouth was in his diocese, which then covered the whole of Devon and Cornwall, for the see of Truro was not created till 1893, but

[1] Caroline frequently uses this word in its older sense of 'immediately.'

Caroline would have had no contact with him ecclesiastically, nor, being in so remote a corner of his diocese, would she be likely to meet him socially. Her Journal consequently only contains two references to him, neither of them based on first-hand experience. 'Wightwick,' she wrote in April 1839, 'has been a great deal lately with the Bishop of Exeter, whom he finds a very interesting well-informed man. He thinks his flattery rather a desire in action of making everyone pleased with themselves, for does he ever flatter a superior, does he ever flatter in the House of Lords?' This may well have been a sound judgement, for Phillpotts was a man of culture, and in his less litigious moods could be agreeable enough. But he had his idiosyncrasies, and Caroline supplies an example of them. This time she owes her information to one L. Dyke, a friend of the Lemon family. 'L. Dyke,' she writes, 'was in the church at Torquay last Christmas Day, when a modest and conscientious clergyman did duty in the presence of the Bishop. In reading the communion service he substituted "condemnation" in the exhortation "He that eateth or drinketh of this bread and this cup unworthily etc." "Damnation" screamed the Bishop in a most effective manner, to the undisguised astonishment of the congregation.' It is not surprising that an average congregation should have been a little startled, but Devonshire churchmen should by 1840 have been reasonably well accustomed to their diocesan's vagaries.

To these eminent men must be added Dr Cumming, who, if he was not precisely eminent, was certainly prominent in the religious world. Caroline was considerably impressed by him when she heard him at different times on public platforms, and she had clearly read, without great edification, some of his apocalyptic writings. A Scotsman by birth, he accepted a call from the National Scottish Church in Covent Garden in 1832, and despite many invitations to fill pulpits in his native land, in London he remained till his death in 1881. He was an impassioned Protestant, and engaged in various public arguments with Cardinal Wiseman. On another side he was intensely philanthropic, raising funds for ragged schools among other good causes. It was, indeed, at a Ragged School Meeting—in 1851—that Caroline first saw him, and he struck her very favourably. 'Attended a Ragged School Meeting,' she wrote in June of that year, 'Lord Kinnaird in the chair, instead of Lord Ashley (who has become Lord Shaftesbury by his father's death). A great deal of good sense was spoken, and encouraging stories told. Dr Cumming was on the platform and made an admirable speech, with perfect ease, choice language and excellent feeling, so as to modify my prejudice against him most notably. He spoke on the mischief of controversy, except in such countries where Error was the law, Truth the exception; and spoke up for the high affirmative course in all possible cases. Described the origin and progress of the Ragged Schools in his parish, and asked the audience for £500, assuring them that at his chapel he always got what he asked for, large sums just as easily as small ones; the great thing being to ask boldly, and you are paid boldly. He is a younger man than I had expected—about thirty-six [a flattering estimate; he was, in fact, forty-three] with dark hair and eyes, rather Jewish, wearing spectacles, and very energetic in voice and manner.' The eloquent doctor's remarks on controversy call for a little qualification, in view of the vigour with which he had thrown himself into the Maynooth argument of 1845 and the protest movement against the so-called 'papal aggression' in 1850.

When Caroline next saw him, in 1853, it was on a Bible Society platform, and again he found favour in her sight. 'Dr Cumming,' she commented, 'was most felicitous in language and illustration.' But Dr Cumming through all these years was going increasingly apocalyptic and prophetic. *Apocalyptic Sketches (three series)*, 1848-50, had been followed by *Prophetic Studies, or Lectures on the Book of Daniel*, 1850, and *Signs of the Times, or Present, Past and Future*, 1854. By 1855, when

Caroline mentions Dr Cumming for the third and last time, her opinion of Dr Cumming had been revised; there was little in common between his vagaries and her steady and level-headed view of life. So it is that she writes to Elizabeth Carne, who would seem to have dallied a little with interpretations of the Book of Daniel and taken *Signs of the Times* seriously: 'If thou and Dr Cumming say that the world is at its last gasp, what is the use of inventing any worldly thing, when either destruction or intuition [1] is so nigh at hand? The dear old world! One certainly fancied it in its very infancy, blundering over BA *ba*, AB *ab*; but it may be dotage, for truly one sees people nowadays quite *blasés* at twenty. Which was its period of manhood? I suppose Kingsley would not hesitate in giving it to the reign of our Elizabeth. But Kingsley is no prophet of mine, however much he may at some times rejoice and at others strike me with awe. Ah! and that would only apply to England; and if I remember rightly, nothing short of the destruction of a world would satisfy Dr Cumming. Oh! the comfort and blessing of knowing that our Future is in other hands than Dr Cumming's; how restful it makes one, and so willing to have the veil closely drawn which separates Now from Then.'

Caroline did not ask to see the distant scene. Dr Cumming did.

Finally, mention must be made of one divine, Edward Irving, in whom Caroline took a deep interest. She never saw him; his brief forty-two years were lived out before she was sixteen. But the closeness of Irving's early association with Jane Welsh and Thomas Carlyle was enough in itself to stir her curiosity about him, and Sterling was there to tell her anything she desired to know. Mrs Carlyle herself, indeed, added a little information one day when Caroline was calling at Cheyne Row. But before she ever saw Sterling she had heard enough, not so much about Irving himself as about what may

[1] So both editions; but the word can hardly be right.

ROBERT WERE FOX, F.R.S. 1789-1877

father of Caroline

PENJERRICK

properly be called (and what Caroline does in fact call) Irvingism, to cause her to listen with some eagerness whenever the eloquent Scotsman's name was mentioned in her presence.

By 1839, when Caroline speaks of Irving first, he had long been famous. Once Canning had taken to attending the Caledonian Church, off Hatton Garden, the preacher who filled its pulpit attracted half the town, including most of the Cabinet of the day and a royal duke. The meteoric rise was by this time being followed by a melancholy descent, but with that Caroline was not concerned. It was the vagaries of the cult that interested her—as well they might. In August 1839, at her Uncle Charles Fox's house at Trebah, she heard (from whom she does not say) a strange story, which the Irvingite writer Robert Baxter has also related, of the family of a Gloucester clergyman who, persuaded that his twin children of seven years old were endowed with the authentic gift of prophecy, implicitly followed all the directions the infants gave, including a behest to leave all and go to Jerusalem and settle there. The story, including the intervention of Irving, who supplied instructions as to how to 'try the spirits,' need not be pursued in detail here. In the end it was decided to treat the preposterous brats as preposterous brats, and Caroline ends her account of the affair with two statements of objective fact: 'By a judicious discipline these two children were rescued from what is considered, with some show of reason, to have been a demoniacal possession. The father, however, became insane ultimately from what he had passed through, and died in that state.'

Later, in talks with Sterling, she heard of the tuition of Jane Welsh by Irving (she would gladly have married him, child though she was, had he not considered himself bound by a half-understanding elsewhere), of the friendship between Irving and Carlyle and of Sterling's estimate of Irving—which was indeed the common estimate—as a man wrecked by an inordinate vanity. Yet Maurice, as has been seen, told her that in his view Irving had a message for his age, and did it on balance more good than harm. He was a strange manifestation. The Catholic Apostolic Church in Gordon Square presents its massive Gothic frontage to the world as witness to the doctrines he proclaimed.

Chapter XV
Science and Invention

I t would have been strange if Caroline had not been interested in science. The predominant atmosphere at Rosehill was the scientific—or rather it was second only to the religious, and in that household no conflict between religion and science was admitted. Certain branches of science occupied Robert Were Fox incessantly. Falmouth was too remote geographically to make attendance at British Association meetings every year practicable, but he went whenever possible—even as far afield as Dublin—and Caroline frequently went with him. She consequently met most of the outstanding scientists of the day, and got to know some of them, like Lloyd and Owen, intimately. Davies Gilbert, moreover, who was for three years President of the Royal Society, was a neighbour at Falmouth and a family friend; his is actually the first name mentioned in the published Journal. It need not be claimed that Caroline was gifted with a naturally scientific mind, but it is clear that, thanks to her father, she could take an intelligent part in any ordinary scientific conversation.

Robert Were Fox was essentially a practical scientist, and all his earlier investigations and inventions were connected with the mining industry—tin and copper—in which he was commercially interested. As early as 1812 he joined another Friend, Joel Lean, in devising means of increasing the power of Watt's steam-engine through high-power steam; he collaborated with the well-known Cornish engineer Richard Trevithick in various mechanical inventions; he made discoveries of substantial importance regarding the earth's temperature by placing thermometers at different depths in mine-shafts; and his researches into local geological conditions bore mainly on mining problems, such as ores and veins. He was made an F.R.S. in 1848. In 1857, at the Dublin meeting of the British Association, he read a paper on temperature in mines, and Caroline, who was there herself, mentions that he was specially complimented by the President of the Section, Lord Talbot de Malahide, who spoke of him as a veteran in the cause of science (though he was at the time still two years under seventy).

But it is for the contribution he made to accuracy in navigation at sea rather than to safety and efficiency in mines that the name of Robert Were Fox is generally remembered. His principal invention was an improved dipping-needle, of which it was written: 'the value of this instrument was at once recognised by the Admiralty as being of great service to the scientific observer, enabling him to ascertain with great accuracy the dip intensity and variation of terrestrial magnetism, resulting in more correct use and adjustments of the compass at sea.' [1] Sir Joseph Hooker, in referring, as President of the Royal Society, to Fox's death in 1877, spoke of him as 'the inventor of some and the improver of other instruments now everywhere employed in ascertaining the properties of terrestrial magnetism.' The dipping-needle was of particular value on Polar expeditions like those of Ross and Nares. Caroline writes in May 1841 that 'today Father received a letter from Captain James Ross, informing him that they have discovered the South Magnetic Pole, a result they could not have attained without Papa's Deflector.' The Deflector had already won high praise at the French Academy, where Fox displayed and explained it when on a visit to Paris (with the eighteen-year-old Caroline, who records the event) in 1838. In 1855 Caroline mentions in the course of a letter to Elizabeth Carne that 'Papa has been busy making bottled compasses for Brunel's great ship, who begged

[1] From a monograph on Robert Were Fox published by the Royal Cornwall Polytechnic Society.

him to get at some magnetic results for him, but Papa must experiment in the neighbourhood of much larger masses of iron than he can scrape together here. One thing, however, he has made out, that a needle suspended in water becomes quiet in its true position wonderfully sooner than when, as usual, hung in air—hence bottled compasses.' [Brunel's ship was the famous *Great Eastern*, by far the largest vessel ever designed up to that time.] Caroline's father was far from being the greatest of the scientists whose words and deeds she records, but it is clearly fitting that in any review of them he should be given the first mention.

Second must certainly come Davies Gilbert, if only because the first words of the Journal in its published form run: '*Falmouth, March* 19,(1835).—Davies Gilbert and others dined here. He was full of anecdote and interest as usual.' There was the tie of proximity as well as of common scientific interests between the Foxes and Gilbert, for he lived at Trelissick, on the River Fal, about half-way between Falmouth and Truro. He was a scientist, primarily a geologist, of considerable note, and sat in the House of Commons as Member, first for Helston and then for Bodmin, from 1804 to 1832. He gave help and encouragement to Sir Humphry Davy in the latter's early days; to Richard Trevithick; and to Telford over the Menai Bridge. He was President of the Royal Society from 1827 to 1830.

Though Caroline always speaks with warm regard of Gilbert (who began life as Giddy, but changed his surname on marrying a Miss Gilbert), her references to him amount to relatively little, partly no doubt because he died in 1839. On the occasion already mentioned, when Gilbert dined at Rosehill, he told one story which Caroline, then fifteen, faithfully chronicled, but it hardly calls for reproduction here. In September of 1836 he was at Rosehill again, in company with Wheatstone (of whom more later), but all Caroline's record on that occasion was devoted to another member of the party. A year later, in October 1837, there comes a much more expansive entry, which loses none of its interest from the fact that its first sentence is not, to me at any rate, quite intelligible. 'Time,' Caroline wrote, 'this evening was very gracious, for it developed its dear impersonate Davies Gilbert. He had been holding his court and dining with his tenants. Soon after his arrival all the other gentlemen had to go off to a committee, so we had him all to ourselves. He repeated the admirable song of Trelawny with true Cornish energy, and gave us interesting accounts of his interviews with George IV, William IV and the Queen; the two former he visited in right of his Royal Society's Presidentship, to get their signatures. To George IV he went and requested that he would confirm the patent as his royal predecessors had done, and pointed out to him several of their signatures. "Would you show me Evelyn's?" said the King. "I have lately been reading his Memoirs with great interest." Davies Gilbert found and showed it, when the King remarked, "He was the founder of the Royal Society." Gilbert said it was His Majesty Charles II who gave the first charter. "Very true," replied the King; "but that was only *ex officio*, any man who happened to be in his situation would have done that; but Evelyn was the real founder, you may depend upon it." On leaving him Davies Gilbert remarked to his friend, Sir Everard Home, "If that had not been the King I should have remarked what an agreeable, intelligent man I have been conversing with," which delighted the King exceedingly on being told of it.' It can hardly be supposed that Gilbert meant that intelligence and urbanity were necessarily incompatible with kingship; possibly he had heard George IV maligned on those heads. Actually that monarch, in spite of the possession of many repellent qualities, could be pleasant enough when he chose, and was never to be mistaken for a fool; no man could be that who was capable of holding his own in conversation on any subject with Charles James Fox and Sheridan.

Curiously enough, Fox and Sheridan happen to be the principal subjects of another conversation with Gilbert—

Gilbert the politician this time—two days later. 'Once,' says
Caroline, 'when in the House of Commons, a bill was brought
forward by Fox to prevent the use of porter pots in Westminster! Davies Gilbert opposed the bill as too absurd, and
said he did not think it could be one that Mr Fox himself
approved, but that he was only bringing it forward in compli-
ance with the wishes of some of his constituents. Fox was not
in the House, but Sheridan immediately rose and declared that
as a friend of Fox's he must entirely deny a charge so injurious
to the reputation of the honourable member. It was Fox's bill,
and worthy of its high origin. Davies Gilbert could only say
that of course he bowed to conviction, and must therefore bear
the weight of the responsibility of differing from Fox. The
next day he met Sheridan, who accosted him. "It was all
perfectly true what you said yesterday, but I thought I must
say what I did to keep up Fox's credit." '

All these contacts were at Falmouth, but in 1838 Caroline
met Gilbert in London. He was no longer President of the
Royal Society, but he seems to have devoted much of his time
to pursuits connected with it; he was living at this time mainly
at Eastbourne, where he had considerable estates which his wife
had brought him. Caroline thus recounts her visit to him: 'At
Davies Gilbert's invitation we went to his "habitat," and were
hailed at the door by the venerable philosopher. After a little
visit to his sister he got with us into our fly, and we drove to
the Royal Society's Rooms at Somerset House.[1] He is very
busy establishing the standard of weights and measures, which
was lost at the recent burning of the Royal Exchange. They
are measured to a thousandth part of a grain. Duplicates are
to be kept in all our colonies and the different European capitals,

[1] Sir Walter Scott was a little pungent on Davies Gilbert as P.R.S. 'Breakfasted at Somerset House with Davies Gilbert, the new preses of the Royal Society,'
he wrote. 'Tea, coffee and bread and butter, which is poor work. Certainly a slice
of ham, a plate of shrimps, some broiled fish or a mutton chop would have been
becoming so learned a body. I was most kindly received, however, by Dr D. Gilbert
and a number of members' (*Journal*, May 8th, 1828).

so that a similar loss need not be feared. He is going today to put the stars in order at Greenwich with Airy.[1] Went first into the Council Room, having summoned the secretary, where was the reflecting telescope made by Newton's own hands, the MS. copy of the *Principia* which went to the publisher, all in his neat hand and with his autograph, and there was an old portrait of him. In the library were two barometers which have just returned with Herschel from his expedition. Their assembly-room is hung round with portraits of their presidents and great members and patrons, dear old Davies Gilbert smiling on his living representative in the centre of the room. A fine bust of Newton here, his face quite full of nervous energy and deep reflection. On the table was a very splendid gold mace, which Gilbert informed us was the identical one which Cromwell ordered away when dissolving the Long Parliament.'

That, it seems, was the last time Caroline and Gilbert met, for the only other entry in her Journal marked the end of all possibility of meeting. 'News arrived today in an indirect manner,' she wrote on December 28th, 1839, 'of the death of poor, dear, long-lived Davies Gilbert; no particulars but that it came suddenly at last.' He had died at Eastbourne four days earlier.

Professor Wheatstone, it has been mentioned, visited Rosehill with Davies Gilbert in September 1836, but on that occasion Caroline no more than mentioned him. It was not till the following year, when she went to the British Association meeting at Liverpool with her father, that she understood, or at any rate described, the then startling invention which enabled two persons far apart to communicate with one another instantaneously. 'Papa,' she wrote then, 'took us to the meeting of the British Scientific Association. Wheatstone came up to us in the gallery and was most agreeable and cordial; he told us of his electric conversations which are conducted by subterranean wires between here and London

[1] Astronomer Royal from 1836 to 1881.

in a second or two. He took us to the Physical Section, where Sir David Brewster and Whewell were discussing some questions about spectrum light.'

Caroline's description suggests the idea of the telephone, but that would be very premature; all that was in question at that time was the telegraph, and Caroline saw its inventor, at precisely the right moment, for it was in that year, 1837, that Wheatstone took out (in conjunction with W. F. Cooke) a patent for an electric telegraph. The next year she had another and fuller demonstration—at the special invitation of Wheatstone, who, hearing that the Foxes were in London, suggested their calling on him at King's College, where he was Professor of Experimental Physics. 'Went there,' says Caroline, 'and found Uncle Charles with the Professor inspecting his electric telegraph. This is really being brought into active service, as last week they began laying it down between London and Bristol, to cost £250 a mile. He then showed us his "Baby," constructed in imitation of the human organs of speech; it can beautifully pronounce some words and can cry most pathetically. He treated it in a most fatherly manner. His "Syren" is an extraordinary little instrument, so called because it will act under water; its object is to measure the intensity of sound. He then played the Chinese reed, one of the earliest instruments constructed, exhibited the harp, or rather sounding-board with additaments, which communicates with a piano two stories higher, and receives the sound from it quite perfectly through a conductive wire. Wheatstone has been giving lectures, and in fact is in the middle of a course. No ladies are admitted, unluckily; the Bishop of London forbade it, seeing how they congregated to Lyell's, which prohibition so offended that gentleman that he resigned his professorship.'

To the statement about the sound transmitted by wire from a piano two storeys higher up Caroline's editor appends a footnote: 'Query. How far was this the origin of the telephone?' The answer appears to be, Not at all, so far as any practical consequences were concerned. All the development in the next forty years was in connexion with the telegraph, though when Alexander Graham Bell did invent the telephone in 1876 it was as the result of experiments very similar to Wheatstone's. Caroline, by the way, was right about the exclusion of ladies from Sir Charles Lyell's lectures at King's College (on the plea that their presence distracted the male students) and the part it played in precipitating the professor's resignation. The Bishop of London and his fellow-Governors were in a position to impose the ban because King's College was an Anglican foundation.

When the Foxes left Wheatstone they promised to come back some time and see more experiments, but it does not appear that they ever did, though Wheatstone survived Caroline. There was, however, another scientific visit six days later, when Caroline, and no doubt the others, breakfasted with Lister. This was Joseph Jackson Lister, F.R.S., father of the more famous Lord Lister. 'He is,' says Caroline accurately, 'a great authority on optics. Showed us varieties of fossil sections through his powerful chromatic—or something—microscope.' Lister was a Friend, and connected with the Gurney circle, which would account for the Foxes' acquaintance with him.

But there was another scientist of note with whom Caroline laid the foundations of a lasting friendship before she had met either Wheatstone or Lister. Henry de la Beche is encountered on the third page of her Journal. He came to lunch at Rosehill with two Falmouth neighbours, Sir Charles Lemon and John Enys, in April 1836. Caroline was then only sixteen, but the conversation was by no means above her head, and she gives a good description of the unfamiliar guest, mentioning that 'he looks about forty'—a guess which, seeing that he was born in 1796, argues some discernment. In those forty years de la Beche had covered a good deal of ground. Educated for the Army, he resigned his commission when 1815 brought peace and the end of active service, and became an ardent student of geology, both in the Alps and in his native Dorset. In 1824 he went out (like John Sterling) to visit a family estate in the West Indies, a subject on which he and Caroline conversed more than once, and on his return to England decided to supplement the one-inch ordnance map which had just been produced by a geological survey of each county, with a geological map as its ultimate objective. He began on Devon and Cornwall at his own expense, but the Government took the project up, and in 1832 put de la Beche in charge of an official survey. In the course of it he initiated the Geological Museum in Jermyn Street.

It was in connection with this survey that de la Beche settled temporarily in Cornwall,—at Redruth, in 1836,—when Caroline first met him, and it was natural enough that in company with Sir Charles Lemon, a great authority on Cornish mines and the geology that concerned them, he should be lunching at the house of Robert Were Fox, a great authority on the geology of Cornwall generally. The conversation begun over the luncheon-table was long continued, but Caroline gives only a brief résumé of it. She describes de la Beche as 'a very entertaining person, his manners rather French [his family had come to England with the Conqueror], his conversation spirited and full of illustrative anecdote. He looks about forty, a handsome but careworn face, brown eyes and hair and gold spectacles. He exhibited and explained the geological maps of Devon and Cornwall which he is now perfecting for the Ordnance. Accordingly he is constantly shifting his residence that he may survey accurately in these parts. Papa read his new theory of "Veins"; de la Beche thoroughly seconds his ideas of galvanic agency, but will not yield the point of the fissures being in constant progression; he says they were all antediluvian. They stayed several hours, and were particularly charmed with some experiments about tin and galvanism.'

That was a good beginning, and the acquaintance developed satisfactorily, for a fortnight or so later de la Beche and his daughter, a girl a couple of years younger than Caroline, had a day's excursion with the Foxes, and at the end of the year one of de la Beche's periodical shifts of residence brought him to Falmouth, where, Caroline mentions, they 'are now settled on our terrace,' which presumably means Wood Lane. They were, she says, 'very merry, Henry de la Beche calling up the memory of some of his juvenile depravities and their fitting punishments,' and in the course of further reminiscences remarking that 'hunting alligators on the Nile is capital fun; they generally spear them, but once de la Beche attempted to shoot one with a long old swivel-gun fastened down to the boat with an iron bar; the machine burst, and the boat, not the alligator, was the victim.'

It was clearly not the professional side of de la Beche that appealed to Caroline most, nor was it the side that he was most in the habit of displaying to his lively young friend. They got on singularly well together. De la Beche was evidently a raconteur of some merit, and in the course of a visit in January 1837 he gave a highly entertaining account of a slightly eccentric character, Sir Richard Vyvyan [1] of Trelowarren, between Falmouth and Helston, at that time M.P. for Helston. A month later, when he appeared one morning at Rosehill for breakfast, Caroline described him as 'a regular fun-engine.' That day they all went off to look for 'faults' in the rocks on Gillanvase beach. Caroline pays due tribute to the serious aspect of the search by mentioning that they 'traced various cross-courses; one ending in little indefinable streaks of quartz was very pretty.' It probably had other qualities than prettiness, 'but,' observed Caroline, 'I am not geological, nor was a great deal of the talk.' It was not. De la Beche 'told innumerable stories, as was his wont'—one (not very powerful) about two Frenchmen who, anxious to air their knowledge of

[1] Owner of the bull with which Caroline had her adventure, pp. 35-6.

English in a London coffee-house, exchanged the observations 'It deed rain tomorrow.' 'Yes, it was.' Examination of 'the castle,' presumably Pendennis Castle, though it is not very close to Gillanvase beach, evoked from de la Beche, who had studied at Sandhurst, a short discourse on the principles of fortification, and at dinner at Rosehill that afternoon, by way of providing further entertainment, he 'drew a cartoon of the results of A. Crosse's system of revivifying the fossil life in an old museum, grotesquely horrible.'

In all this geology is well in the background, and so it remains as far as Caroline is concerned. But in relation to Robert Were Fox the case is different, as Caroline indicates when she mentions that the morning after the day at Gillanvase de la Beche 'wandered in at breakfast to give Papa the two first fossil remains that have been found near a lode, which he drew forth from their hiding with his own authentic hands. One is the vertebra, the other the body, of an encrinite. He read us some of a report he is now drawing up for the Government, in which he does Papa all manner of honour.' Why the conversation should then have turned to Greek vases is not clear, but it did, Caroline recording that 'he says that all the beautiful Greek vases are formed of a series of ellipses, and he has sent for patterns from Mr Phillips of the Woods and Forests, to give the Cornish better ideas of forms for their serpentine and porphyry vases.' Why Greek vases should come within the purview of the Woods and Forests is again not clear, but perhaps Mr Phillips of that Department was approached in his personal capacity.

A week or two later de la Beche's friend John Enys threw some light on his humanitarian instincts. De la Beche, he told the Foxes, 'had spent some time in the West Indies, and tried to ameliorate the condition of his slaves, and abolished the practice of flogging, though the power was still vested in the overseer; he established a system of education, and did much good. He was warmly opposed by the planters, but he

pursued his way, and they theirs. On his return to England
he had many troubles, which accounts for his low view of
mankind, and for the artificial spirits in which he so often
seems to be veiling his griefs and disappointments.' Caroline's
description of de la Beche as a regular fun-engine and other
similar references hardly suggest that his high spirits were
artificial.[1] As for his slaves, they must have ceased to weigh
on him by the time this conversation took·place, for slavery in
all British colonies had been abolished for ever more than two
years earlier.

Throughout the summer of 1837 de la Beche not only
dominates but almost monopolises Caroline's pages. He and
his family dined with the Foxes in April, and after a varied
conversation on Ireland, the West Indies, the Protestant and
Roman Catholic Churches, education and phrenology, there
came a revulsion to riddles and anecdotes, the latter including
one of a lady who had asked de la Beche the name of a pet
plant supported by a piece of whalebone. 'Oh,' he said, '*stay-
bonia pulcharia*,' and a little while later had the satisfaction of
seeing it so labelled. He was in contact with the Foxes again
in June, when he denounced the tomfoolery of wearing mourning (as he was doing himself) for a monarch whose decease
inspired so little regret as William IV's; and once more in
July, when, in spite of the presence of a geological student, the
talk ran off on the West Indies, negroes and mosquitoes. In
addition, 'he told us of a spectral illusion which had once
befallen him, when he saw a friend whom he had attended on
his death-bed under very painful circumstances. He reasoned
with himself, but all in vain; whether his eyes were shut or
open the apparition was ever before him. Of course he explains
it as a disordered stomach. He gave me a mass of autograph

[1] Cf. Sir Archibald Geikie, in a chapter on de la Beche in his *Life of Sir Andrew
Ramsay* : ' Over and above all shone his bright cheery nature, his irrepressible
merriment, his helpful sympathy and that inexhaustible enthusiasm which not only
supported his own untiring efforts but, like a contagion, affected and stimulated all
who were associated with him.'

letters and bestowed his solemn benediction on us at parting, as they leave Falmouth on the 31st'—a slightly premature leave-taking, for the date was then only the 10th.

It was eleven months before Caroline met the geologist again. This time it was in London, at the Athenaeum (that sedate institution had been founded by John Wilson Croker in 1824, fourteen years earlier; did it even then admit ladies, or was the portico the limit for Caroline?), and there was a crowd there intent on seeing all that could be seen of Victoria's coronation. De la Beche talked about many things. Caroline summarised the conversation thus: 'The de la Beche West Indian property is in a very flourishing state, thanks to the beautiful changes there. He has long used free labour, and found it answer well, though he was mightily persecuted for carrying out this system. A great deal of thoughtful talk on things as they are and things as they should be, on human nature, human prejudices, self-love and self-knowledge. Whilst the Royal party were in the Abbey we wandered across the Park to see the ambassadors' carriages which were ranged there. They were very magnificent, the top of one being covered with what de la Beche called crowns and half-crowns; Soult's, one of the old Bourbon carriages, richly ornamented with silver; the Belgian very grand, but part of the harness tied together with string! The servants had thrown off their dignity and were sitting and standing about, cocked hats and big wigs off, smoking their pipes. It was an odd scene.'

The next, and last, contact was in more academic surroundings, at the Plymouth meeting of the British Association in 1841. (Both now, and in her account of her talk at the Athenaeum three years earlier, Caroline curiously refers to her friend as 'Sir' Henry, though he was not in fact knighted till 1848; even if, looking through her Journal in later years, she had inserted the title, it is not easy to see why she should have done that in these two cases only.) De la Beche was President of the Geological Section, but, as usual, geology was the last subject he was inclined to discuss in his social moments. 'This evening,' Caroline writes, 'as we were taking tea at Colonel Mudge's, he wandered in, and was forcibly reminded of old times in seeing us all.' He talked of education in general and popular education in particular, and expressed strong approval of Carlyle's *Chartism*. A few days later, Caroline sat next him at dinner, when 'he talked of the all-importance of an honest belief. I see he is very careful not to give his opinion until he has really studied the subject, he so dreads and deprecates untrue statements both of opinion and fact.'

That, so far as the Journal testifies, was the last time Caroline saw de la Beche. It was mainly by chance that they had met in the past, and it was no doubt by chance that they did not meet in the future. But she mentions one occasion when his name came up in conversation. It was in connexion with Florence Nightingale. Miss Nightingale sat next to de la Beche, and set herself, very properly, to draw him out on geology. That went very well; she 'charmed him by the boldness and breadth of her views, which were not common then.' Unfortunately 'she accidentally proceeded into regions of Latin and Greek, and then our Geologist had to get out of it. She was fresh from Egypt, and began talking with W. Smyth about the inscriptions etc, where he could do pretty well; but when she began quoting Lepsius, which she had been studying in the original, he was in the same case as Sir Henry [*Sir* Henry once more]. When the ladies left, the latter said to him, "A capital young lady that, if she hadn't so floored me with her Latin and Greek!"' Miss Nightingale, it may be mentioned, was at this time in the late twenties. The original tongue of Lepsius was neither Latin nor Greek, but German.

The two scientists with whom Caroline was on the most intimate terms, Professor (subsequently Sir Richard) Owen and Professor Lloyd, afterwards Provost of Trinity College, Dublin, she met for the first time in the same week, in August 1841.

Science and Invention

As the British Association meeting at Plymouth had ended a few days before, it is a reasonable inference that both of them had come on to Falmouth from there; Owen certainly had. Professor and Mrs Lloyd appeared at Rosehill after breakfast one morning, and the party 'took shipping and went to Trelissick' [on the Fal; the former home of Davies Gilbert, who had died in 1839]. In the course of a general conversation Lloyd told a story of an excursion he had taken in Ireland with Sir John and Lady Franklin and the Sabines, in the course of which a difficult climb had to be negotiated. 'Professor Lloyd was with them, and vastly amused at Lady Franklin again and again saying "John, you had better go back, you are certainly giddy." At last, poor woman, she had to change her feint and could proceed no farther. Sir John found it advisable to carry her back, and asked Col. Sabine to assist him. The Colonel thought it nervous work, and hesitated, until encouraged in a grave matter-of-fact way by the excellent husband: "Don't be afraid, Sabine; she never kicks when she's faint." '

The next day Caroline took a walk alone with Lloyd, in the course of which he gave an estimate of Whewell.[1] In the evening ghosts were among the topics. Lloyd's 'own belief in ghosts extends thus far —At the moment at which the soul is separated from the body, he thinks the spirit may range for any definite purpose, our comprehension of which is by no means necessary for its reality.'

Two days later Owen was encountered, at Grove Hill, the home of Caroline's uncle George Croker Fox. She described him as 'a very interesting person, his face full of energetic thought and quiet strength. His eye has in it a fixedness of purpose, and enthusiasm for that purpose, seldom surpassed.' A couple of days later again comes an interesting story. Colonel Sabine (the explorer, later Sir Edward Sabine, K.C.B.) was at breakfast at Rosehill, Lloyd also being present. Caroline gives a lively account of a striking conversation. 'Breakfast,' she

[1] See p. 282.

writes, 'made joyous by Colonel Sabine announcing that he had got glorious news for us, which he set us to guess. His wife looked keenly at him, and asked, "It is about Captain Ross?" Such is the sympathy between these married magnetists; for in very truth it was about Captain Ross—that he had reached 78° South Lat., being 11° further than anyone before him. He had discovered snow-capped mountains. Twenty-two years since (in 1818) Colonel Sabine and he had stood upon the North Pole ice, and the former said "Well, Ross, when you become a post-captain and a great man, you must go through the same work at the South Pole." Colonel Sabine's excitement is delightful, and the spirit of reverent thankfulness with which he receives the tidings truly instructive. They are so charmed at the coincidence of the news arriving here, when Lloyd, Sabine and Fox are assembled together.' Lloyd's association with Ross I cannot trace. Francis Were Fox's arose from the fact that Ross was on that voyage using his dipping-needle, or magnetic deflector, and had succeeded, thanks to it, in discovering the South Magnetic Pole.[1]

Later in that month Lloyd and Owen, still at Falmouth, were both staying with Sir Charles Lemon at Carclew, and Sterling was invited there to meet them. 'John Sterling,' Caroline writes on August 30th, 'is extremely pleased with his visit to Carclew, and the society there of two men of European celebrity. He characterises Lloyd as a highly cultivated and naturally refined abstract thinker, living and dreaming in his abstractions, feeling "the around him" as nothing and "the beyond him" everything; his course, therefore, very naturally takes the direction of pure mathematics. Owen, with his strong perceptions, vigorous energy and active will, chooses organic matter for his investigations, and dwells rather in what is and what has been than in what may be. It is interesting to observe how these antithetical characters have alike arrived at the fact of the extreme importance of analogies.' It may be

[1] See p. 254.

further remarked of these antithetical characters that each of them became in later years a President of the British Association, Lloyd at Dublin in 1857, and Owen at Leeds in 1858.

The two scientists and the Foxes were much together in the next few days, an arrangement that gave obvious pleasure on both sides. Barclay Fox and others shot a seine for Owen's benefit on Meudon beach, but it yielded no better harvest than a single cuttle-fish. Then they settled down on the beach, and Sterling read Tennyson aloud. Caroline found Owen 'very delightful; he is such a natural creature, never affecting the stilted "philosophe," and never ashamed of the science which he so ardently loves. He is passionately fond of scenery; indeed all that the Infinite Mind has impressed on Matter has a charm and a voice for him. A truly Catholic soul. He is delighted with the Cornish character of independence, kind-heartedness, intelligence and energy.' A day or two later a question from Mrs Lloyd to Sterling as to what Kant thought brought the immediate answer: 'he thought fifteen octavo volumes.' In one of the conversations of those pleasant days Mrs Owen took a leading part. She was the daughter of William Clift, Conservator of the Museum of the Royal College of Surgeons, to whom Owen was first assistant and then successor; Clift, in his youth, had been amanuensis to John Hunter, the great surgeon, who laid the foundations of the museum.

On one of the early days of this September of 1841 'Mrs Owen gave us many sketches of her own life and experiences. She has been a great deal with the Cuvier family, and considers Cuvier an infinitely great man—so great, indeed, that you could never approach him without feeling your own inferiority. Her husband strongly recommends Cuvier's *Eloges* as very beautiful pieces of biography. He thinks him the greatest man since Aristotle, not to be repeated for two thousand years. He has great faith in cycles applied to great men; such regular intervals occurred between the Epic Poets. Mrs Owen told us about her education, which was very much left to herself. She said

"I determined to get to myself as much knowledge as possible, so I studied languages, even Russian; music, drawing and comparative anatomy. My father being Curator at the College of Surgeons, I had great facilities for this latter branch. I determined I would never love any but a very superior man, and see how fortunate I have been." She is a very perfect little Fact in the great history of the world.'

The next day it was Professor Owen who held the field; he talked about phrenology, he talked again about Whewell, he talked about Carlyle, and speaking of Carlyle's message of sympathy with the whole human race said he dissented from it because he agreed with Johnson in liking a good hater. Later on he 'gave us the individual adventures of different specimens of heads and a foot of the Dodo now existing in this country, the history of the Oxford one traceable from Elizabeth's time. In Ashmole's time it was a whole bird, but his executors, finding it dusty, broke off the head and burnt the rest, and successive naturalists have chanted a loud miserere. He gave a lecture on going to bed early; the two hours before midnight the most important for health.'

Another morning they spent at Pennance Rocks, with Sterling talking about 'Wordsworth, Carlyle and collateral subjects.' Which of them it was who contributed an anecdote which Caroline appends here is not stated, but it has merits of its own in any case. 'Lady Holland has established a sort of tyranny over matters of literature and criticism. Henry Taylor dining one day at Holland House, Lady Holland asked him what he was doing now. "I am writing a review of Wordsworth for the *Quarterly*." "What!" exclaimed her Ladyship, "absolutely busied about the man who writes of caps and pinafores and that sort of thing!" Taylor replied in the gravest, quietest way, "That is a mode of criticising Wordsworth which has been obsolete for the last ten years." And Taylor has not since been invited to Holland House.' In the course of the ensuing conversation Owen expressed the view that 'Coleridge had a

Science and Invention

bad effect on the young literary men about him, in teaching them to speak, instead of write, their thoughts.' This seems a little surprising. Coleridge certainly never taught anyone to speak while he was holding the floor, and that was almost always; it must have been tuition by example.

Now Professor Lloyd in his turn comes to the fore, giving a lecture on Light, apparently in the Rosehill drawing-room, with the Owens and the Sterlings among his listeners. Caroline conscientiously reports it, but her résumé may be left undisturbed. Owen took notes diligently, finding Lloyd's explanations, according to Caroline, more acceptable than Whewell's theories. The next day there was a drive, in the course of which Owen told some 'capital stories' about Irish landlords. Then his visit to Falmouth ended, and almost all Caroline's future contacts with him were at his museum at the College of Surgeons, a visit to which fascinating institution became a regular feature of sojourns in London at Yearly Meeting time. The first of these was in the next year, 1842, Caroline writing on May 17th: 'to the College of Surgeons to meet Professor Owen, who showed us over their Museum, and added infinitely to its interest by his luminous expositions. The things are arranged altogether physiologically on the idea which Hunter first struck out and worked on, that there is a certain analogy of structure running throughout Nature, vegetable as well as animal; a hyacinth, for instance, has its fibres, but no internal stomach, so the earth in which it is embedded acts as one. Owen believes that no animal has sensation unless furnished with a brain, therefore the cuttle-fish is the lowest creature which can be effectively treated with cruelty. Examined a long series of skulls; those of babies so much phrenologically better than grown persons—which Owen thinks quite natural, as they came uncontaminated from the Author of all Goodness, and degenerate after contact with the world.' Later that year Caroline noted in her Journal a tribute paid to Owen by Carlyle in a letter to Sterling. He

271

had, he said, 'been greatly interested by two interviews with Professor Owen, from whom, he says, he has learnt more than from almost any other man. He is charmed by his naturalness, and the simplicity he has preserved in a London atmosphere.'

The 1843 visit to the museum had a particular interest, for it was the last time Caroline ever saw Sterling. He was there, with John Mill, W. E. Forster and Barclay Fox. But there was general interest over and above that. 'Here,' says Caroline, 'we saw the great bone—the actual bone—of a bird which a sailor brought to Owen from Sydney, and out of which he has mentally constructed an immense ostrich. And we saw the series of vast bottles, each filled with a fixed Idea. Sterling said he was quite awe-struck at the thought of being with a man who knew them all! Owen gave us a little lecture on the brain: that when it is much worked a certain portion is actually lost; adding that *Strafford* [Sterling's tragedy], he supposed, cost its author about two ounces. He and Sterling then got into a delicate little discussion upon Dr Johnson's taste for a good hater. Mrs Owen supposed that differences in opinion would be settled by definition, so Sterling defined it as the sort of feeling which Owen would entertain towards Sir Everard Home, who destroyed John Hunter's papers; he would not do him any harm, but he would not go out of his way to prevent his being well punished. This led to discussion on the wicked waste of Thought which Home had thus committed. Facts and results of positive worth have been irrevocably lost.' These last few lines refer to a historic scandal in the scientific world. Sir Everard Home, Hunter's brother-in-law and pupil, subsequently his assistant and his executor, took charge of all the great surgeon's manuscripts in 1799 (Hunter having died in 1793), kept them till 1823, drawing on them freely during that period for his own lectures and dissertations, and then burnt them, alleging that Hunter had charged him to destroy them after his (Hunter's) death. Owen could speak with authority on all this, and so, still more, could Mrs Owen, for she was the daughter of William Clift, who had as a boy been Hunter's devoted amanuensis, and had fortunately preserved copies of some of the manuscripts. These Owen edited and published in 1861.

After a three-years interval, May 1846 found Caroline again in London and again at Owen's museum; she went there, with others of her family, on May 23rd, the day before her twenty-seventh birthday. Owen was at home, and talked on a variety of subjects. 'On looking at the Dodo,' Caroline reports, 'he said that he believes the Dutch, on their way to Amboyna, used to call at New Zealand and lay in a stock of these birds; that the poor natives used themselves to eat them, and when they were all gone they were reduced to feed on each other. He talked genially about Cromwell: long since he had founded a high notion of him from Milton's Sonnet, which he once triumphantly repeated to a party who were considering the propriety of erecting Cromwell's statue, as a monument likely to outlast the House of Commons and other tangibilities.' This Cromwell incident had, in fact, been rather more embarrassing to Owen than he indicated. The question was raised by Lord Clarendon in a distinguished company—no less, indeed, than 'The Club,' Johnson's Club—to which Owen had only lately been admitted, and when opinions were being collected he was appealed to first, as being the youngest. Taken aback for a moment, he quickly regained his presence of mind and made an effective and rather non-committal reply by quoting immediately 'Cromwell, our chief of men, . . .' and the rest, and observing that in that the Protector had a monument already in the hearts of men.

Owen had a great admiration for Cromwell, and when the Foxes called on him next he showed them his recently arrived portrait of the Protector. 'It was,' said Caroline, 'as of one resting after a long hard fight, and in the calmness of his evening recalling and judging some of its stern incidents. The Carlyles had been to see it, and spent a characteristic evening there; he grumbling at all Institutions, but confessing himself convinced by Owen's "Book on Fossils." ' Caroline says nothing of the history of the picture, though it would be surprising if Owen failed to tell her about it. When he was at Florence in 1845 he got permission from the Grand Duke to have a copy of the portrait of Oliver Cromwell, which hung as a pendant to that of Charles I in the room, or gallery, of the Pitti Palace assigned to Portraits of Great Generals. The copy was made, at the recommendation of the Grand Duke, by Michele Cortezzi. It arrived at the end of April 1846, and Carlyle and various other people came to see it. Owen records all this in his own diary, adding 'More people to see Cromwell. He has held quite a levee.'

Another three years and the museum was disclosing its treasures to the Foxes once more, this time no less noteworthy a treasure than the skeleton of a veritable sea-serpent. 'He showed us,' Caroline wrote, without a hint of scepticism, 'some of the vertebrae of the genuine sea-serpent; the commonly reported ones are really a very long species of shark, and when a pair are following each other, and appearing from time to time above water, they look of course wondrously long. Thirty feet is in reality their general length, but he has had evidence of one of sixty feet. Gave a little exposition of his bone and limb theory, the repetition of the same thing under all sorts of modifications. For the arm of a man, the fore-leg of a beast, the wing of a bird, the fin of a fish, there is first one bone; this passes into two, and ramifies into any number necessary, whether it be a bat's wing for flying or a mole's paw for grubbing. The ideal perfection is most nearly approached by fishes, their construction being the simplest and most conformable to the perfect arch. He spoke of the impossibility of any living creature capable of existing in the Moon, because they must do without air or water; but, he added, there is no physiological reason against Ezekiel's beasts existing in some of the Planets.'

How seriously this last observation is to be taken seems debatable. But Caroline would not be likely to doubt Ezekiel's beasts.

Once more a three-years interval, and Caroline and Owen meet for what is apparently the last time. She gives the fact no more than a bare mention, though it was at a British Association meeting (at Dublin in 1852), where there must have been plenty of opportunities for renewing a friendship and exchanging reminiscences. In the Ethnological Section a paper was being read on the fauna of the Arctic regions, and the discussion centred round the fate of Sir John Franklin, from whom news had long been awaited in vain. 'Murchison, Owen, Sabine and Prince de Canino,' writes Caroline briefly, 'all expressed themselves most earnest that the national search should be continued. It was a great treat to be present at this discussion, and to watch the eager interest with which they claimed their friend's life from science and from England.' (Though they did not know it, the intrepid explorer had already been dead five years—as Caroline herself learned, and recorded in her Journal in 1859,[1] when the rescue expedition reported.) It seems strange that Caroline's last reference to Owen should be so casual, but she could not, of course, know when she wrote it that it would be the last. Whether she never saw him again during the remaining eighteen years of her life, after seeing him so often in the preceding eleven, and if so why that should be, there can now be no means of knowing.

Of Lloyd, after her report of his lecture on Light at Rosehill in 1841, Caroline says nothing till five years later, when he came to Falmouth again, this time with his Dublin friend Robert Ball, the naturalist. Lloyd was at the Foxes' twice in September and twice in October. In the course of one of the earlier visits he entertained the company with views on, and anecdotes of, Whately, who was Archbishop of Dublin from 1831 till his death in 1863. Caroline's entry for September 3rd runs: 'Dr Lloyd with us: he threw out many of his own

1 See p. 293.

large comprehensive views and feelings on religious matters; his untractarian and unsectarian convictions, and his broad charity, which longs for all to enter the fold. He has introduced Mill's *Logic* into the Dublin College, and thinks he has, more than any other, shown the worth of Bacon, but also that he is wanting in the deductive department. Bacon would make all reason from Facts upward. He is much interested in Mill's chapter on Free-Will, and does not see the evil which some suspect in it, but feels it the simple statement of a Fact, that there are definite laws governing the Moral as well as the Physical world. He talked of Whately, who is much injured by being the centre of a clique who flatter and never contradict him, hence he becomes very despotic. He is a most generous creature and full of knowledge. He wriggles his limbs about in an extraordinary manner, and once pronounced the benediction with one leg hanging over the reading-desk in Church; and in society he will sit balancing his chair, occasionally tipping over backwards. One of his chaplains, during a walk with him, stated that fungus was very good eating, upon which the Archbishop insisted on his then and there consuming a slice, which the poor chaplain resisting, the Archbishop jerked it into his mouth. A Doctor who was with them was in ecstasies of mirth at the scene, which the Archbishop perceiving, said "Oh, Doctor, you shall try it too; it is very important for you to be able to give an opinion." "No, thank you, my lord," said the Doctor, "I am not a clergyman, nor am I in your lordship's diocese." '

About the two October visits, on successive days, Caroline says less, but both the entries have their interest. 'Dr Lloyd,' the first of them runs, 'rejoined us this evening. He looks at science with the ardour of a lover and the reverence of a child. He accepts the Incomprehensible and waits for clearer vision; thus he can be no scoffer, no denier, but a teachable, and therefore a taught, disciple of very Truth itself, whether speaking through outward Nature, inward conviction, or the written message of God to man. His face glows with a sublime faith when he unfolds to others some glimpses of the mysteries of existence, and helps them to an intelligent love for the things seen and the things not seen. Talked much of Humboldt,[1] a universal man, who lives in reality far longer than others, as he takes but three hours and a half for sleep out of the twenty-four, and is always in a high state of mental excitement. He talks any language you please, and upon any subject.' And the second: 'A luminous talk with Dr Lloyd on men and books. He holds Butler's *Analogy* as second only to the Bible; values Wilberforce's *Practical Christianity* and all Paley's works, except his *Moral Philosophy*. He wants us to know his friend Aubrey de Vere, a poetical, pure-minded, high-souled creature.'

In the next year, 1847, Caroline was in Dublin, and at dinner at the Lloyds' had a conversation which clearly gave her great enjoyment with Dr Anster, the learned and literary Professor of Civil Law at Dublin University. Everything she reports him as saying is of interest. 'Dined at Mrs Lloyd's,' she wrote, 'met amongst many others Dr Anster, the admirable translator of *Faust*, who fell to my share, and we had plenty of talk on German and other matters. He is weary of translations, and thinks that except S. T. Coleridge's *Wallenstein*, no poem has ever come of such attempts. Talked of Bailey's *Festus* and other natural children of *Faust*. He objects to *Festus* on poetical, not theological, grounds, for somehow he could not hit on the fine passages. He is an enthusiast for Goethe, and thinks him as selfish for others as for himself, earnest at all costs that they should get their meed. But he pretends to discover vast selfishness in *Iphigenia*, in her steady adherence to what she felt to be right, whatever it might cost others. He likes Carlyle's translations better than his originals, except his *Cromwell*, which he receives with great deference. Speaking of the "Young Man in Business Who Wrote Essays at

---

[1] Alexander von Humboldt, author of *Cosmos*, the more distinguished of two distinguished brothers.

Intervals," [1] he said, "He seems not to think more than other people, which is a great comfort." Dr Anster is a great burly man, awkward in his ways, occasionally making a deep utterance, the voice rising from the lowest depth within him. There is some beauty in his profile and in the sudden lighting up of his countenance. He seems warmly interested in the sufferings of the poor people around him.'

Lloyd himself, fertile in anecdotes as ever, produced another when Caroline met him two days later. The story he told was that 'one night, during the British Association Meeting in Dublin, when he was utterly fagged with his duties as Secretary and had fallen into an intense sleep, he was aroused by tremendous knocking, and in came Sir William Hamilton with "My dear Lloyd, I'm so sorry to disturb you, but this Norwegian noble and I have become great friends, and he must not leave Dublin until we have had a glass of wine together. Unluckily I have none left; will you lend me a bottle?" So the poor Doctor had to turn out to promote friendly relations between scientific bodies.'

In 1848 the Lloyds were back at Falmouth, and this time they stayed with the Foxes at Rosehill. The quiet assurance with which Caroline records the Professor's learned, almost erudite, conversation is a notable, though of course unconscious, tribute to her own intellectual capacity: 'Had a stroll with the Professor; he was on the heights where he breathes most freely. He spoke of a little pet speculation of his own—of the unity of Force which governs the material Universe. Faraday's theory of forces is a sort of repetition of Boscowitz's, which is a charming bit of Berkeleyism. Talked of Fichte's character with delight, though he was doomed to illustrate the melancholy truth that Ontology was not for man.' Every day during Lloyd's visit there was something for Caroline to record. One day he talked of Whewell and Whately; on another he told stories of Captain Ross; on another of Humboldt; on another

[1] Sir Arthur Helps, author of *Friends in Council*.

of Jenny Lind; and on another recalled an anecdote, quoted elsewhere in this volume,[1] of Sir William Hamilton and Airy.

Four years later the Foxes returned the visit, going to stay with the Lloyds in Dublin in August 1852. Caroline has strangely little to tell about her host on this occasion, though in writing to Elizabeth Carne after her return home she speaks of him with great warmth, likening him to 'the most beautiful of Greek philosophers, with the purest, most loving, Christianity superadded. He dwells in regions where all high things meet and are harmonised, where music, mathematics and metaphysics find themselves but several expressions of one Law, and the Lawgiver the object of our simplest faith. His wife is a lovely young creature; a steady thinker where that is needed, but playful, graceful, fascinating with those she loves.' Caroline saw Lloyd once more at Dublin, at the British Association over which he presided there in 1857. He told of a happy turn which Lord Carlisle gave to an incident before the first British Association meeting at York.[2] 'A coin had been found, whose inscription they could not read, until on applying heat out came the words "Deo Gloria." "Thus," said Lord Carlisle, "when the torch of Science is faithfully applied to dark subjects 'Deo Gloria' is always the result it brings." '

It is surprising, in view of the comparative frequency of Caroline's contacts with the Lloyds, that she should, to all appearance, never have seen them again in the remaining thirteen years of her life. Possibly she did. This is not the only case in which her Journal maintains an unexpected silence. But the entries from this time on are very sporadic, and none of them mentions the Lloyds.

Among the many scientists of her acquaintance Adam Sedgwick, for over fifty years Woodwardian Professor of

[1] See p. 287.
[2] In 1831. The Lord Carlisle in question was George William Howard, the 7th Earl, Lord Lieutenant of Ireland 1855-58 and 1859-64.

Geology at Cambridge, evoked Caroline's admiration in a special degree, as combining extensive scientific knowledge with orthodox Christianity, and refusing resolutely to admit any antagonism between religion and science. An example of that, at the British Association meeting at Liverpool in 1837, she relates with enthusiasm. It was the closing meeting of that year's series. Various papers were read and discussed. 'Then came forward our glorious chairman,[1] Sedgwick [Caroline had had some talk with him the day before and found him "very delightful"], who, after saying many soft things to the soft sex, gave the moral of the science, that if he found it interfere in any of its tenets with the representations or doctrines of Scripture, he would dash it to the ground, gave the whys and the wherefores in his own most admirable method, and sat down; the Synod was dissolved, and Sedgwick had disappeared.'

This was not the first time Caroline had met Sedgwick, for in September of the previous year, intent on geological investigation, and no doubt well acquainted with so ardent a geologist as Robert Were Fox, he had made an unexpected appearance at Rosehill. 'Just after tea,' the seventeen-year-old diarist had written then, '"a gentleman" was announced, who proved to be nothing less than Professor Sedgwick. He had unluckily unpacked at the inn, and so preferred keeping to those quarters. He goes tomorrow with Barclay to Pendour Bay in search of organic remains, which he fully expects to find there, and does not think the Cornish have any cause to boast of their primitive rocks, as he has discovered limestone with plenty of organic remains, and even some coal in the east of the county.' The next day Barclay Fox took Sedgwick off on an expedition productive of limestone, but not of organic remains, and brought him back to dinner, a meal enlivened by the arrival of a note from Sir Charles Lemon, expressing with rather laborious

---

[1] Not of the whole Association—he had been that in 1833—but of the Geological Section.

humour the hope that the Professor (a confirmed bachelor) would, next time he came to Falmouth, stay at Carclew and bring Mrs Sedgwick with him. It may well be that he did go to Carclew, for he was often in Cornwall, studying the geology of the county intensively. In 1839 Caroline picked up from a visitor a story of how 'some years ago a Miss James, an eccentric lady, was walking from Falmouth to Truro, and fell in with a very intelligent man in a miner's dress. She entered into conversation, and concluded by giving him a shilling. In the evening she dined out to meet Professor Sedgwick, and was not a little astonished to recognise in the Professor her morning's friend of the pickaxe.'

Sedgwick was one of the many public characters of whom Sterling at one time or another passed judgement in conversation with Caroline. A Trinity man himself, he linked for comparison two Trinity men not very much senior to him, Whewell (of whom more in a moment) and Sedgwick, rivals incidentally at a later date for the Mastership of that great college.[1] 'He called Whewell (with whom he is well acquainted) a great mass of prose, a wonderful collection of facts. Whewell once declared that he could see no difference between mechanic and dynamic theories, and yet the man reads Kant, has domesticated some of his ideas, and thinks himself a German. Sedgwick he owns to be of a different stamp, a little vein of genius running through his granite.' At the time of this conversation, 1841, Sedgwick was a Canon of Norwich. He had exhaustively investigated the geology of Devonshire, and given the name Devonian to the slates, grits and limestones of that county, Cornwall and West Somerset, as he later gave the name Cambrian to the oldest rocks of the palaeozoic era. Caroline only saw him once more, at Cambridge in 1864, when she found him 'looking very aged.' He was then seventy-nine,

[1] The present Master of Trinity has written ' He [Whewell] and his friend and fellow-northerner Adam Sedgwick did in their day more than anyone else to promote the new scientific studies at Cambridge ' (*Trinity College*, by G. M. Trevelyan).

but lived nine years more, having held his chair at Cambridge since 1818.

His friend Whewell, though a Lancashire man, had early associations with Cornwall, for in 1826 and 1828 he joined Airy in experiments regarding the density of the earth at Dolcoath mine. While remembered principally as a forceful Master of Trinity, thoroughly reactionary in both college and university affairs, he was prominent as scientist and philosopher, and it was entirely appropriate that Caroline should have first met him at a British Association meeting (in 1837) where, in the Physical Section, he and Sir David Brewster 'were discussing some questions of spectrum light.' He had at this time held, and resigned, the Professorship of Mineralogy, and was in the following year, 1838, to be appointed to the Chair of Moral Philosophy. In 1840 Caroline mentions seeing him among the audience at one of Carlyle's lectures on Heroes, and in 1841 —the year in which he married, became Master of Trinity and was President of the British Association—she heard Sterling speak of him in the language just quoted. Professor Lloyd gave her another opinion of Whewell a few months later, but it is too concisely summarised to be very instructive. She speaks of having a walk with Lloyd, 'in which he beautifully analysed Whewell's character, sermons and scientific standing. To each the objections are rather negative than positive, but nevertheless they are objections.' With that may be compared a judgement given to Caroline in the following month by Lloyd's friend Owen: 'Talked enthusiastically of Whewell, and his *Philosophy of the Inductive Sciences*, a book which he thinks will live by the side of Bacon's *Novum Organum*. He considers him as deep as he is universal. A rare eulogy.' Some years later came another brief *obiter dictum* from Lloyd on the same subject: 'On Whewell: his want of humility one grand barrier to his real intellectual elevation, his talents rather agglomerative than original.'

If Caroline's first and only meeting with Whewell was long

deferred, at least it was well prepared. It took place in 1859. Whewell, then seventy-four, was staying with Sir Henry Lemon at Carclew, and Caroline, who was forty, went there for a couple of days too. A great deal of ground must have been covered in those two days, and it could be wished that Caroline had devoted more space than she did to them. But what she does write is worth writing. 'We spent two days at Carclew,' she records, 'with Dr Whewell and his wife Lady Affleck. [Whewell had married in 1858 as his second wife the widow of Sir Gilbert Affleck; she continued to be known as Lady Affleck.] He was as urbane and friendly as needs be, and seemed determined to live down Sydney Smith's quiz about Astronomy being his forte and Omniscience his foible; [1] for he rarely chose to know more about things than other people, though we perseveringly plied him with all manner of odds and ends of difficulties. There is a capital element of fun in that vast head of his; witness his caricatures of Sedgwick in his Cornish Sketch-book. He made me notice the darkness of sky between two rainbows, a fact only lately secured, and a part, he says, of the whole theory of the rainbow. Speaking of some book he had written with a touch of Architecture in it, he said, "There are many wise things in it, but I'm wiser still," which he hoped was a modest way of stating the case. He declines throwing light on the axe-heads which are making such a stir, thinking there is no need for such hurry, and only tossing to one the theory of the greater age of man than is now admitted.'

Then the conversation went off—or more probably another conversation took place—on adult education. 'Of the Working Men's College at Cambridge, he is quite sure it is doing the teachers great good, whatever it does to the learners. He does not see what is to come of the middle-class examinations; they are not a step to anything by the direct method, and one man who got a high certificate was quite astonished at having some trusty situation offered him, never dreaming that it was in

[1] Sydney Smith said ' Science,' not ' Astronomy.'

consequence of this. "But won't some further career be opened for these meritorious people?" "I don't find people in general very good judges of their own merits." "Well, then, won't the lookers-on open some ways for them?" "I don't see much good comes of spectators. Why, already there are so many half-starved curates; what are you to do?" F. D. Maurice comes down sometimes, and there is a great sensation; or Mr Ruskin, who astonished them all highly the other day, only he flew rather over the people's heads.'

Then one or two isolated topics. 'Papa got from him a formal contradiction of the choice story about Chinese Music, which was a pity; but he says he never wrote on the subject, only on Greek Music.' It was a pity. The commonly accepted version of the story is that some of the Trinity Fellows conspired to floor Whewell with an abstruse question on the subject of Chinese music. He at once gave a learned answer, on which they commented with satisfaction that it was at variance on several points with the article on the subject in the *Encyclopaedia Britannica*. 'Ah, yes,' said Whewell, 'but my views on the subject have changed considerably in the years since I wrote that article.'

Finally, 'he told of a talk he had had with Martin [1] among his pictures, which he assured him were the result of the most studied calculation in perspective; he had been puzzled how to give size enough to an angel's hand, and at last hit on the expedient of throwing a fold of his garment behind the sun.'

Whewell had many qualities, not all of them equally attractive. Caroline evidently caught him in an urbane mood. Or was it that she had on the old gentleman the mollifying effect which her personality so frequently produced?

[1] John Martin (1789-1854), painter of ' Belshazzar's Feast ' and many other pictures on Biblical themes.

Chapter XVI
Searchers of Sky and Sea

There was no reason why Caroline should have taken a special interest in astronomy, nor is there any evidence that she did, but fortune happened to bring her in contact at different times with three of the most famous astronomers of the day—Sir George Airy, who was Astronomer Royal from 1835 to 1881; John Couch Adams, the discoverer of the planet Neptune, who was invited to succeed Airy but declined; and Lord Rosse, who, besides being an observer of the heavens, was a manufacturer of telescopes.

Airy came to Falmouth in 1845. He had then been Astronomer Royal for ten years, and was still engaged in re-organising Greenwich Observatory, the condition of which when he got there was deplorable. He had before that been Plumian Professor of Astronomy at Cambridge. Caroline met him at Penmere, which was subsequently the home of Alfred Lloyd Fox, her first cousin. Who was living there in 1845 Caroline does not indicate, but the question is not of great consequence, for if the host took any part in the conversation she felt it unnecessary to report him, devoting her whole attention, no doubt rightly, to Airy. She must have looked forward to meeting him, for she had heard something of him before. Eight years earlier, when she was calling on Sir Charles Lemon at Carclew, Airy's name came up. Sir Charles said he had invited him to come and stay at Carclew, and talked about him a good deal. 'Airy, he said, was so shy that he never looked a person in the face. A friend remarked to him "Have you ever observed Miss ——'s eyes? They have the principle of double refraction." "Dear me, that is very odd," said the philosopher, "I should like to see that; do you think I might call?" He did so, and at the end of the visit begged permission to call again to see her eyes in a better light. He, however, found it a problem which would take a lifetime to study, and he married her.' If the story is to be accepted, the blank which Caroline substitutes for the lady's name can be filled in—with the monosyllable Smith. But the statement about calling again must be widely interpreted, for the solid fact is that Airy proposed unsuccessfully in 1824 to Miss Richenda Smith, daughter of the Rev. Richard Smith, rector of Edensor, near Chatsworth, and in 1830 she changed her mind and accepted him.

With the Carclew conversation in mind, Caroline met Airy at Penmere in 1845. His talk was less astronomical than might have been desired, but it was not the less interesting for being comprehensive. 'His subjects,' Caroline explained, 'were principally technical, but he handled them with evident power and consciousness of power. Perhaps his look and manner were sometimes a little supercilious, but his face is a very expressive and energetic one, and lights up with a sudden brightness whilst giving lively utterance to clear expressive thoughts. He spoke with evident astronomical contempt of the premature attempts of Geology to become a science; all but mathematically-proved Truth seems to him a tottering thing of yesterday. He delights in the Cornish miners, whom he has long known, and attributes their superior intelligence and independence partly to their having themselves an interest in the mining speculations and adventures of their employers —an arrangement unknown in other parts. The virtues of the dousing-rod he wholly attributes to the excitability of the muscles of the wrist. He totally ignores all inhabitants of the Moon, and says there is no more appearance of life there than in a teacup. And he seems to shun everything like undemonstrable hypotheses. He says the difference which Herschel's telescope [this great instrument had been completed in 1789] makes in the appearance of the Moon is by giving it shade, and therefore the globular, instead of the flat, look, which it has through ordinary glasses.' Airy's reference to Cornish miners was no doubt based on knowledge derived from familiarity with them when he was conducting experiments into the earth's density at Dolcoath mine, near Camborne, in 1826 and 1828. He was unsuccessful on both occasions, from causes outside his control.

Caroline mentions no other meeting with Airy, but three years later Professor Lloyd told her an anecdote about him which suggests that a fair measure of self-confidence might have been included among the qualities which her analysis of his character revealed. 'When in Dublin,' Lloyd recounted, 'Sir William Hamilton mentioned to Airy some striking mathematical fact. He paused a moment. "No, it cannot be so," interposed Airy. Sir William mildly remarked, "I have been investigating it closely for the last few months and cannot doubt its truth." "But," said Airy, "I've been at it for the last five minutes, and cannot see it at all." '

Adams was a younger man than Airy. He was, indeed, almost the same age as Caroline, and was Cornish like her, but as he was born at Laneast, near Launceston, at the opposite end of the county, there was no particular reason why they should ever have met. They actually did meet in 1847, at Carclew, where Caroline had listened to stories about Airy ten years before. In 1847 Adams, though only twenty-eight, was already famous throughout the world, for two years earlier he had discovered a planet which it was decided to name Neptune. The story of how the French astronomer Leverrier discovered it almost simultaneously (though Adams was a few weeks ahead of him) is familiar enough, but it was newer in 1847, and Caroline tells it well. 'Adams,' she says, writing of the evening at Carclew, 'is a quiet-looking man, with a broad forehead, a mild face, and a most amiable and expressive mouth. I sat by him at dinner, and by gradual and dainty approaches got at the subject on which one most wished to hear him speak. He began very blushingly, but went on to talk in most delightful fashion, with large and luminous simplicity, of some of the vast mathematical Facts with which he is so conversant. The Idea of the reversed method of reasoning, from an unknown to a known, with reference to astronomical problems, dawned on him when an Undergraduate, with neither time nor mathematics to work it out. The opposite system had always before been adopted. He, in common with many others, conceived that there must be a planet to account for the disturbances of Uranus; and when he had time he set to work at the process, in deep, quiet faith that the Fact was there, and that his hitherto untried mathematical path was the one which must reach it; that there were no anomalies in the Universe, but that even here, and now, they could be explained and included in a Higher Law. The delight of working it out was far more than any notoriety could give, for his love of pure Truth is evidently intense, an inward necessity unaffected by all the penny trumpets of the world.'

It must have been a satisfaction to this brilliant and shy young man of twenty-eight, when once the ice was broken, to unfold his doctrines to a hardly less intelligent young woman of his own age, whose interpretation of his words shows how fully she was capable of entering into his thought. Her demonstration of his devotion to pure science was a necessary prelude to the story of how that science was so decisively applied. To that she now turns. 'Well, at length he fixed his point in space, and sent his mathematical evidence to Airy, the Astronomer Royal, who locked the papers up in his desk, partly from carelessness, partly from incredulity—for it seemed to him improbable that a man whose name was unknown to him should strike out such a new path in mathematical science with any success. Moreover, his theory was that if there were a Planet it could not be discovered for 160 years; that is, until two revolutions of Uranus had been accomplished. Then came Leverrier's equally original, though many months younger, demonstration; Gall's immediate verification of it by observation; and then the astronomers were all astir. Professor Adams speaks of those about whom the English scientific world is so indignant in a spirit of Christian philosophy, exactly in keeping with the mind of a man who had discovered a planet. He speaks with warmest admiration of Leverrier, specially of his exhaustive method of making out the orbits of the comets, imagining and disproving all tracks but the right one—a work of infinite labour. If the observer could make out distinctly but a very small part of a comet's orbit, the mathematician would be able to prove what its course had been through all time. They enjoyed being a good deal together at the British Association Meeting at Oxford, though it was unfortunate for the intercourse of the fellow-workers that one could not speak French nor the other English! He had met with very little mathematical sympathy, except from Challice [Challis] of the Cambridge Observatory; but when his result was announced there was noise enough and to spare. He was always fond of star-gazing and speculating, and is already on the watch for another planet. One moon has already been seen at Liverpool wandering round Neptune. Papa suggested to him the singularity of the nodes of the planets being mostly in nearly the same signs of the Zodiac, a matter which he has not considered, but means to look into.'

So much for Adams himself. Under the same date Caroline adds a few lines about him, quoting Burnard, the Cornish sculptor, to the effect that 'when Professor Adams came from Cambridge to visit his relations in Cornwall he was employed to sell sheep for his father at a fair.' That not very momentous piece of information would hardly be worth mentioning but for the interest it derives from a pencilled note in the margin of a copy of the Journal now at Penjerrick. Against the passage on Adams selling sheep for his father some commentator, perhaps

Anna Maria Fox, has written 'Adams says he never could have been entrusted with such transactions'—which suggests that Adams, who lived till 1892, may have read the Journal, with Caroline's description of himself. If so, it must have given him pleasure to see her entry on the day after the Carclew conversation, an entry which indicates, like so many others, her instinctive tendency to draw spiritual lessons from conversations that impressed her. 'Professor Adams' talk yesterday,' it ran, 'did me great good, showing in living clearness how apparent anomalies get included and justified in a larger Law. There are no anomalies, and I can wait until all the conflicts of Time are reconciled in the Love and Light of Heaven.'

Caroline's acquaintance with Adams must have developed in ways not recorded, for in 1864 she went to stay with him at Cambridge, where he was Lowndean Professor of Astronomy and Director of the Observatory. 'Have just returned,' she wrote in July of that year, 'from a visit to Professor Adams at Cambridge. He is so delightful in the intervals of business, enjoying all things, large or small, with a boyish zest. He showed and explained the calculating-machine (French, not Babbage) which saves him much in time and brain, as it can multiply or divide ten figures accurately. We came upon an admirable portrait of him at St John's College before he accepted a Pembroke Fellowship and migrated thither.' (Adams, *pietas* compels me to emphasise, was a Johnian first and foremost. He entered St John's as an undergraduate, and was a Fellow of St John's when he discovered Neptune. It was seven years after that, when the college statutes precluded further re-election to his Fellowship, that he received, and accepted, an invitation from Pembroke.)

Caroline's third astronomer-acquaintance was that distinguished Irishman, Lord Rosse, who did invaluable pioneer work in the construction of specula, but is almost better known to the present generation as the father of Sir Charles Parsons, whose name is inseparably associated with the early development of both the motor-car and the turbine engine. A great six-foot speculum was Rosse's supreme achievement. This was made at the Rosse family seat at Parsonstown, King's County, with workmen recruited locally, and ovens, furnaces, etc., built on the spot. The next thing was to construct a telescope large enough for the speculum; the result was a tube 58 feet long and 7 in diameter, so that it is not surprising that Caroline was able to walk about in it. Rosse, who succeeded to the title in 1841, had sat for King's County in the House of Commons from 1821 to 1834. Caroline saw him at the British Association meeting at Dublin in 1852; he was at that time President of the Royal Society. She owed her introduction to him to her friend Professor Lloyd, and her entry for August 3rd, 1852, tells of a very interesting day among the telescopes at Parsonstown. 'Went to Parsonstown'; she writes, 'Lord Rosse was very glad to see the Lloyds, and very kind to all the party. It was a great treat to see and hear him amongst his visible powers, all so docile and obedient, so facile in their operations, so grand in aim and in attainment. We walked about in the vast tube, much at our ease, and examined the speculum, a duplicate of which lies in a box close by: it has its own little railroad, over which it runs into the cannon's mouth. There are small galleries for observers, with horizontal and vertical movements which you can direct yourself, so as to bring you to the eye-piece of the leviathan. The telescope takes cognisance of objects fifteen degrees east and west of the meridian, which is more than usual in large instruments, but observations near the horizon are worth little on account of the atmospheric influences. The three-and-a-half-foot telescope goes round the whole circle, and there is a third instrument at hand, under cover, for the more delicate results.'

Such were the finished objects, but hardly less notable than the instruments themselves was Rosse's skill and success in constructing them. The story of that process Caroline heard—

and tells. 'Then Lord and Lady Rosse showed us the foundry, the polishing shop, etc., and Professor Lloyd gave the story of the casting, under the very tree which caught fire on that occasion, and by the oven where the fiery flop was shut up for six weeks to cool, before they could tell whether it had succeeded or not. Lord Rosse's presence of mind in taking a sledge-hammer and using it when a moment of hitch and despair arrived in the casting was a beautiful feature. We had tea, and were shown a multitude of sketches of nebulae taken on the spot. Sir David Brewster was there, with his sagacious Scotch face, and his pleasant daughter. Whilst we were over our tea news came of a double star being visible; so we were soon on the spot and gazing through the second glass at the exquisite pair of contrasted coloured stars, blue and yellow. The night was hazy, and the moon low and dim, which was a disappointment; but Lord Rosse kindly showed us a cluster of stars and a bit of the Milky Way through the great telescope; the very movement of its vast bulk in the darkness was a grand sight. After the British Association a little party are coming here to enquire into the geology of the moon, and compare it with that of the earth, and in six weeks Otto Struve is expected, when they mean to begin gauging the heavens.'

Clearly a day to be remembered, and small wonder that Caroline should comment: 'We left after midnight full of delight.' She ended with one or two stories of Lord Rosse— 'of his conduct as a landlord, his patriotic employment of a multitude of people in cutting for an artificial piece of water, because work was very scarce; of his travelling in England long ago as Mr Parsons, visiting a manufactory, and suggesting a simpler method of turning, so ingenious that the master invited him to dinner, and ended by offering him the situation of foreman in his works!' It is not surprising that Caroline, writing to her friend Elizabeth Carne an account of her Irish experiences, should have mentioned Rosse's paper on the nebulae, and the visit to his telescopes, as among the most memorable incidents of the British Association week. Stirred by them to a new interest in the heavens, she put in a visit to the Armagh Observatory as well, and 'saw Saturn as we had only guessed him before.' Airy and Adams Caroline had only talked to in drawing-rooms; Rosse she saw in the midst of the instruments he had constructed, and she makes no attempt to conceal the thrill it gave her.

From exploration of the skies to exploration of the seas is no great step. Caroline was always interested in the latter, partly perhaps because at least two Arctic explorers relied on her father's dipping-needle. We have seen how the prevalent anxiety about the fate of Sir John Franklin formed one of the subjects of her brief entries during the British Association meeting at Dublin in 1857, and it is clear that, though she seems never to have met him,[1] the famous explorer made a great appeal to her imagination. It was in 1845 that he sailed off with the *Erebus* and *Terror* to find the North-West passage, a mission from which he never returned. Expedition after expedition was sent in search of him, but it was not till 1859 that the mystery of his death, which had taken place as long before as 1847, was solved. Caroline mentions a curious incident that took place a little before he sailed. 'C. Enys told us,' she writes at the end of 1851, 'of Sir John Franklin, shortly before leaving home the last time, lying on a sofa and going to sleep. Lady Franklin threw something over his feet, when he awoke in great trepidation, saying, "Why, there's a flag thrown over me; don't you know that they lay the Union Jack over a corpse?"' Even in 1851, though Caroline did not know it, Franklin had been dead four years. When authentic news of his ill-fated expedition did arrive, in 1859, she set down in her Journal the gist of what there was to tell. 'The little *Fox*,' she recorded, 'has gained her quest, and brought distinct tidings of Franklin's death in 1847; the vessel crushing

---

[1] She did go and call on 'poor Lady Franklin' in London in 1849 but found her out.

in the ice in 1848; multitudes of relics found in various cairns, which were their posts of observation around that dreary coast: Bibles with marked passages and notes, clothes, instruments, all sorts of things of most touching interest, so preserved by the climate; many skeletons they found, and some they could identify by things they had about them. It is a comfort to believe that they were not starved, as thirty or forty pounds of chocolate was found with them, and Sir John Franklin may have died a quite natural death a year before the catastrophe.'

In spite of her interest in such matters there was only one explorer of note with whom Caroline appears to have been personally acquainted—Captain, afterwards Sir James, Ross, who had in 1831 determined the position of the North Magnetic Pole; he took part later, in 1848, in the first Franklin Relief Expedition. Caroline heard a good deal about him before she met him. Early in her Journal days—in 1836—Captain Belcher, later Sir Edward Belcher, who commanded the Franklin Relief Expedition of 1852, was one of the guests at a large dinner-party at Rosehill. He had sailed with Ross in the *Hecla* in 1827 to Spitsbergen, with the idea of reaching the Pole from there by travelling over the ice, and he entertained the company with some of his reminiscences. 'Captain Belcher,' Caroline wrote that day, 'an admirable observer of many things, was very amusing. In 1827, when among the Esquimaux with Captain James Ross, they were treated in a very unfriendly manner; he and five men were wrecked and their boat sunk, and they were obliged to betake themselves to the land of their enemies, twenty-four of whom, well armed with clubs, came down to dispute their proceedings. They had only one brace of percussion pistols among them, and one load of powder and ball. The natives were aware of the terrible effect of these instruments, but not of their scarcity, so Captain Belcher went out of his tent just before their faces, as if looking for something, put his hand in his pocket and drew out a pistol as if by accident and hurried it back again. The other sailors, by slightly varying the ruse, led the natives to imagine the presence of six pairs of pistols, and so they did not venture on an attack. Shortly after this, having been repeatedly harassed, they were thankful to see their ship approaching; the Esquimaux now prepared for a final assault, and came in great numbers demanding their flag. Seeing the helplessness of his party, Captain Belcher said, "Well, you shall have the flag, but you must immediately erect it on the top of that hill." They gladly consented, and Captain Belcher fastened it for them on a flag-staff, but put it Union downwards. The consequence was that the ship's boats put off and pulled with all their might, the natives scampered off, the flag was rescued and the little party safely restored to their beloved ship. I should like to hear the Esquimaux' history of the same period. Captain Belcher has invented a very ingenious instrument for measuring the temperature of the water down to "bottom soundings." He is a great disciplinarian, and certainly not popular in the navy, but very clever and intensely methodical.'

There is, it is true, much more Belcher than Ross here, but the expedition of which Belcher talked was under Ross's command, and, her interest in the latter thus kindled, Caroline naturally welcomed the opportunity of an introduction to him at the British Association meeting at Liverpool in the following year. A couple of months after that Ross appeared at Falmouth, and of course at the Rosehill dinner table, where he proved almost more copious in anecdote than Belcher. Caroline reports him at pardonable length, but it will do her no injustice to summarise a little here. Ross pronounced Polar exploration healthy, justifying his view by asserting that on ordinary expeditions the average of deaths would be thirty-seven, while on the northern voyages it was twenty-five. He then embarked on an admirable sailor's story of one of his expeditions. 'He described the first appearance of the *Isabella*. After an absence of five years, throughout which they managed to keep up hope, Captain Ross said to the look-out man, "What's that dark

object in the distance?" "Oh, Sir, 'tis an iceberg; I've seen
it ever since I've been on watch." Captain Ross thought so
too, but he could not be satisfied about it, and sent for his
glass; he had no sooner viewed it than his best hopes were
confirmed, and at the top of his voice he cried "A ship, a ship!"
Not one of the crew would believe him until they had seen it
with their own eyes. They were soon in the boat, but a little
tantalising breeze would come and drive the ship on two or
three miles and then cease, and this frequently repeated. In
spite of all their signals they were too insignificant to be seen,
until Captain Ross fired off his musket half a dozen times, and
at last it was heard and a boat was lowered. As soon as the
ship's boat met these forlorn objects, twenty in number, un-
shaven skin-clad sinners, they said, "You've lost your ship,
gentlemen?" "Yes, we have," replied Captain Ross, "but
what ship is this?" "The *Isabella*, formerly commanded by
Captain Ross," was the reply. "Why, I am Captain Ross."
"Oh, no, Sir, that's impossible; Captain Ross has been dead
these five years." Dead or alive, however, they brought them
to Hull, where they felt the most miserable anxiety as to what
changes might have taken place in their absence; and Captain
Ross added that in the following week he was the only one
of the party not in mourning.' There were more stories:
then 'Captain Ross had an experimental evening with papa,
and left us at ten'—dinner having presumably been about
three.

Soon after this, in 1839, Ross was off again, this time to the
Antarctic, and it was on this voyage that he sent a message to
Robert Were Fox telling him of the discovery of the South
Magnetic Pole, thanks to the Fox dipping-needle. From that
journey he returned in 1843. There is no record of Caroline's
ever meeting him again, though he lived till 1862, but in 1848
she heard more stories about him from the Lloyds, when they
came to stay at Rosehill. 'He told them such pleasant things
about some of the Greenlanders who had come under missionary

influence. He had asked a large party to dine on board his ship, and they came in full native costume, and when they assembled at the table they all stood for a while and sang a Moravian hymn, to the delighted surprise of their hosts. He finds some vestiges of what he supposes to be a traditional religion amongst the most remote Esquimaux, a sense of right and wrong, and an expectation of a future state, though this takes the grossest form of enjoyment—"plenty of whales." One of his sailors married a Greenlander, and as she approached England she was very curious to learn if seals were to be found there. "Yes, a few, but you will hardly meet with them." This was sad; however, she tried the country for a time till the *mal du pays* and the longing for seals seized her so fiercely that there was no comfort but in letting her return home.'

Caroline must have had more to tell about Arctic expeditions than she did tell. She knew, for example, Sir Edward Sabine, who presided over the Belfast meeting of the British Association meeting which she attended in September 1852. He had been on expeditions with both Ross and Parry, and spent some time carrying out scientific investigations on Spitsbergen. But Ross's and Belcher's stories are the only ones Caroline retails at length. There was, however, one historic voyage of discovery with which she was brought into some association. 'On the 2nd of October,' wrote Charles Darwin in *The Voyage of the Beagle*, 'we made for the shores of England; and at Falmouth I left the *Beagle*, having lived on board the good little vessel for nearly five years.' In the first sentence of the same book he had written: 'After having been twice driven back by heavy south-western gales, Her Majesty's ship *Beagle*, a ten-ton brig, under the command of Captain FitzRoy, R.N., sailed from Devonport on the 27th of December 1831.' It would be satisfactory to be able to narrate that the first thing the great naturalist did on reaching Falmouth was to seek out Caroline's family. Unfortunately he did not do that. But Captain Fitzroy, who was a much more interesting person than is commonly realised, did.

His visit occupies the whole of Caroline's not very lengthy entry for October 3rd, 1836. 'Captain Fitz-Roy,' she records, 'came to tea. He returned yesterday from a five-years voyage in H.M.S. *Beagle*, of scientific research round the world, and is going to write a book. He came to see papa's dipping-needle deflector, with which he was highly delighted. He has one of Samby's on board, but this beats it in accuracy. He stayed till after eleven, and is a most agreeable gentlemanlike young man. ["Young": thirty-one as seen by seventeen.] He has had a delightful voyage, and made many discoveries, as there were several scientific men on board. Darwin, the "fly-catcher" and "stone-pounder" [he had at this time published nothing] has decided that the coral insects do not work up from the bottom of the sea against wind and tide, but that the reef is first thrown up by a volcano, and they then surmount it, after which it gradually sinks. This is proved by their never finding coral insects alive beyond the depth of ten feet. He is astonished at the wonderful strides everything has made during the five years afore-passed.'

What strides the observant sailor had noted in his first twenty-four hours in port it would be interesting to learn, but Caroline does not tell us. (Why, incidentally, did Darwin, referring to a voyage which both began and ended in the reign of William IV, write of *Her* Majesty's Ship?) This appears to have been the nearest Caroline ever got to contact with Darwin, and the only time she actually saw Fitzroy, but years later, in 1843, a Lieutenant Hammond, who dined at Rosehill, spoke of him with admiration. Mentioning the lieutenant's visit, Caroline continues: 'He was with Captain Fitz-Roy on the *Beagle*, and feels enthusiastically towards him. As an instance of his cool courage and self-possession, he mentioned a large body of Fuegians, with a powerful leader, coming out with raised hatchets to oppose them: Captain Fitz-Roy walked up to the leader, took his hatchet out of his hand, and patted him on the back; this completely subdued his followers.' On

Fitzroy's (this seems to be the correct spelling, though it is neither Darwin's nor Caroline's) subsequent career—he became a Member of Parliament, Governor of New Zealand and an F.R.S. and was promoted to Admiral—it is tempting to enlarge, but the story would be irrelevant here.

Chapter XVII
Sculptors and Painters

Caroline's interest in art and sculpture was developed in her early days largely by the activities of the Falmouth Polytechnic (for so it is most convenient to describe the Royal Cornwall Polytechnic Society). There may have been no great pictures, and no great sculpture, there, but local talent was sufficient to keep interest in the arts alive. Anna Maria sketched assiduously, and was a regular prize-winner at the Polytechnic, which also was the scene of the first successes of a Cornish sculptor, Nevill Burnard, who subsequently established a not inconsiderable position in London. Caroline devotes more space to him than she does to greater craftsmen. That is natural enough in view of his history, for Burnard, who was born at Altarnun, in the centre of Cornwall, first made a name for himself by exhibiting at the Falmouth Polytechnic in 1836 a 'Laocoon' which he had carved in Cornish slate. Sir Charles Lemon, M.P. for Helston, helped the young craftsman by taking him to London and putting him in touch with Chantrey. As a consequence he was soon distinguished by the receipt of a commission to execute a bust of the Prince of Wales (King Edward VII), who, as Duke of Cornwall, might more fittingly sit to a Cornish sculptor than to any other. He had a successful professional career, but being unpractical in business matters he died (in 1878) in straitened circumstances.

Burnard was naturally known to Caroline through the Polytechnic, but it is not till 1847, when he was twenty-nine and she a year younger, that she mentions him first. In October of that year 'Burnard, our Cornish sculptor, dined with us.

He is a great powerful pugilistic-looking fellow of twenty-nine; a great deal of face, with all the features massed in the centre; mouth open, and all sorts of simplicities flowing out of it. He liked talking of himself and his early and late experiences. His father, a stone-mason, once allowed him to carve the letters on a little cousin's tombstone which would be hidden in the grass; this was his first attempt, and instead of digging in the letters he dug around them, and made each stand out in relief. His stories of Chantrey very odd: on his death Lady Chantrey came into the studio with a hammer, and knocked off the noses of many completed busts so that they might not be too common— a singular attention to her departed lord. Described his own distress when waiting for Sir Charles Lemon to take him to Court: he felt very warm, and went into a shop for some ginger-beer; the woman pointed the bottle at him, and he was drenched! After wiping himself as well as he could, he went out to dry in the sun. He went first to London without his parents knowing anything about it, because he wished to spare them anxiety, and let them know nothing until he could announce that he was regularly engaged by Mr Weekes. He showed us his bust of the Prince of Wales—a beautiful thing, very intellectual, with a strong likeness to the Queen—which he was exhibiting at the Polytechnic, where it will remain.'

The sculptor, who was responsible for the story about John Couch Adams selling sheep for his father,[1] added a few more anecdotes a week later, telling what Caroline calls 'amusing stories of his brother-sculptors, and their devices to hide their ignorance on certain questions. Chantrey, after sustaining a learned conversation with Lord Melbourne to his extremest limits, saved his credit by "Would your lordship kindly turn your head on the other side and shut your mouth." Spoke of Bacon, the sculptor, after having given up his craft for twenty-five years, resuming it, at the request of his dying daughter, to make her monument, and finding himself as much

---

[1] See p. 289.

at home with his tools as ever.' In 1849 came news of Burnard from a source which gave it added interest, in the form of a note to Caroline from Carlyle, who reported that he had seen 'my gigantic countryman, Burnard, and conceives that there is a real faculty in him; he gave him advice, and says he is the sort of person whom he will gladly help if he can.' Burnard himself wrote too, enclosing 'in great triumph, the following note he had received from Carlyle with reference to a projected bust of Charles Buller: "February 25, 1849. . . . Nay, if the conditions *never* mend, and you cannot get that Bust to do at all, you may find yet (as often turns out in life) that it was *better* for you you did not. Courage! Persist in your career with wise strength, with silent resolution, with manful, patient, unconquerable endeavour; and if there lie a talent in you (as I think there does) the gods will permit you to develop it yet.— Believe me, yours very sincerely, T. Carlyle." '

At this time, and for many years hereafter, Burnard was leading a diligent and successful life, carrying out numerous commissions, and exhibiting for four years (this was a little later) at the Royal Academy. After that, as has been stated, he was beset with financial difficulties, and his closing years were considerably clouded by them. But Burnard, important though he might be in Cornwall, was no very prominent figure in the larger world of art, certainly in no way the equal of men like Flaxman or Westmacott, Flaxman's successor in the Professorship of Sculpture at the Royal Academy. Caroline never knew Flaxman; he died when she was only seven; but she took a great interest in his work. Her estimate of him was no doubt due in part to Sterling, who told her he considered Flaxman the head of English art. She heard more of Sterling's views during a visit she paid with him in 1842 to Sir Richard Westmacott's studio in South Audley Street. Westmacott at this time had held his Professorship of Sculpture for fifteen years, and his fame was fully established by the numerous products of his art, among which the most generally familiar today are the

Achilles statue at Hyde Park Corner and the Duke of York on his column in Waterloo Place. Caroline describes the visit and the conversation. 'We then went to Westmacott's studio, introduced by Fanny Haworth. He is a man of extreme energy and openness of countenance, real enthusiasm for his art, and earnest to direct its aim as high as heaven. He and Sterling had several spirited discussions on Greek feeling for Art, and how far we may benefit by studying from such models. Westmacott thinks that our enthusiasm for Greek forms is merely the effect of education, because their mythology has given place to something so far higher and purer. Sterling maintained that it was their embodiment of all that was worshipful and venerable, and in so far as they succeeded it must be venerable to all Time and to universal man. The highest conquest of Art is to combine the purest feelings with the highest forms, and if this is effected we need not be fastidious about the medium, or be deemed profane for reverencing a head of Jupiter. Westmacott delights in Flaxman, and pointed out a bas-relief of his Mercury and Venus "as a little piece of music." "A most pagan illustration by a most Christian artist," said Sterling. "I cannot desire further confirmation of what I have said." '

Hearing Flaxman's successor on Flaxman was, no doubt, the next best thing to hearing Flaxman himself, and seeing his work the next best thing to seeing Flaxman. Caroline did indeed see one example of it at Westmacott's studio, but it was not till 1849 that she saw a representative collection. The first sentence in her entry on the subject—'F. Newman joined us, to show us their new treasures of Flaxman's bas-reliefs'—calls for some little explanation. Why Francis Newman? What does 'their' mean? And why new or newly-acquired? The mystery is, in fact, not very profound. Francis William Newman, the Cardinal's brother, had since 1846 been Professor of Latin at University College, Gower Street, and that institution had, through the agency of Flaxman's sister-in-law,

Miss Denman, acquired a large collection of casts from his studio sketches. To Gower Street, accordingly, Caroline went, and found there Miss Denman herself. 'Finding us enthusiastically disposed, she most graciously invited us to go home with her and see his most finished works. She was very communicative about him, as the Star which had set in her Heaven, and it was a most serene, mild and radiant one, and those who came under its influence seemed to live anew in a Golden Age. He was ever ready with advice and friendship for those artists who needed it; his wife was his great helper, reading for him in poetry and history, and assisting him by wise and earnest sympathy. Miss Denman would have liked to found a Flaxman Gallery and leave it to the Nation, but no fit freehold could be purchased. At her house are choice things indeed,—a little world of Thought, Fancy and Feeling, "music wrought in stone," devotion expressed in form, harmony, grace and simplicity. We saw the illustrations of the Lord's Prayer; lovely young female figures clinging to their Guardian Angel, going out into Life, and saying by every look and attitude, "Lead us not into temptation." And the "Deliver us from evil" was full of terror and dismay, but yet of trust in an Infinite Deliverer.'

Here Caroline's acquaintance with sculptors and their work seems to have ended, but she saw something of various leading painters, and one of them is associated with the visit to the Flaxman bas-reliefs. The last two lines of the Journal entry that day run: 'We looked in on Laurence on our way home, and admired his sketch of Aunt Backhouse, which looks hewn out of granite.' (This was Hannah Backhouse, wife of Jonathan Backhouse, of Darlington, whose daughter Jane had married Caroline's brother Barclay; Hannah Backhouse was an active Minister of the Society of Friends.) Caroline had reason to know Laurence, for in 1846, when she was twenty-seven, she sat to him for her portrait—that portrait which, etched by Herkomer, appears near the beginning of this volume. Laurence was one of the leading portrait-painters of the day; there are several examples of his work in the National Portrait Gallery, his Whewell is at Trinity College, Cambridge, and his Thackeray at the Reform Club, Pall Mall. By 1846, the year in which he painted Caroline, he had already become known through his portraits of Carlyle and Sir Frederick Pollock and his crayon drawings of Dickens and Professor Sedgwick; F. D. Maurice (as Caroline mentions) had just been sitting to him. For whom this portrait of Carlyle, which was executed in 1842, was intended was discovered by Caroline later in the year, when Laurence told her he had given it to Carlyle's old mother. Meanwhile Anna Maria Fox, as Caroline notes in November 1842, had commissioned Laurence to make a copy of the portrait, and had presented it to Jane Welsh Carlyle. Caroline's references to Laurence are brief, though one phrase she uses suggests that she had intended writing more about him, but never did. Two entries at the time she was being painted say simply: 'To Samuel Laurence's studio to be drawn. Admirable portraits in his rooms of Hare, Tennyson, Carlyle, Aubrey de Vere and others. Of Laurence himself more anon.' And on the next day: 'Interesting time with Laurence. Tennyson strikes him as the strongest-minded man he has known. He has much enjoyed F. D. Maurice's sittings lately, and dwelt especially on the delicate tenderness of his character.' Caroline's sittings, which began in May, were interrupted by a visit to the Continent, but she resumed them in August. It was on this occasion that she mentioned that 'He has given the portrait of Carlyle to Carlyle's old mother. He thinks Mrs Carlyle fosters in him the spirit of contradiction and restlessness. He regrets the jealous feeling existing among so many artists, keeping them apart, and leading them to deprecate [? depreciate] each other like petty shopkeepers. He spoke on the growth of things and people, adding, "What is growth but change?"' Laurence makes only one other appearance in the Journal. In 1849, when Caroline was in

London, she went to his studio once more and was taken by him to see Samuel Rogers's pictures. The banker-poet (he was offered the laureateship, before Tennyson, on Wordsworth's death) was a great patron of the arts, and filled his house in St James's Street with pictures. Caroline says little about them—simply that 'he has some capital drawings, a letter of Milton's, and his rooms are decorated with all sorts of curiosities' —but to visit Rogers's luxurious and costly house must have been worth while in itself. Its owner, it would seem, was not at home.

Two other painters of whom Caroline says something are Richmond (whose portrait of Elizabeth Fry is well known) and Landseer. Her two references to Richmond are interesting, because one quoted Sterling on Richmond and the other Richmond on Sterling. In 1841 she wrote (of Sterling) that he 'knows George Richmond well: he is painting portraits till he can afford to devote himself to historical painting and live in Italy. He has lately done one of Christ and the disciples at Emmaus, but there is not incident enough in the scene to explain itself without the words—an essential consideration.' It was not till 1847 that Caroline met Richmond herself. She was taken to his studio by Baron de Bunsen, whom he had lately painted. Of the artist she said, 'George Richmond is a mild, unassuming, easy, agreeable man, with a large open eye, and a look of as much goodness as intelligence. He talked of John Sterling and his merits [Sterling had been dead three years] and he regrets that he never got even a sketch of him.' Richmond, a friend and disciple of Blake and later a friend of Ruskin, was a man of strong religious convictions—which may have accounted for Caroline's impression of his look of goodness.

At Landseer's studio in 1846 there was a strange encounter. Caroline devotes to it little more than half a dozen words: 'Count d'Orsay was with him when we came.' Anything more incongruous than a meeting between the sober young Quakeress

306

from the provinces and the admired and accepted arbiter of
London fashion is difficult to imagine. Caroline knew all about
the Count—thanks once more to the volume and variety of
Sterling's conversation. In the course of a long talk in 1840
he had 'described Count d'Orsay coming to sketch Carlyle: a
greater contrast could not possibly be imagined; the Scotch
girl who opened the door was so astonished at the apparition of
this magnificent creature that she ran away in a fright, and he
had to insinuate himself the best way he could through the
narrow passage.' It is not surprising that the girl was startled.
Jane Carlyle has left a description of the visitor's attire: 'He
was as gay in his colours as a humming-bird—blue satin cravat,
blue velvet waistcoat, cream-coloured coat, lined with velvet
of the same hue, trousers also of a bright colour, I forget what;
white French gloves, two glorious breast-pins attached by a
chain, and length enough of gold watch-guard to have hanged
him in.'[1]

That was how d'Orsay appeared in 1840 or thereabout, but
it is not the vision that broke on Caroline's eyes at Landseer's
studio. The perfection of the Count's art was that he suited
his apparel to his years, as Mrs Carlyle (if I may be forgiven
for quoting a few lines more from her), pointed out with some
acuteness. Her description of the discomfited servant-maid was
written after another visit from the Count in 1845. On that
occasion, 'in compliment to his five more years, he was all in
black and brown, a brown velvet waistcoat, a brown coat some
shades darker than the waistcoat, lined with velvet of its own
shade, and almost black trousers, a large pear-shaped pearl set
into a little cup of diamonds and only one fold of gold chain
round his neck, tucked together right in the centre of his
capacious breast with one magnificent turquoise. Well! that
man understood his trade; if it be but that of dandy nobody
can deny that he is a perfect master of it, that he dresses himself with consummate skill! A bungler would have made no

[1] J. W. Carlyle, *Letters and Memorials*, vol. i, p. 300.

allowance for five more years at his time of life; but he had the fine sense to perceive how much better his dress of today sets off his slightly enlarged figure and slightly worn complexion than the humming-bird colours of five years back would have done.' It was no doubt this subfusc d'Orsay of 1845 whom Caroline encountered in 1846. There may have been a touch of disappointment that the expectations kindled by Sterling were not completely fulfilled; but even so the Count was no doubt something such as she had never seen before. Nothing seems to have passed between them. She came, he went; but she had one unusual memory to take back to Falmouth.

D'Orsay gone, Landseer could turn his attention to his latest visitors. Caroline frankly did not take to him. He 'did not greatly take my fancy' is how she puts it, proceeding: 'Someone said he was once a Dog himself, and I can see a look of it. He has a somewhat arrogant manner, a love of contradiction and a despotic judgment. He showed us the picture he has just finished of the Queen and Prince Albert in their fancy ball-dresses. He deeply admires the Queen's intellect, which he thinks superior to any woman's in Europe. Her memory is so very remarkable that he has heard her recall the exact words of speeches made years before, which the speakers had themselves forgotten. He has a charming sketch of her on horse-back before her marriage. His little dogs went flying over sofas, chairs and us—brilliant little oddities of the Scotch terrier kind. Count d'Orsay was with him when we came; Landseer's ambition is to make a picture for the next exhibition of Count d'Orsay and John Bell, in the same frame, as Young England and Old England. Saw the Fighting Stags, the Belgian Pony, and a capital sketch of his father done at one sitting.' Caroline mentions, by the way, that she was taken to Landseer's by Jacob Bell. He was a Friend, which was no doubt why Caroline knew him, and a lifelong friend of Landseer's, which is no doubt why he took her to Landseer's studio: he was also a well-known London chemist, the founder of the

Pharmaceutical Society and the *Pharmaceutical Journal*, and for a short time a Member of Parliament.

Later in life, a little perhaps to her surprise if she had not kept abreast of the movements in art, Caroline found herself unexpectedly in contact with a leading Pre-Raphaelite. In September 1860 (a notable month, for Tennyson and Palgrave had come and gone less than a week before) Holman Hunt and Val Prinsep appeared suddenly at Rosehill out of nowhere, and Caroline had an engrossing day. They were younger than she was, Prinsep much younger (Caroline 41, Hunt 33, Prinsep 22), but Hunt had already painted his famous picture 'The Light of the World.' Naturally enough, Caroline gives all her space to him; Val Prinsep she speaks of as an artist, but he was an artist of the future, for his first exhibit at the Royal Academy was not till two years later. Her whole entry reveals the delight the visit gave her. 'Holman Hunt,' she writes, 'and his big artist friend, Val Prinsep, arrived, and we were presently on the most friendly footing. The former is a very genial, young-looking creature, with a large, square, yellow beard, clear blue laughing eyes, a nose with a merry little upward turn in it, dimples in the cheek, and the whole expression sunny and full of simple boyish happiness. His voice is most musical, and there is nothing in his look or bearing, spite of the strongly-marked forehead, to suggest the High Priest of Pre-Raphaelitism, the Ponderer over such themes as the Scapegoat, the Light of the World, or Christ among the Doctors, which is his last six years' work. We went to Grove Hill, and he entirely believes in the Leonardo being an original sketch, especially as the head of our Lord is something like that of one of Leonardo's extant studies; he is known to have tried many, and worked up one strongly Jewish one, but not of a high type, which at last he rejected. Holman Hunt entirely agrees with F. D. Maurice about the usual mistaken treatment of St John's face, which was probably more scarred with thought and inward conflict than any of the other Apostles, and why he should ever have been represented with a womanish expression is a puzzle to him.'

The talk then became more discursive. 'He spoke of Tennyson and his surprise at the spirited, suggestive little paintings of strange beasts which he had painted on the windows of his summer-house to shut out an ugly view. Holman Hunt is so frank and open, and so unspoiled by the admiration he has excited; he does not talk "shop," but is perfectly willing to tell you anything you really wish to know of his painting etc. He laughed over the wicked libel that he had starved a goat for his picture, though certainly four died in his service, probably feeling dull when separated from the flock. The one which was with them by the Dead Sea was better off for food than they were, as it could get at the little patches of grass in the clefts; still it became ill, and they carried it so carefully on the picture-case! but it died, and he was in despair about getting another white one. He aimed at giving it nothing beyond a goat's expression of countenance, but one in such utter desolation and solitude could not but be tragic. Speaking of lionising, he considers it a special sin of the age, and specially a sin because people seem to care so much more for the person doing than for the thing done.'

That is the last reference in the Journal to art or artists, except a line in 1868 to the effect that 'we have had Mr Opie (great nephew of a great uncle!) painting a very successful portrait of my dear father.' The words in brackets signify 'Edward Opie, nephew of John Opie, R.A.,' the latter being the husband of Amelia Opie, née Alderson, novelist and poet, a friend of the whole Gurney circle at and around Norwich.

One great painter Caroline failed to see. In 1849 she and Anna Maria 'drove to J. M. W. Turner's house in Queen Anne's Street and were admitted by a mysterious-looking old housekeeper, a bent and mantled figure, who might have been yesterday released from a sarcophagus.' The artist was not there; he rarely was in those closing days. But they viewed his handiwork.

Chapter XVIII
Dark Visitors

Falmouth's importance as a packet-station was, as has been seen, responsible for the passage through the port of a constant stream of interesting visitors of all nationalities, either embarking on their outward or landing on their homeward journey, and G. C. Fox and Co. were likely to come in contact with most of them in a business capacity. Several of these with whom Caroline struck acquaintance (all, as it happens, in the early days of her Journal) were Asiatic or African notabilities. It was perhaps because of the interest attaching to the unfamiliar that she devoted so much space to them.

One, Edhem Bey, the Egyptian Minister of Public Instruction, has already been encountered in company with Dr Bowring,[1] who brought him to Falmouth, and no more need be said about him here. But the Begum of Oudh, whose intelligence and idiosyncrasies made a lively impression on the seventeen-year-old Caroline, will repay some attention. According to Caroline, the lady, who was leaving England by way of Falmouth in 1836 to go on pilgrimage to Mecca, was 'aunt to the present, sister of the late, and daughter of the former King of Oude.' Her name was Marriam, and her husband was Molvé Mohammed Ishmael [? Ismail], described by Caroline as Ambassador of the King of Oudh in London. In the light of indications so numerous and so explicit the identification of the Begum ought, it might be supposed, to be a simple matter. It has, in fact, proved extremely difficult,

_____
[1] See p. 203.

and I am much indebted to Sir Atul Chatterjee and Sir Richard
Burn, who have investigated the records and conclude that the
Begum must have been a daughter of Saadat Ali Khan (a ruler
of Oudh at the end of the eighteenth century), a sister of his
successor, Ghaziuddin Haidar, and aunt of Nasiruddin Haidar,
who reigned from 1827 to 1837, and was therefore King when
the Begum was at Falmouth in 1836.

However all this may be (and it matters very little), the
Begum was evidently a lady of parts, who thought for herself
and expressed her thoughts without inhibition. When the
Foxes went to Pearce's Hotel to call on her they found her out,
but being told by her Hindustani maid that she had 'gone down
cappin's' they followed her to Captain Flavel's (the commander,
I take it, of the packet by which she was to sail), and there
found her 'seated in great state in the midst of the family
circle, talking English with great self-possession in spite of her
charming blunders. Her dress was an immense pair of trousers
of striped Indian silk, a Cashmere shawl laid over her head,
over a close covering of blue and yellow silk, two pairs of
remarkable slippers, numbers of anklets and leglets, a great
deal of jewellery, and a large blue cloak over all. She was very
conversable, showed us her ornaments, wrote her name and
title in English and Arabic in my book, and offered to make an
egg curry. At the top of the page where she wrote her name
she inscribed in Arabic sign "Allah," saying "That name God
you take great care of."' She promised Mrs Clavel and her
daughter a cashmere shawl apiece, adding 'I get them very
cheap, five shillings, seven shillings, ten shillings, very good,
for I daughter king, duty take I, tell merchants my, make
shawls, and I send you and miss.' In spite of this outburst of
generosity Caroline has no scruples about observing that 'her
face is one of quick sagacity but extreme ugliness.'

This was only a proem. Solid contributions in the fields
of politics and theology came twenty-four hours later. 'The
next day,' Caroline states, 'we found her squatting on her bed

on the floor, an idiot servant of the Prophet in a little heap in one corner, her black-eyed handmaiden grinning us a welcome and a sacred kitten frolicking over the trappings of Eastern state. We were most graciously received with a shriek of pleasure. She told us of going to "the Court of the King of London.—He very good man, but he no power.—Parliament all power.—King no give half-penny but call Parliament, make council, council give leave, King give half-penny.—For public charity King give one sovereign, poor little shopman, baker-man, fish-man, barter-man also give one sovereign. Poor King! King Oude he give one thousand rupees, palanquin mans with gold stick, elephants, camels; no ask Parliament."

'She and Papa talked a little theology; she of course began it. "I believe but one God, very bad not to think so; you believe Jesus Christ was prophet?" Papa said, "Not a prophet, but the Son of God." "How you think so? God Almighty never marry! In London everyone go to ball, theatre, dance, sing, walk, read; never go Mecca. I mind not that, I go Mecca, I very good woman." She took a great fancy to Barclay, declaring him very like her son. She offered him a commission in the King of Oude's army and £1200 a year if he would come over and be her son; she gave him a rupee, probably as bounty money. There are 200 English in her King's service, two doctors and three aides-de-camp. She showed us some magnificent jewellery, immense pearls, diamonds and emeralds, tied up so carelessly in a dirty handkerchief. Her armlets were very curious, and she had a silver ring on her great toe, which lay in no obscurity before her. Then a number of her superb dresses were displayed, gold and silver tissues, satins, cashmeres, muslins of an almost impossible thinness, which she is going to give away at Mecca. She is aunt to the present, sister of the late, and daughter of the former King of Oude. She has a stone house in which she keeps fifteen Persian cats. It is a great virtue to keep cats, and a virtue with infinite reward attached to keep an idiot; the one with her she discovered in

London, and was very glad to appropriate the little Eastern mystery. Aunt Charles' bonnet amused her; she wanted to know if it was a new fashion; she talked of the Quakers, and said they were honest and never told lies.'

The next day the Foxes for some reason absented themselves from this particular felicity, but the day after that saw them waiting on her again. She was in her theological mood. 'Today,' says Caroline, 'the Begum began almost at once on theology, asking mamma if she were a *religieuse,* and then began to expound her own creed. She took the Koran and read some passages, then an English psalm containing similar sentiments, then she chanted a Mohammedan collect beautifully in Arabic and Hindustani. She made mamma write all our names, that she might send us a letter, and then desired Aunt Lucy [Mrs George Croker Fox] to write something, the purport of which it was not easy to divine. At last she explained herself, "Say what you think of Marriam Begum, say she religious, or she bad woman, or whatever you think." Poor Aunt Lucy could not refuse, and accordingly looked sapient, bit her pen-stump, and behold the precipitate from this strong acid: "We have been much interested in seeing Marriam Begum, and think her a religious lady." I think a moral chemist would pronounce this to be the result of more alkali than acid, but it was an awkward corner to be driven into. She was coming to visit us today, but had to embark instead, after expressing hopes that we should meet again in Oude.'

The hopes were not destined to be realised, but there was to be one echo of Marriam. A little more than three weeks later, her husband, who had not gone to Mecca (detained, no doubt, by his mission to the 'King of London'), appeared at Falmouth. He might more fittingly have arrived earlier to see his spouse off; Caroline does not explain that lapse. What she has to say about the 'ambassador' is: 'On coming home this morning found Molvé Mohammed, the Begum's husband, in the drawing-room. He has a sensible face, not totally unlike his wife's, and was dressed in the English costume. On showing him the Begum's writing in my book, he was much pleased at her having inserted his name as an introduction to her own. "Ha! she no me forget, I very glad see that." He added some writing of his own in Persian, the sense of which was, "When I was young I used to hunt tigers and lions, but my intercourse with the ladies of England has driven all that out of my head."' With that rather singular observation—not greatly improved by Caroline's next sentence, 'he is said to be by no means satisfied with bigamy, and it is added that one of the motives of the Begum's English visit was to collect wives for the King of Oude'—the record of the conversation ends. In view of the nature of the Begum's quest it seems surprising that she did not invite Anna Maria and Caroline to return with her to Oudh as well as Barclay. Perhaps she did.

The next dark visitor, some three years later, hardly perhaps deserves that description, for Turks are no more than swarthy, and not always even that. This particular Turk, who walked into the Rosehill drawing-room one day in January 1840, was named Nadir Shah, and is introduced by Caroline as 'this interesting *soi-disant* son of the late Sultan'—a description which covers a multitude of what in Falmouth might be called sins, but in the Ottoman Empire mere habits. The late Sultan must have been the enlightened reformer Mahmoud II (1785-1839), but Nadir Shah himself I have not succeeded in identifying; perhaps he was too *soi-disant* to find a place in history. It is evident that Caroline had seen him before, for she remarks that 'he does not look nearly so distinguished as in native costume.' That is partially explained by an entry on the same date in Barclay's journal, running: 'After dinner had a visit from a Turkish prince, Nadir Bey, returning a call from me three months ago. A remarkably acute and well-informed man, good manners, fluent and interesting conversation.' It looks, therefore, as if Nadir Bey (probably a more accurate designation than Caroline's Nadir Shah) had landed at Falmouth on his arrival in England and been called on by Barclay and thus got to know the family, whom he naturally sought out again on sailing from Falmouth for home.

His conversation, apart from some account of the methods he employed in learning English, was mainly political. 'He talks English beautifully,' Caroline testified, 'having been here three times, and described the manner in which he learned it in five months: took an English professor, made himself master of the alphabet, but resolutely resisted the idea of spelling, told his master "I'll pay you ten times as much if you will teach me in my own way. I understand that Milton and Shakespeare are the finest writers in English, so you nust now teach me in them." The plan succeeded, to the astonishment of the professor. He is acquainted with Edhem Bey, but speaks of his plan for artificial inundations of the Nile as not feasible, in consequence of its having so many mouths, each of which would require a separate embankment. The idea has been before started. Spoke of Mahomet Ali as a capital general,[1] and a character of great penetration—able, though not an original genius himself, to see and appreciate the talents, opinions and advice of others, as useful a quality as originality. He shrugged his shoulders when Russia was talked of, and said he should act in the same manner as Nicholas if he had the power: he should try and extend his possessions. Spoke of the wonderful libraries they have in Turkey, old Arabic and Persian manuscripts; the Austrian Government has employed people to copy those in the various public collections for its own use, not for publication.'

This record may be supplemented by one or two quotations from Barclay Fox's journal. After reporting, like Caroline, the Bey's achievements in the acquisition of English, Caroline's brother continues: 'Had no fault to find with England except the weather and the cab-drivers. Talked with much accumen [*sic*] of the positions of Egypt and Turkey. A lady in Town

---

[1] This was a moment when the operations of Mahomet Ali, the Pasha of Egypt, against his Suzerain the Sultan of Turkey were exercising all the Cabinets of Europe.

accusing the Turks of worshipping the sun, he replied "So would you, madam, if you ever saw it." So detests steamers that on one of his voyages, being sick beyond endurance, he attempted suicide with a pistol, but was prevented by the captain. Took leave of him at the Meeting House door, when he shook my hand warmly, and said "I am going to pray for you and I hope you won't forget me. We don't worship in the same house, but I hope we serve the same God."'

This was clearly very edifying, but it is not quite the whole story. The next day, January 6th, Barclay is found writing: 'Called on my worthy friend the Bey before his leaving by the steamer. He lost last evening, he says, a pocket-book containing notes to the value of £300 to £400, with letters and a picture which he values more. Had it immediately cried and posted, offering a reward of £100.' That produced news of two children who had been seen to pick up a pocket-book in the street. The clue was, of course, followed up, but it was immediately complicated by a cross-scent. Barclay and a friend, while hot in pursuit of the children, ran into two constables, who reported that they had seen the *soi-disant* scion of the Sultan the previous evening in company with two notorious thieves. The latter's 'roost' was accordingly searched, but without result, and the children who had found a pocket-book turned out to have found the wrong one; theirs belonged to the under-boots at Selley's Hotel. Barclay concludes with an observation which credits Robert Were Fox with some cynicism or some shrewdness, probably the latter: 'Returned fruitless; my father doubts the existence of the book.'

And so to Africa. Whatever might be the case with the Turk, there could be no question about the hue of two visitors who appeared at Rosehill in April of the same year, 1840. In Princes William Quantamissa and John Ansa, Caroline introduces us to two entertaining characters. There is more to be said about them than she says, or probably was in a position to

Dark Visitors

say. Their visit to Falmouth, which she describes in detail, was an episode in a brief interlude between an eventful past and an interesting future. A good deal of history underlies Caroline's opening sentence: 'In the evening the Rev. T. Pyne was announced, introduced by the Buxtons, who proved to be the tutor and travelling companion of William Quantamissa and John Ansale, Princes of Ashantee, whose father had killed Sir C. MacCarthy (a particular recommendation).' She is not quite accurate in implying that both the Princes were sons of the ruler of Ashantee, or that he murdered Sir Charles McCarthy, the Governor of Cape Coast Castle. The boys were cousins, not brothers, the one the son, the other the nephew, of Ossi Bonsu. Sir Charles was killed in battle, in 1824, and though it is true that his heart was subsequently eaten and his skull used at Kumasi as a royal drinking-cup, that does not convert death in battle into common murder. Relations between the King of Ashanti (in the middle of what is now the Gold Coast Colony) and the British on the coast, who were protecting the tribes in that region, remained tense for some years, but in 1831—and here we get back to the young Princes—a treaty was signed, one of whose terms provided that two boys of the Royal Family of Ashanti, named Ossoo Ansa and Ossoo In Quantamissa (sometimes Inkwantabissa) should be delivered to the British Governor of Cape Coast for a term of six years as hostages for the keeping of the peace. The treaty was kept, and the boys were sent to be educated in England.

That phase of their careers was getting near its end when they paid their visit to Falmouth. It was on April 17th, 1840, that Caroline penned the sentence already quoted. She went on: 'They had just arrived at Falmouth and came to consult about plans, so Papa recommended them to go on tomorrow to Penzance and return here to stay next week. They are youths of seventeen and nineteen, tolerably intelligent, quite disposed to be haughty if that spirit is fostered, have been educated in England, and are now travelling with their eyes wide open. But more anon of "these images of God cut in ebony."' (Caroline at this time was less than two years older than the elder of the visitors.) Four days later, the trip to Penzance having no doubt intervened, their education was broadened by introduction to a tin-mine. Caroline describes the process. 'Met their Royal Highnesses and many others at Consols Mine; they were much delighted with the machinery. In Ashantee they have copper mines as well as gold and silver, but they are not much worked. Yesterday they went sixty fathoms down Huel Vean and were much tired, but their Cornish exploration has charmed them. Each one keeps a journal, and a certain red memorandum-book which occasionally issues out of Mr Pyne's pocket as a capital check on our little members. The Princes have unhappily imbibed the European fashion of sticking their hands through their hair, which, says Dr Calvert, they might just as well try to do through velvet. Everyone was pleasant and witty according to their measure.'

The next morning the party went up the River Fal to Tregothnan; after that came a lively day at Glendurgan, the home of the Alfred Foxes, and they spent the last day of all at Pendennis Castle, at the end of the peninsula on which Falmouth stands. Here are the details:

'*April 24th.*—Our Ashantee friends enjoyed themselves thoroughly at Glendurgan, playing at cricket and leap-frog, and fishing. In the evening many joined our party, and all were amused with galvanism, blow-pipe experiments and such-like scientific pastimes until between eleven and twelve. The Princes concocted some autographs and were much amused at the exploit, adding to their names "Forget-me-not" at William Hustler's instigation. They talked a great deal about Ashantee and what they meant to do there on their return, the schools they are to found, and the people they are to send to England for education. Their remembrances of their own country are, I should fancy, rather brighter than the actual fact. They

speak of their father's palace as a magnificent piece of architecture, and of the costume of the ladies being generally white
satin! They really seem very nice intelligent lads, gentlemanlike and dignified. When too much puffed up, Quantamissa
refuses to take his tutor's arm, which sorely grieves T. Pyne!'

'*April* 25.—We were a large party at breakfast, after which
we had a capital walk to Pendennis. Mrs Coope was in her
chair, which the Princes seized and galloped off with up the
steep hill. They mightily enjoyed playing with the cannon-
balls; their own Ashantee amusements consist in watching
gladiatorial combats. They laugh in a knowing manner when
slavery is alluded to, and they left us this afternoon after a really
pleasant visit.'

There, so far as Caroline is concerned, the Princes disappear.
But their subsequent fortunes are of some interest, and it is
worth while following them a little further. Most of the
information about their return to their native land emanates
from the Rev. Thomas Birch Freeman, a mulatto Wesleyan
Methodist missionary (his father was a negro gardener who had
settled near Winchester and married a Hampshire woman), who
was the first Englishman of that vocation to enter Kumasi, and
who fortunately, like Caroline, kept a journal. The Princes
made their entry into the capital with him. They had travelled
out from England in one of the ships of the ill-fated Nigerian
expedition of which Caroline speaks [1] in connexion with its
originator, Sir Thomas Fowell Buxton. Leaving England in
April 1841, they reached the African coast in late August or
September. Mr Freeman sends home news of their arrival in
the words: 'With the Niger Expedition came the Ashanti
Princes, and I am glad to find them promising young men.
They will be exposed to many dangers on their arrival at
Kumasi. O God, preserve them!' Arriving there in
December, after travelling up-country not only with Mr
Freeman but with a carriage (wheeled vehicles were of course

[1] See p. 227.

unknown in Ashanti) which the Missionary Society was sending out as a gift to the King, the Princes were warmly received, but the Rev. Mr Freeman was gloomily agitated by finding that some occasion of joy or sorrow was being celebrated by human sacrifices. It was a new King who was on the throne, an uncle of both the boys—so that neither of them stood in the direct line of succession.[1]

There is not much more to add. William Quantamissa died a year or two after his return to Ashanti. John Ansa, to all appearance fully reabsorbed in the life of his country, lived some forty years longer, dying ultimately with a good deal of political intrigue to his credit. Memories of Rosehill and Glendurgan must have seemed a little distant and a little strange, if his thoughts ever ranged back to those green slopes and lawns.

[1] ' He (His Majesty) stopped opposite us for some little time and surveyed the Princes Quantamissah and Ansah from head to foot (as they stood in their English military dresses, one on my right hand and the other on my left) under the influence of considerable emotion. He appeared affected ; it was indeed a noble scene. Yes ; the King of Ashantee is capable of feeling some of those sensations which delight the heart, on a happy and auspicious meeting after a long separation. If this be felt by the King of Ashantee, surrounded as he is by ignorance and gloom, O what must be the feelings of those happy spirits who meet to part no more in the realms of glory ! But whither am I wandering ? I am still in the vale of tears ' (*Second Journal of the Rev. T. B. Freeman*, London, 1844).

Chapter XIX
Varied Company

Many of Caroline's friends or less intimate acquaintances it is possible to classify appropriately—the writers, poets, divines, explorers, scientists and others. But there are many who, while they fit into no such category, call decisively for mention, for they are of interest both in themselves and by reason of the interest they aroused in Caroline. One function of her Journal, indeed, is to start a dozen hares which it is almost impossible not to chase, though so far as this present volume is concerned the chase must be but brief. With three or four exceptions—Lawrence and J. A. Froude and Elizabeth Fry and Borrow—the company gathered here consists of half-forgotten men and women. All of them were noted in varying degree, and in different circles, in their time, and all are worth recalling, if only for a moment, to a generation that has hardly heard their names. Caroline came across them at various places, many of them at Falmouth, whither several, like William Cooper and George Dawson and Elihu Burritt and Clara Balfour, came to lecture at the Polytechnic, while others were there on more personal errands.

The first among the more familiar figures to find a place in Caroline's pages was John Lawrence. On May 10th, 1841, she began her entry with the words: 'Amusing day. J. Sterling has a friend and connection here, a Mr Lawrence, an Indian judge, and he brought him to call.' From this description one of the greatest figures in the history of British India might not be immediately recognised, for John Lawrence, the future Mutiny hero and Viceroy of India, was at this time only a simple judge, or, as Barclay Fox put it rather more accurately in his journal entry of the same date, a magistrate and collector of the revenue. When he came to Falmouth, Lawrence, who was then thirty, had done just ten years' service, and in 1840 had been sent home on sick leave after two severe attacks of fever. What brought him to Falmouth Caroline does not say, but Barclay does, and his diary provides much better justification for the application to Lawrence's visit of Caroline's adjective 'amusing' than Caroline's own. Referring to a Bible Society meeting at the Town Hall, Barclay adds: 'Sterling's friend Lawrence there; his object at Falmouth is "Love, all love," in the shape of a very pretty, simple girl, a Miss Gresley, who is staying with the Dawsons. How to get an interview puzzled him, he not knowing the D's. I offered to take him there and introduce him to the Lieut., for which he was profoundly obliged.' The series of shifts and expedients invoked to bring the gentleman and lady together make an entertaining story, but Caroline had no part in it. The suit was unsuccessful, and it would seem either that Lawrence never really had his heart in it or that his powers of resilience were considerable, for less than three months later he had married a lady from Donegal, with the happiest future results.

Barclay Fox met Lawrence at Sterling's the day before Caroline first saw him, and quotes him as putting Clive on the same level as the Duke of Wellington, and asserting that 'the secret of our power in India is that we keep discipline and confidence in our troops through the magic of punctual payment. The Rajahs' and Nawaubs' forces are always a year's pay in arrears.' Then came the visit to Rosehill which Caroline found so amusing, though her record of it hardly bears out that description. Here it is. 'India the principal topic. Lawrence was describing an illness he had, in which he was most tenderly nursed and borne with by his native servants. "Yes," said Sterling, "Patience, Submission, Fortitude are the virtues that characterise an enslaved nation; their magnanimity and heroism is all of the passive kind." Lawrence (a man of strong religious convictions himself) spoke of the stationary kind of progress which Christianity was making amongst them. When a native embraces this new creed he retains his old inveterate prejudices, and superadds only the liberty of the new faith. This Lawrence has repeatedly proved—so much so that he would on no account take one of these converts into his service; all his hope is in the education of the children, who are bright and intelligent. The Indians will, from politeness, believe all you tell them; if you speak of any of Christ's miracles they make no difficulty, but directly detail one more marvellous, of which Mahomet was the author, and expect your civility of credence to keep pace with theirs. If you try to convince them of any absurdities and inconsistencies in the Koran, they stop you with, "Do you think that such an one as I should presume to understand it?" Sterling remarked, "Have you never heard anything like that in England?"'

How Lawrence was a connexion of Sterling's is not explained, but that they should be acquainted with each other was natural enough, since they were both at this time living at Clifton; both, moreover, had had associations with Londonderry. Lawrence stayed on at Falmouth for most of the month, and Caroline mentions him casually once or twice more. On May 16th she notes, 'Pleasant visit from Sterling and Lawrence,' and on the 24th (her twenty-second birthday) Calvert and Lawrence dined with the Foxes. Earlier that day, as Caroline records briefly and Barclay at greater length, Joseph Bonaparte, the ex-King of Spain, Napoleon's elder brother, put in to Falmouth, and Barclay and Lawrence both boarded his ship, the *Iberia*, and talked to the exiled monarch. On the 28th, Lawrence and Calvert (the elimination of Sterling is due to the fact that he had gone back to Clifton to fetch his family) rode over to Penjerrick,—possibly a p.p.c. call on Lawrence's part, for hereafter the future Baron Lawrence of the Punjab and

Grateley vanishes from the Falmouth scene. Events to come made him in retrospect a distinguished visitor.

After Lawrence, Froude. It is not to be claimed that Caroline knew the historian intimately. She saw him twice in 1842, and apparently only once again—in 1848, though there are one or two references of some interest to his writings at later dates. James Anthony Froude in January 1842, when Caroline first met him, was twenty-three, just over a year older than Caroline herself. An unhappy childhood had been followed by an uneasy five years at Oxford, where his kinship with Richard Hurrell Froude, his elder brother, had carried him naturally into the Tractarian circle. He sat under John Henry Newman at St Mary's, but soon fell into perplexity over belief in miracles, and into more perplexity when in 1840 and 1841 he spent some time as tutor in an Irish household, and found that the evangelicalism to which the family of his pupil adhered could produce a purity and integrity of life which he had till then believed to be the fruit of Anglo-Catholicism alone.

Whether Froude was actually on his way back from Ireland to Oxford when he came to lunch with the Foxes in January of 1842 is not quite clear, but he did return to Oxford at the beginning of that year, won the Chancellor's Prize for an English essay on the influence of political economy on the development of nations, and was a few months later elected to a Fellowship at Exeter College. It was just before these stabilising successes were achieved that Caroline, out of the wisdom of her twenty-two years, recorded her verdict on the young Oxonian. 'Anthony Froude a very thoughtful young man, with a wonderful talent for reading lives in written characters. To John Sterling he spoke of the beautiful purity of the early Christian Church; Sterling answered, "If any of those early Christians were to appear now, I rather think we should disclaim fellowship."' No more than that. But Caroline mentions that the luncheon-party was large—'there were too many to enjoy any thoroughly'—so it is likely enough that she got no individual conversation with Froude at all. The reference to reading lives in written characters is not as clear as it might be, but it suggests that Froude was a graphologist, and the next mention of him in the Journal confirms that.[1]

In October of the same year Froude was in Falmouth again, and Caroline met him at the Polytechnic. She once more applies to him the adjective thoughtful—he was 'thoughtful, speculative and agreeable'—and again he was interested in analysing character. 'From Sterling's handwriting he calls him enthusiastic but not sanguine, rather desponding; an amazing flow of ideas and great choice of language.' There is nothing peculiarly striking about the characterisation, which would fit a great many people besides Sterling—whom, it must be remembered, Froude had met at least once before, on the occasion mentioned by Caroline nine months earlier. This time Caroline, now twenty-three, and Froude do seem to have had some talk together, and she discovered to her satisfaction that 'he is as delighted with Arnold as I am.' (The great headmaster, appointed Regius Professor of Modern History at Oxford in 1841, had died in June 1842, four months before this conversation; Froude himself was appointed to the same chair exactly fifty years later.) But the delight with Arnold was not universal, for Caroline continues: 'On his (Froude's) remarking to Dr Pusey on the beauty of Arnold's comparing the Church and State to the Soul and Body, Pusey quietly but most solemnly said "I consider the Church belongs to a much higher Body."' The Journal entry is brief, but in its single paragraph it illuminates accurately the two influences disputing for Froude's soul, history and the love of truth, Tractarianism and the demands of faith.

By the time he next met Caroline the contest had been decided. The date was March 1848, and much had happened

---

[1] Caroline had, two years earlier, written of John Mill that ' he can always judge from handwriting whether the writer's character is a natural or artificial one.'

to Froude in the interval. He had found belief in the infalli-
bility of the Tractarians impossible when in 1845 Newman
had gone to the Church of Rome and Keble stayed in the
Church of England. In that year Froude himself took deacon's
orders, as every Fellow of an Oxford College was expected to
do. But doubts thickened. He read Emerson and Carlyle and
Goethe. His orders, from which there was no escape, were a
strait-jacket. He did preach an occasional sermon, but all the
intellectual revolt which found expression in *The Nemesis of
Faith* was boiling up. That work, however, was not published
till 1849. It was early in 1848 that Caroline met him, at
dinner at Penmere, the home of one of the Molesworths.
'Who should appear,' she writes, 'but Mr Froude? The
only thing specially characteristic of his name that fell from
him was a solemn recognition of the vitality existing in the
Church of Rome, or rather, that if the Pope succeeds in maintaining his spiritual supremacy in conjunction with all these
remarkable reforms [this was the year of revolution in Europe],
it will prove that a real vitality must exist.' That was not
quite all the conversation. Caroline adds one sentence which
brings yet another more than half-forgotten figure momentarily
to life. 'He also spoke of Miss Agnew's second work, *The
Young Communicant*, as likely to be a still more perplexing and
influential book than *Geraldine*.' No one, I imagine, reads
Emily Agnew's rather saccharine religious novels now. She
was a sister of Sir Andrew Agnew, the Sabbatarian, and her
principal work *Geraldine, A Tale of Conscience*, was published
in 1839. What is surprising is to find a man like Froude
taking her novels so seriously.

That, as has been said, seems to have been the last time
Caroline talked to Froude. But she talked of him, and wrote
of him, at least twice in later years. In March 1849 'S. Sutton
[probably the Rev. Schuyler Sutton, Vicar of Penwerris, near
Falmouth, but possibly Sarah Sutton] came in, and we had a
talk about Anthony Froude's astonishing book *The Nemesis of*

Faith, which has made an ugly stir, and has been publicly burnt at Oxford and so on. I guess it is a legitimate outcome of the Oxford party's own dealings; for I remember how a few years since he was warmly associated with them, soon afterwards employed in writing some of the lives of the Saints, then by degrees growing disgusted at the falseness of their *modus operandi.* All this must have given what was good and Truth-seeking in him a terrible shake, and now out comes this *Nemesis,* which is a wild protest against all authority, Divine and human.' This entry shows how well abreast of current literature Caroline kept herself. *The Nemesis of Faith* was not published till the early part of 1849; at any rate it was dated 1849, though Froude, writing to Kingsley on New Year's Day of that year, seemed to suggest that Kingsley might already have seen and bought it. By March 21st Caroline had apparently read the book and had heard all about the episode at Exeter College, when a copy was solemnly burned by the Senior Tutor, the Rev. William Sewell, in the College Hall. She is, moreover, perfectly correct about earlier events. Newman enlisted Froude as an associate in the production of a series of *Lives of the Saints,* with special emphasis on the miracles they performed. But the more Froude read of the saints the more sceptical he became about their miraculous powers, and when he concluded his study of St Neot with the observation 'That is all, and perhaps rather more than all, that is known of the blessed St Neot,' it became obvious that the series as planned would fare better without his collaboration.

Caroline's only other reference to Froude creates an odd literary coincidence. She was writing in 1854 to her friend Elizabeth Carne, of Penzance, of a recent visit to Torquay, where she had met Kingsley for the first time. In the course of the letter she remarked: '*Yeast* is the book which is written with his heart's blood; it was the outcome of circumstances and cost him an illness. Thou knowst that Anthony Froude, the author of the burnt *Nemesis,* has become his brother-in-law.' Curiously enough, though Caroline could not have known it, Froude had written to Kingsley at the beginning of 1849 about the *Nemesis*, 'There is something in the thing. I know, for I cut a hole in my heart, and wrote with the blood.'

It was a pity that Caroline and Froude never discussed Carlyle together, for their respective estimates of him would have been singularly interesting. But their last conversation was in 1848, and Froude did not make Carlyle's acquaintance till 1849.

None of Caroline's own relatives holds a more honoured place in the social history of England than Elizabeth Fry. 'Cousin Elizabeth' was, in fact, Caroline's first cousin once removed and of a different generation from her. She was one of the Gurneys of Earlham, a first cousin of Caroline's mother, and married Joseph Fry, banker and merchant, in 1800. There could be no frequent contact between Foxes and Gurneys, for it was a far cry in pre-railway days from East Anglia, where the Gurney homesteads were scattered thick, to West Cornwall, but all well-concerned Friends went every two or three years, if not every year, to Yearly Meeting in London, and the Fox-Gurney cousins of different degrees must have met there from time to time.

It is not till early in 1842 that Elizabeth Fry is first mentioned by Caroline. By that time she was well advanced in life, and had for nearly thirty years been carrying on that prison-visitation by which she will always be remembered. Newgate was the scene of her first ministrations, but since then she had visited prisons in Scotland, France, Holland and Germany. At home the young Queen Victoria had already expressed interest in various branches of Mrs Fry's work, and sent her a donation of £50. In 1841 the then Lord Mayor, Sir John Pirie, whose wife was among the ladies who had worked with Elizabeth Fry at Newgate, arranged a Mansion House gathering to enable Mrs Fry to meet Prince Albert, the Duke of Wellington and the principal Ministers of the Crown. She had only just returned from a wearing Continental journey, and accepted the invitation with some hesitation and

misgiving. But everything went well, and Mrs Fry sent a full
account of the proceedings to Falmouth, where she had two
first cousins, Caroline's mother, formerly Maria Barclay, and
Lucy Barclay, who had married George Croker Fox. It was
no doubt meant for the whole family, and Caroline transcribes
it in full—fortunately, for it contains a very notable summary
of conversations with persons of importance.

'Cousin Elizabeth Fry,' Caroline wrote, 'sends a simple and
characteristic account of her dinner at the Mansion House, on
the occasion of Prince Albert's laying the foundation-stone of
the Royal Exchange.—"I think you will be interested to hear
that we got through our visit to the Mansion House with much
satisfaction. After some little difficulty that I had in arriving,
from the crowd which overdid me for the time, I was favoured
to revive, and when led into the drawing-room by the Lord
Mayor I felt quiet and at ease. Soon my friends flocked around
me. I had a very satisfactory conversation with Sir James
Graham [Home Secretary at the time], and I think the door
is open for further communication on a future day. It appeared
most seasonable, my then seeing him. I then spoke to Lord
Aberdeen [Foreign Secretary] for his help, if needful, in our
foreign affairs. During dinner, when I sat for about two hours
between Prince Albert and Sir Robert Peel [Prime Minister]
we had deeply interesting conversation on the most important
subjects. With Prince Albert upon religious principle, its
influence on Sovereigns and its importance in the education of
children; and upon modes of worship, our views respecting
them—why I could not rise at their toasts, not even at the one
for the Queen, why I could rise for prayer; also on the management of children generally; on war and peace; on prisons and
punishment. I had the same subjects, or many of them, with
Sir Robert Peel. The kindness shown me was extraordinary.
After dinner I spoke to Lord Stanley [Colonial Secretary] about
our Colonies, and I think I was enabled to speak to all those in
power that I wanted to see. I shook hands very pleasantly with

the Duke of Wellington, who spoke beautifully, expressing his desire to promote the arts of peace and not those of war; he said he was not fond of remembering the days that were past, as if the thought of war pained him. Although this dinner, as numbers I have been at, may not in all respects accord with my ideas of Christian simplicity, I have felt and feel now, if on such occasions I seek to keep near to my Guide and in conduct and conversation to maintain my testimony to what I believe right, I am not out of my place in them, when, as it was the other day, I feel it best to go to them." '

The story of what she naturally felt to be a memorable occasion is told by Mrs Fry in her own journal in much the same language, but she makes it clear there that her little homily on the upbringing of children had a more personal application than the letter to Falmouth indicates. The Queen and the Prince Consort had at this time two children, the Princess Royal and a three-months-old baby who was one day to be King Edward VII. 'With the Prince,' Mrs Fry writes, 'I spoke very seriously upon the Christian education of their children, the management of their nursery, the infinite importance of a holy and religious life; how I had seen it in all ranks of life: no real peace or prosperity without it.' As the mother of nine children herself, Mrs Fry could speak with authority on this subject, and there can be little doubt that she was sympathetically heard.

A few days later Elizabeth Fry was in contact with royalty again, this time with the King of Prussia, Frederick William IV, who had come to England to stand sponsor at the christening of the infant heir to the Throne. Mrs Fry had already met him in Berlin, when he was Crown Prince. An account of his visit to Newgate reached Falmouth in a letter from one of her daughters. Either it was brief or Caroline abbreviates it, for all she writes is: 'Bessie Fry sends an account of the King of Prussia's visit to Cousin Elizabeth Fry. They spent the

morning at Newgate,[1] where Cousin Fry read with the women,
and then prayed for them and for the King, which greatly affected
him; he knelt all the time.   Bunsen went with him to Upton,
where all the small Fry were introduced to him, and he did
them the honour to wash his hands and to eat their luncheon.'
Upton was the Frys' Essex home, and the King's insistence on
going there seems to have upset his official time-table, which had
been otherwise arranged.   There was much more to tell about his
visit, but as Caroline does not tell it there is no place for it here.

Later in the same year Caroline was in a position to write
of her kinswoman at first-hand.   Whether it was their first
meeting is not clear; at any rate it is the first recorded in the
Journal.   The Fox family were in London, evidently for
Yearly Meeting, and two of the incidental engagements, so
far as Caroline was concerned, were a call on the Carlyles at
Cheyne Row and a visit to Coldbath Fields Prison with
Elizabeth Fry a few days later.   The one proved an appropriate
prelude to the other, for Carlyle, in the course of a wide-ranging
conversation, 'told us of having once been with Elizabeth Fry
at Newgate, where she read the story of Mary Magdalene in
those silver tones of hers; it went from the heart, and therefore
to the heart; there was nothing theatrical about it.   Mrs Fry
and one or two Quakeresses who were with her looked like a
little spot of purity in a great sweltering mass of corruption.'

That was on June 6th (1842).   On June 11th 'Elizabeth
Fry,' wrote Caroline, 'took us to Coldbath Fields Prison.'
This gaol, which was built in 1794 and closed in 1875, was
situated just off Farringdon Road, close to Mount Pleasant.
It accommodated from 1200 to 1400 prisoners of both sexes,
and in spite of Coleridge's reference to it [2] had many good

---

[1] Greville, who says Coldbath Fields, is clearly wrong.

[2]   ' As he went through Coldbath Fields he saw
             A solitary cell ;
             And the Devil was pleased, for it gave him a hint
             For improving his prisons in Hell.'

                                        The Devil's Thoughts.

features as things went in that day.   Caroline continues:
'Asked her concerning her experience of solitary confinement:
in one prison, where it was very limitedly used, she knew six
who had become mad in consequence of it.   Met the Duchess of
Saxe-Weimar (sister to our Queen-Dowager), her two pretty
daughters and Lady Denbigh.   The survey of the prison was
exceedingly interesting.   It is on the whole the best of our
Houses of Correction, though a severe one, as whipping and
the treadmill are still allowed.   It was sad to see the poor
exhausted women ever toiling upward without a chance of
progress.   The silent system is enforced with as much strictness
as they can manage, but of course it is sometimes evaded.   It
was beautiful to hear Cousin Fry's little conversations with
them; her tone of sympathy and interest went to their hearts.
She had no reading, owing to the High Church principles of
the directors and chaplains of the prison, but she craved leave
to tell them a story of the effect of one passage from the Bible
on a poor prisoner, which melted many of them to tears.   The
tact with which she treated the two chaplains who went round
with us was inimitable, telling them that if the Duchess was
very anxious for a reading, she would propose to turn out all
the gentlemen except her brother, for they had said it would
be impossible to be present at worship which they did not
conduct.   The Duchess was much pleased, and with her
unaffected daughters drove off to Chiswick.'

Here ends Caroline's last contemporary record of Mrs Fry.
There is indeed one more entry regarding her, but it is a retrospective reference, and indirect at that.   It is of interest none
the less as linking the Quaker philanthropist with a man of
world-wide fame, Alexander von Humboldt, the author of
Cosmos.   In September 1848 Professor Lloyd and his wife were
staying at Rosehill, and in the course of conversation mentioned
that 'when Humboldt came through Paris to see them he spoke
of Elizabeth Fry having been in Berlin, and that she had a
religious service there, and herself addressed the company,

when, Humboldt said, he had the honour of translating for her, which was, he added with a twinkling sense of incongruity, *"très bon pour mon âme."* ' The date of this visit is of no great consequence, but it would appear to have been in 1841.

From Elizabeth Fry to George Borrow is no such abrupt transition as it may seem. For one thing, Mrs Fry was among the founders of the Bible Society, which Borrow served for so many years. For another, he lived near Norwich and was acquainted with the whole Gurney circle. Caroline, with the singular knack she possessed of making contact with any interesting personage available wherever she might be, finding herself at Norwich in 1843, inevitably went off to see Borrow. That remarkable man was then living at Oulton Broad, some twenty-five miles from Norwich and two from Lowestoft, having three years earlier married Mary Clarke, a widow nine years older than himself. In 1833, at the age of thirty, he had entered the service of the Bible Society—one of its most distinguished and most unlikely agents—and travelled on its behalf in Russia and Spain and most of the countries lying between them. One fruit of his journeying, *The Bible in Spain*, appeared in the year 1843, in which Caroline went to see him. *Lavengro* and *The Romany Rye* and *Wild Wales* were still to come.

Caroline no doubt knew all about Borrow. To begin with, he was of Cornish extraction, his father, Thomas Borrow, hailing from St Cleer, near Liskeard. He had, incidentally, sailed from Falmouth for Spain in 1838, but there is no record of his being in touch with the Foxes. That is rather surprising in view of his close association with the Foxes' kinsmen the Gurneys. It was to one of their circle that he owed his first introduction to the Bible Society, though which member of the family it was is not quite certain. Andrew Brandram, the secretary of the Society, told Caroline (as will be seen) that it was Joseph John Gurney, but the balance of testimony seems to point to the Rev. Francis Cunningham, Vicar of Lowestoft, who was the husband of J. J. Gurney's sister Richenda. However that may be, there is no doubt who introduced Caroline to Borrow; it was Catherine Gurney, the eldest of the family, who had become the guardian and guide of her numerous brothers and sisters after their mother's early death.

Caroline describes the visit in her Journal under date October 21st (1843): 'Catherine Gurney gave us a note to George Borrow, so on him we called—a tall, ungainly, uncouth man, with great physical strength, a quick penetrating eye, a confident manner, and a disagreeable tone and pronunciation. He was sitting on one side of the fire, and his old mother on the other. His spirits always sink in wet weather, and today was very rainy, but he was courteous and not displeased to be a little lionised, for his delicacy is not of the most susceptible. He talked about Spain and the Spaniards; the lowest classes of whom, he says, are the only ones worth investigating, the upper and middle class being (with exceptions, of course) mean, selfish and proud beyond description. They care little for Roman Catholicism, and bear faint allegiance to the Pope. They generally lead profligate lives, until they lose all energy and then become slavishly superstitious. He said a curious thing of the Esquimaux, namely that their language is a most complex and artificial one, calculated to express the most delicate metaphysical subtleties, yet they have no literature, nor are there any traces of their ever having had one—a most curious anomaly; hence he simply argues that you can ill judge a people by their language.' This reference to the Esquimaux is an example of the astonishing range of Borrow's knowledge of foreign languages, but it is one I am unable to account for, since Borrow's travels never took him farther north than St Petersburg. It is possible, of course, that he studied the language of the Esquimaux as a recreation without ever visiting the people who speak it.

That was all that Caroline saw of Borrow himself, but in the following year Andrew Brandram, the Bible Society secretary, came to Falmouth to address a Bible Meeting. He appears to have stayed at Rosehill. At any rate, he was at breakfast there on the morning after the meeting and entertained the family with recollections of many interesting people. 'J. J. Gurney,' Caroline reports him as saying, 'recommended George Borrow to their Committee; so he stalked up to London, and they gave him a hymn to translate into the Manchow language, and the same to one of their own people to translate also. When compared they proved to be very different. When put before their reader, he had the candour to say that Borrow's was much the better of the two. On this they sent him to St Petersburg to get it printed, and then gave him business in Portugal, which he took the liberty greatly to extend, and to do such good as occurred to his mind in a highly executive manner.' Caroline said advisedly that Borrow 'stalked' to London; according to his own account, immediately on receiving the introduction from Mr Cunningham (or J. J. Gurney) he set off on foot, covering the 112 miles in 27 hours, with a total expenditure of $5\frac{1}{2}$d. on food and nothing on lodging. On one point Caroline has gone a little astray. It may well be asked how it came about that Borrow was already versed in Manchu when he appeared at the Bible Society's offices. The answer is that he was not. When he stalked to London he was asked whether he would care to learn Manchu—for which six months would be allowed—and then go to St Petersburg and supervise the printing of a Manchu Bible. It was at the end of the six months that he came a second time to London and proved so decisively superior to the rival candidate.

With Borrow may fitly be associated a character still stranger, who, like the author of *Lavengro*, spent many years travelling abroad for the spread of Christianity. Joseph Wolff appears on Caroline's first page, and with him is associated another unusual personality, notorious in the east, Lady Hester Stanhope, whom Caroline never had an opportunity of meeting, since that eccentric and masterful lady had betaken herself to her Lebanon fastness three years before the diarist was born. 'Heard at breakfast,' Caroline records on March 30th, 1835, 'that the famous Joseph Wolff, the missionary, had arrived at Falmouth. He gave an interesting lecture on the subject of his travels in Persia etc. He has encountered many dangers, but "the Lord has delivered him out of them all." Lady Georgina Wolff [*sic*; Joseph Wolff had married in 1827 Georgiana, daughter of the second Earl of Orford, Sir Robert Walpole's eldest son] is at Malta, as she does not like the sea.' The next day Wolff came to Rosehill to dinner (at the then normal hour of 4 p.m.) and talked at length of his experiences, particularly of a visit he had endeavoured to pay to Lady Hester Stanhope in her stronghold at Djoun.

Of Lady Hester (best known to the world through the chapter devoted to her in Kinglake's *Eothen*) more in a moment. First a word on Wolff himself. Who was he, and what was the story he had to tell on the platform and at the dinner-table? As things have turned out, Joseph Wolff is largely forgotten, while his son, Sir Henry Drummond Wolff, diplomatist and politician, fellow-member with Arthur Balfour and Randolph Churchill of the historic 'Fourth Party' in the eighties of last century, is still at least a name, if not much more. It is convenient to remember him for another reason, for his Christian names recall Henry Drummond, the Irvingite banker, through whom Joseph Wolff first met his future wife—in the period when he was involved temporarily with the Catholic Apostolic circle at Albury in Surrey. Before that happened, Wolff's religious and other vicissitudes had been numerous. When Caroline made his acquaintance in 1835 he was in his fortieth year, having been born near Bamberg in Germany in 1795. His father was a Jewish Rabbi, of the tribe of Levi, but young Joseph, who moved about considerably with his family to get out of the conquering Napoleon's way, soon forsook the traditions of his house, and at the age of seventeen (with Goethe's encouragement) was baptized a Christian at the Abbey of Emaus, near Prague. From that time he began to cultivate assiduously both languages and theology—among the former Latin, Greek, Hebrew, Persian and Arabic. He was at this period a Roman Catholic, but after finding his way to London, and thence to Cambridge, where he came under the highly Protestant influence of Charles Simeon, he changed his faith again. It was consequently as an orthodox member of the Church of England that he set off on his first missionary journey to the East in 1821. This took him through Egypt, Palestine and Persia, and no doubt supplied part at least of the material for the Falmouth lecture which Caroline attended.

On getting home, in 1826, he met, and married, Lady Georgiana Walpole, and in 1828 started off once more, this time to find the lost ten tribes. After being shipwrecked at Cephalonia, off the mouth of the Gulf of Corinth, he undertook a circuitous journey through Armenia to Khorasan, where he was made a slave. From that status he was rescued, to pursue his way via Bokhara to Kabul, travelling for six hundred miles through Central Asia (according to his own account) completely naked, as the result of an encounter with bandits. Ultimately he reached India, where, having acquired apparel, he was entertained by the Viceroy, Lord William Bentinck, and turned homeward by way of India and Malta. At Malta he found Lady Georgiana, who, however, did not return to England with him. That is clear from Caroline's statement that 'Lady Georgina is at Malta, as she does not like the sea.'

Later in the same year (1835) Wolff appeared at Falmouth again, walked in on the Fox family at breakfast-time and discoursed on his relations with the Irvingites. He had had traffickings with them (through Henry Drummond, the banker, whom he met in Rome) but thought better of it. 'Their want of Christian love,' he explained, 'speaks strongly against them, and their arrogating to themselves the titles of angels, prophets and apostles shows a want of Christian humility.' This may have been Caroline's first introduction to Irving's church, but she showed considerable, though quite academic, interest in it later. As for Wolff, 'he embarked soon afterwards,' Caroline mentions, 'on his way to Timbuctoo, and perhaps we shall never see him again.' There is no evidence that they ever did. It was not quite to Timbuctoo that he was going, but to Abyssinia. What happened to him between that time and his death in 1862 (at Iles Brewer, Somerset, of which he had been vicar since 1847) is no part—unfortunately—of the story of Caroline Fox.

But what Wolff had to say about Lady Hester Stanhope clearly is, in view of the entertainment Caroline, then aged sixteen, derived from the story. What she knew already of the unattractive eccentric who was granddaughter of Lord Chatham, and chatelaine for her uncle, Pitt the younger, in the last three years of his life, and four years after his death left England for ever to settle down on the slopes of Lebanon as an imperious semi-chieftainess of the Druses round her convent of Djoun—how much of that singular and engrossing adventure Caroline had already heard there is no means of knowing. But she writes of 'Lady Hester as of a familiar figure in reporting Wolff's account of a visit he paid or, rather, attempted to pay, to the famous Lebanon convent in 1822. 'When at Mt Lebanon he sent a message with which he was charged to a lady staying with her [presumably Lady Hester's companion, a Welsh lady named Miss Williams]. On which Lady Hester sent him a most extraordinary but clever letter, beginning "How can you, a vile apostate, presume to hold any intercourse with my family? Light travels faster than sound, therefore how can you think that your cracked voice can precede the glorious light of the Gospel, which is eventually to shine naturally in these parts?" He returned an appropriate answer, but he noticed that the servant he had sent with it came back limping, having been actually kicked and beaten by her ladyship *in propria persona*.'

There, so far as direct contact is concerned, Caroline takes leave of Joseph Wolff, but he appears twice more in her pages, in one case, as it happens, in connexion again with Lady Hester. Dr Bowring, when he saw the Foxes at Falmouth in 1838, spoke of Wolff, and the strictures Lady Hester had passed on him.[1] That led to a little more on the noble lady herself. Bowring it seems, like Wolff, had failed to secure an interview with her, but he had not failed to pick up a good deal of local gossip about the notorious Englishwoman. From that it was to be gathered that 'everybody in her neighbourhood laughs at her, except her numerous creditors, who look grave enough.[2] All consider her mad. One of her last delusions was that under a certain stone, guarded by a black dragon, governed by a sable magician under her control, all the treasures of the earth were concealed; the query being, why she did not give the necessary orders and pay her debts.' For whatever reason, she never did.

In 1839 the Falmouth circle had its information regarding Wolff brought up to date. Caroline, visiting her friends the Lemons at Carclew, hears from Elizabeth Lemon, Sir Charles Lemon's sister, that Joseph Wolff 'is now Doctor, and has a parish near Huddersfield.' (A D.D. degree had been conferred on him in America, and in 1837 he had been instituted rector of Linthwaite, in Yorkshire.) Miss Lemon had been Lady Georgiana Wolff's bridesmaid, and described the wedding as an odd affair. Lady Georgiana's comment on her future husband, after seeing him for the first time, was: 'I met the most interesting, agreeable, enthusiastic, ugly man I ever saw.' All the adjectives appear to have been justified. One manifestation of Wolff's enthusiasm took the form of an attempt to embrace

[1] See p. 205.
[2] So grave that Lord Palmerston, as Foreign Secretary, had to take the matter up and capitalise part of her pension to meet their demands.

Caroline's father, Robert Were Fox, the first time he met him, at Falmouth in 1835.

Wolff had come to Falmouth in the first instance to lecture at the Polytechnic, and the same errand brought several other interesting personalities within Caroline's orbit. To one of them, Clara Balfour, she devotes what today seems a singularly disproportionate amount of her space, for Mrs Balfour, whose name is hardly known in these days, was a competent and successful lecturer on such subjects as temperance and woman's place in society, but had no larger claim to distinction. She lived in Chelsea, near the Carlyles, with whom she was very friendly. Her husband, who was a civil servant, was not connected with any of the Balfours known to fame in later years. Why Caroline should have included in her Journal pages of reports of Mrs Balfour's lectures is not obvious, for while the lectures were no doubt interesting they displayed no special merit. Was it perhaps that as the friend of so many men of note she thought and cared more about woman's position in the intellectual world than she ever revealed?

The conversation when Mrs Balfour called at Rosehill is of greater value. She talked a good deal about Alexander Scott, a one-time associate of Edward Irving, and then, in response to a question of Caroline's, said something about her own work. Wasn't the lecturing a great effort? Caroline asked. No, she replied, it came gradually and without pre-meditation, and her interest in the subject carried her through. 'Carlyle once asked her, "Well, Mrs Balfour, have ye got over your nervousness over that thing (i.e. lecturing)?" "Oh, no, and I believe I never shall." "I'm very glad to hear ye say so," he replied.' She had got to know Carlyle through proof-reading an article of his on Mirabeau for the *London and West-minster Review*. 'Her press-correcting superior was a very matter-of-fact man, who held Addison the immutable standard in English writing, so anything of Carlyle's drove him half-mad, and he was thankful enough to make it over to his subordinate. Her temperance friend, Mr Dunlop, is a cousin of Carlyle's, and he asked her if she had ever seen the *French Revolution*. "No, but she longed to do so." The next day, to her delighted surprise, Mrs Carlyle called on her, with the volumes under her arm; and this was the first of an untiring succession of acts of kindness and consideration.' At this point Caroline resumes her reporting of the lectures, which, with all respect, we may leave her to pursue unaccompanied.

It was in 1849 that Clara Balfour appeared at Falmouth. Two other lecturers who came a little later, George Dawson and Thomas Cooper, deserve a moment's attention, one of them in particular, for both of them were men of some note in their day. Dawson was at Falmouth early in 1850, and Caroline disposes of him rather summarily,—thus: 'Heard many thoughts and things of the times discussed in the evening by George Dawson in his lecture on the tendencies of the age. It consisted of a string of weighty and brilliantly illustrated truths, which very few are in a sufficiently advanced condition to call truisms. He is a little black-eyed, black-haired, atra-bilious-looking man, full of energy and intensity, with an air of despising, if not defying, the happiness which he wished to make us all independent of.' Perhaps Caroline meant this to be appreciative. On the whole it should have been, for the Rev. George Dawson did educational work of considerable value on public platforms. He was pastor of an unsectarian church at Birmingham, and active in local and national politics, particularly in the field of social reform. As a lecturer on literary and historical subjects he was very successful in spreading knowledge of the works of Shakespeare, Carlyle and Emerson, and in stimulating his hearers to read for themselves.

A much more noteworthy figure than either Clara Balfour or George Dawson was Thomas Cooper, the ex-Chartist. Here is a remarkable man, whose memory is well worth reviving. His autobiography, published in 1872, tells an

impressive story of his astonishing achievement in self-educa-
tion (he was the son of a working dyer, who died when the
boy was four, leaving him and his mother penniless), an effort
which he pursued with such success that in later years his
acquaintance was welcomed by men like Disraeli and Carlyle
and W. E. Forster. After stormy experiences in the Chartist
movement, which cost him at one time two years in prison,
he became a lecturer (rather of the type of W. J. Fox, with
whom he was closely associated) on a wide variety of subjects,
literary, historical, ethical and religious. Referring to a period
from June 1858 onwards, Cooper writes: 'I entered Cornwall
for the first time, and preached and lectured at Falmouth,
Penryn, Penzance, Redruth and Truro.' It was then, in
November 1858, that Caroline heard him, and she devoted to
him a few well-packed paragraphs.

'Heard Thomas Cooper lecture on his own vagaries,' she
writes, 'practical and speculative, and their solution. He began
by an autobiographical sketch, dwelling on the mischief done
by inconsistent professors, who seemed to have badgered him
out of Methodism into scepticism; then, seeing the cruel
wrongs of the stocking-weavers of Leicester, drove him into
Chartism; he was in the thick of a bad riot, much of which
he encouraged, but he did not intend the incendiary part of it.
However, he was taken up and convicted of sedition, and
imprisoned for two years. Then and there he sank the lowest,
in loveless, hopeless, unbelief. His study of Robert Owen, and
discovery of the fallacy of his reasonings, seemed to do much
to bring him round again; and then going round England
with Wyld's Model of Sebastopol [1] seemed to have had some
mysterious influence for good; and here he is—Convert,
Confessor and Reasoner. He is a square-built man, with a
powerful, massive face; he walks up and down the platform

[1] James Wyld, who was Geographer-General, and sat as M.P. for Bodmin for
sixteen years, exhibited a ' Great Globe,' 60 feet high and lit by gas, in Leicester
Square from 1851 to 1862. His large-scale map of Sebastopol was made to illustrate
the Crimean War.

and talks as if he were in a room, with extreme clearness, excellent choice of language and good pronunciation, considering that he was formerly a poor shoemaker, and had to teach himself the much that he has learnt.' This summary supplies an outline of Cooper's career, but it hardly does it full justice. He had at this time written one or two novels of small importance and a long poem called *The Purgatory of Suicides*, which Disraeli and Douglas Jerrold among others helped him to publish. That has no doubt had such vogue as it deserved; the Autobiography, on the other hand, deserves more than it has had, though it ran through several editions in the year or two after publication.

Another visitor, resembling Cooper in one respect at least, an incredible capacity for acquiring facility in foreign languages, was Elihu Burritt, the so-called 'learned blacksmith,' American by birth, long resident in England, and one of the earliest interpreters of the two countries to one another. Growing up in Connecticut and Massachusetts, he pursued his studies to such purpose while working as a blacksmith that at thirty he was reputed to be able to speak fifty languages. He developed a passion for peace and universal brotherhood, agitating in particular (sixty years before that reform was achieved) for cheap transatlantic postage. The Congress of the Friends of Peace which he organised in Brussels in 1848 was followed by similar congresses in Paris, Frankfort, London and other British cities. Burritt was American consul in Birmingham for five years after the Civil War. He then returned to his own country, and died there in 1879 at the age of sixty-nine. Everything Burritt stood for would naturally appeal to Caroline, who first met him at Wandsworth (at whose house I cannot discover) in 1849, when his peace movement was in full vigour, and he was particularly full of the motion on Arbitration which Cobden had introduced in the House of Commons a week before.

One of Burritt's activities is an interesting example of the art of propaganda a century ago. He had for some years run a weekly paper called *The Christian Citizen* at Worcester, Massachusetts, and when he came to Europe he conceived an enterprise called 'The Olive Leaf Mission.' 'This,' he explains (in the preface to his book, *Thoughts and Notes At Home and Abroad*), 'was the monthly insertion in about forty continental journals of a column of short articles and paragraphs on the subject of peace, extracted from the speeches and writings of eminent men of different countries. This column was called an "Olive Leaf for the People"; and it appeared monthly in newspapers printed in seven languages, from Madrid to St Petersburgh, and from Stockholm to Vienna. The whole sum paid to all these journals was about £300 a year. This amount was contributed by the ladies of the United Kingdom, who formed over a hundred associations for this purpose.' The papers, it will be observed, instead of paying for the column, were paid for inserting it.

But to return to Caroline's contacts with Burritt: the first, as has been said, was in London in June 1849. She wrote of it: 'To Wandsworth, and met Elihu Burritt at dinner. Exceedingly pleased with him; his face is strikingly beautiful, delicately chiselled, bespeaking much refinement and quiet strength. He is a natural gentleman, and seems to have attained the blessed point of self-forgetfulness, springing from ever-present remembrance of better things. That Cobden evening was the happiest in his life; he felt it a triumph, and knew how it must tell on Europe that in the midst of all the wars and tumults of most nations the greatest legislative body in the world should put all their policies aside, and for hours be in deliberation on a vast moral question. Cobden got a larger number of votes than on the introduction of any other of his great subjects,[1] and yet he came out of the House after his speech earnestly apologising for having done so little justice to their subject.'

[1] The previous question was carried by 176 votes to 79.

Varied Company

Three years later, in 1852, Elihu Burritt came to Falmouth, and Caroline met him at Bank House, the home of her grandmother, Mrs Robert Were Fox senior. Burritt was still exhilarated by various events of the previous year, such as 'the Great Exhibition, the Peace Congress, the linking of London with all the great capitals of the continent by the submarine telegraph.' Caroline said of him this time: 'At the Bank House, when enter Elihu Burritt, looking as beautifully refined an American Indian as ever. He has formed a little Peace Society here, with meetings, funds, books and a secretary; and has cleverly managed to persuade the editors of many influential foreign newspapers to give constant insertion to its little "Olive Leaf," which is well. He gave a lecture at the Polytechnic on the extension of the penny-postage system. It was conclusively argumentative and well buttressed with facts, statistical, financial and social.' She concludes with a rather unexpected testimonial: 'Our ragged boys in the gallery quite agreed with him, and the feeling of the meeting crystallised into a petition.' Elihu Burritt, like so many of Caroline's acquaintances, is worth summoning for a moment out of the past. He has his modest place both in American and in English history, and did something appreciable to associate the two.

What shall I more say? For the time would fail me to tell of a score of secondary figures who flitted across the stage of Caroline's consciousness, each leaving some small deposit in her receptive mind—people like Dr Guggenbühl, the founder of an institution for cretins near Interlaken; or Mrs Schimmelpenninck, wife of a Dutch merchant and a friend of the Gurneys, who, having been born a Friend and subsequently savoured Roman Catholicism, ultimately settled down with what was an eclectic faith, but mainly Moravian; or Amelia Opie, wife of the Royal Academician, author of novels and poems, who combined quite naturally the simplicities of the Quakerism she had embraced with a love of a lively and intellectual society in

346

which she claimed the Kembles and Mrs Siddons, Godwin and Mary Wollstonecraft and Sheridan, as her friends. On all these and many others Caroline has some shaft of light to throw. Her life gained something from them all. She realised it, and was quietly grateful.

Yet one more paragraph should be added to this chapter. Caroline never met Thackeray, but she read him; her verdict on *Vanity Fair* has already been recorded.[1] And in 1851 she went to hear him. In that year—on successive Thursdays in May, June and July—he delivered for the first time his six lectures on English Humourists of the Eighteenth Century. On June 12th Caroline attended the third of them, on Sir Richard Steele, and gives a description of the event in a few sentences which have their interest still. 'Went,' she writes, 'to Thackeray's lecture on the "Humorists" at Willis's Rooms. It was a very large assembly, including Mrs Carlyle, Dickens, Leslie and innumerable noteworthy people. Thackeray is a much older man than I had expected; a square, powerful face, and most acute and sparkling eyes, greyish hair and eyebrows. He reads in a definite, rather dry manner, but makes you understand thoroughly what he is about. The lecture was full of point, but the subject was not a very interesting one, and he tried to fix our sympathy on his good-natured, volatile and frivolous Hero rather more than was meet. "Poor Dick Steele," one ends with, as one began; and I cannot see, more than I did before, the element of greatness in him.'

Addison, the subject of the previous lecture, might have appealed to her more.

[1] p. 32.

Chapter XX
Valedictory

Such was Caroline Fox. Such rather—the qualification is necessary—is the portrait of her that emerges from such materials for delineation as exist. They are not abundant. Apart from a few surviving letters, like those to her cousin Lucy Hodgkin from which I have quoted from time to time, and one or two articles, written after her death, or Anne Maria's, in Quaker publications, there is nothing but the Journal, and of that, as has been seen, distressingly little has been preserved in relation to what has been destroyed. What does remain, moreover, covers Caroline's life unevenly. The record for the nine years 1836-1844 is full and detailed, for the remaining twenty-seven by comparison scanty and fragmentary. The Caroline of the first decade of the Journal—Caroline from sixteen to twenty-five—has a clear-cut and consistent personality, and one which inspires both respect and, to one at least who has studied with some diligence the narrative of her life and tried to understand her satisfactions and her sorrows, a warmer feeling which may almost be called affection.

Was her whole life of the same texture? Her editor thinks 'it is worthy of notice how rapidly Caroline Fox's character forms itself; attracting, reflecting and assimilating from the stronger natures around her all that is noteworthy, high-toned and deep-souled.' I do not myself detect that rapidity of change. Every human being, no doubt, shows some signs of growing mental maturity through the procession of the years that lie between the second decade and the sixth, but what impresses me much more in Caroline is the stability of her character and the persistence of its principal traits throughout her life. She had her religious crises and was the better for them. She had her personal sorrows, and may in some sense have been the better for them too. But from the first entry in her Journal to the last, as girl and as woman, she is essentially the same personality, warm-hearted, alert in mind and apt in speech, unwaveringly sincere, quietly spiritual and as quietly sympathetic, soundly critical, but with criticism of persons tempered always by charity, quick in assimilating what was worth assimilating in the life around her, and modestly confident in her capacity to discuss literature or philosophy or science or religion intelligently with men whose distinction in one or other of those fields is universally acknowledged. The series of letters to her friend Elizabeth Carne spread over the last fifteen years of her life, so far from reflecting the sobriety of advancing years, are as lively, as lightly satirical and as pungent in many of their comments as anything to be found in the earlier Journal entries. Caroline, it must be remembered, was never old ; she died before she was fifty-two.

Yet while all that is true, it is impossible not to be conscious of a certain break in Caroline's life. It was different in many respects after 1844 from what it had been. The five years that ended then had enriched her life immensely, but to all the enrichment, or nearly all, there had come an early end. Sterling had appeared at Falmouth at the beginning of 1840; what his friendship meant to Caroline readers of this volume can estimate for themselves; but he went from Falmouth in the summer of 1843, and he went from life in the autumn of 1844. His friend Dr Calvert, wise, learned, mellow of mind, quickly became a friend of Caroline's too; they seemed made to understand one another; but less than two years after she saw him first she was writing of his funeral. John Stuart Mill came into her life at the same time, and here again the friendship struck was swift and close. He gave her autographs, he made her a Calendar of Flowers, he showed her a side of himself of which the world had seen little, and little is revealed in his published works. And then suddenly he went out of her life. 'We have had no intercourse with J. S. M. for many years,' she wrote to Lucy Hodgkin in 1863. It was, in fact, all twenty years; Caroline seems never to have seen Mill after 1844, the year in which Sterling died, and for eighteen months before that their contacts had been rare and casual.

In 1844, too, Caroline had to suffer another impoverishment of a different kind. She says nothing of it, but it must have been very real. In October of that year her brother Barclay was married. That in itself was an occasion of rejoicing rather than sorrow, for his family unreservedly approved his choice, but the ties between Caroline and her only brother had been very close—I have quoted already that little poignant cry after his death, 'For whom should I record them now?'— and that his marriage brought the old companionship to something near an end is certain. Barclay was deeply absorbed in his new home, some miles from Rosehill and Penjerrick, and his growing family; that is revealed unmistakably in the sudden shrinkage of his own diary entries from the day when he left Falmouth to travel north for his wedding. In many ways 1844 was a sad year for Caroline—and a year in which, apart from a loss of friends by death or distance, the sense of intellectual stimulus withdrawn must have been strong.

That no doubt explains why after 1844 Caroline was a less diligent diarist (though it must be remembered that her editor was likely to quote less liberally in respect of later years, when entries would be liable to refer to many people still living when his edition of the Journal appeared). But in the last ten years of her life, at any rate, there were other reasons. Barclay had died in Egypt in 1855, and his widow in France in 1860. From that time Caroline and her sister took charge of their four orphan nephews and brought them up at Grove Hill, which had belonged to Barclay for some years, and Penjerrick. (The fifth child, a girl, was adopted by an uncle and aunt,

Edmund and Juliet Backhouse.) That changed the routine of life for Caroline considerably, but changed it on the whole very happily. She enjoyed the charge thus suddenly laid on her, though she was disappointed that at one time her eldest nephew, Robert, displayed insufficient appreciation of Grove Hill as his heritage. (Robert Fox, as I remember him in his vigorous later sixties, had fully outlived any such deficiency.) But apart from that the rhythm of her life was quiet and even, the winter months spent usually at Rosehill, the summer at Penjerrick, where the original pair of cottages had been renovated, and a farm developed, by Barclay Fox, so that he could write in his journal in September 1839: 'The family settled for the first time at Penjerrick "as a home." '[1] Though the two houses were no more than three miles apart, their surroundings were completely different, Falmouth essentially marine, Penjerrick, with its lanes and woods, essentially rural.

One word is requisite on Caroline as a diarist. Except in journals avowedly or secretly intended for publication—of which there was not the remotest idea in this case—little in the shape of literary style is to be looked for in such documents. Events are recorded, thoughts given expression, in the first words that come to hand. But it is clear that Caroline had it in her to be a writer. Crisp turns of phrase like the description of the sculptor Burnard, 'a great deal of face, with all the features massed in the centre,' or the characterisation of Borrow, 'his delicacy is not of the most susceptible,' or the striking passage in which she tells of the effect the Chevalier Neukomm's playing had on her, testify to the competence her pen might have developed if she had taken up writing seriously. She had a marked capacity for fastening on the outstanding passages in someone's conversation and summarising them or reporting them verbatim.

As it was, she was content to write her Journal (and nothing

---

[1] i.e. the Rosehill family. Penjerrick had been occupied long before this ; George Croker Fox the first had died there in 1781.

else except one or two tracts) and to live her life. She collected her autographs, she visited the Sailors' Home and various old people, she read, she was interested, as various entries in the Journal show, in rather out-of-the-way sciences or semi-sciences like phrenology—though, for that matter, phrenology, thanks to George Combe and Rumball and others, was very much the *dernier cri* in the eighteen-forties. There is no sign that she played any outdoor games—there were very few, indeed, that women did play a century ago—nor that she ever danced. Dancing was not universally eschewed in the Society of Friends; the Gurney girls at Earlham danced like the Congress of Vienna; but there is no evidence of any dancing among the Foxes of Falmouth. Exercise was provided by walking and riding, principally riding, which was the only means of travelling any substantial distance unless a carriage was to be ordered out. Caroline does not seem to have been a great walker. Even the short journey between Rosehill and Penjerrick was usually made on a horse or behind one.

* * *

I am very conscious of the imperfection of the picture of Caroline presented in these pages. The method adopted has not permitted the inclusion of casual and occasional entries which often illuminate one facet or other of Caroline's character or tastes—such, for example, as the two notes on consecutive days in October 1848:

'A wet day and all its luxuries.'
'A fine day and all its liabilities';

or sidelights on history like the remark in January 1840 (on the introduction of penny postage), 'Received my last frank today from Sir Charles Lemon. What a happiness for the M.P.'s, that daily nuisance being superseded'; or irrelevant but entertaining records such as: 'October 9th [1839].—Snow Harris lunched with us; much pleasant conversation

on different modes of puffing. He mentioned that Day &
Martin used to drive about in a gig in their early days all
over the country, one as servant to the other, and at every
inn the servant would insist on having his master's shoes
cleaned with Day & Martin's blacking, "as nothing else
was used by people of fashion," and so induced large orders.'

For all that recourse must be had to the Journal itself. As
Caroline's own record of her experiences, and the mirror of her
mind and thought, nothing, of course, could replace it. Its
defect is the absence of background, such as could be taken for
granted when the words were written but is a necessity for
readers of today. That I have endeavoured to supply, as well
as to gather scattered threads into skeins by grouping the various
entries referring to particular persons or subjects. At the
end of it I take leave of Caroline with a certain melancholy,
as of a companion by whom life has been sensibly enriched. It would be the highest reward if some readers
should share that sentiment.

Index

Index

Index

Fry, Elizabeth, 22, 113, 216, 223, 235, 329-334
Fry, Joseph, 231, 329
Fuller, Margaret, 119

Gentleman's Magazine, 74
George III, King, 213
George IV, King, 256
Gilbert, Davies, 47, 244, 255-258
Gillman, Dr, 63, 172, 175
Gladstone, W. E., 132, 189
Glendurgan, 25, 30, 319
Goethe, Johann Wolfgang, 78, 79, 113, 162
Gorham Case, 247
Graham, Sir James, 330
Grasmere, 43, 82
Great Western Railway, 24
Greville, Charles, 47, 91, 204, 226, 332
Grote, George, 145
Grove Hill, 185, 267, 309, 350
Guizot, 145, 160, 227, 229-234
Gurney, Catherine, 335
Gurney, Hannah, 222
Gurney, Joseph John, 22, 50, 194, 334, 336
Gurney, Sarah, 192
Gurneys of Earlham, 14, 329, 334

Hallam, Henry, 84, 184, 234
Hamilton, Sir William, 278, 287
Hare, Augustus, 14
Hare, Julius, 60, 61, 63, 127-129, 181, 239, 267, 268
Harris, W. Snow, 352
Helps, Sir Arthur, 278
Hoare, Gurney, 176
Hoare, Mrs Samuel, 176
Hodgkin, Dr Thomas, 24, 26, 41, 42
Hodgkin, Mrs Thomas, 44, 348, 350
Holland, Lady, 270
Home, Sir Everard, 272
Hooker, Sir Joseph, 254
Howitt, Mary, 206, 237
Hudson, George, 136
Humboldt, Alexander von, 200, 277, 333
Hunt, Holman, 185, 309, 310
Hunt, Leigh, 205
Hunter, Dr John, 269, 272

Irving, Edward, 72, 109, 120, 250, 251

Jesuits, 80
Jewsbury, Geraldine, 119, 120, 130

Keble, John, 327
Kekewich, Dorothy, 14
Kent, Duchess of, 214
Kestner, Augustus, 195
Kinglake, A. W., 337
King's College, 235, 236, 240, 259
Kingsley, Charles, 130, 241, 242, 250, 328

Lamb, Charles, 72, 148, 169
Landseer, Sir Edwin, 306, 308
Lane, E. W., 204
Latour, Mlle, 231, 232
Laurence, Samuel, 117, 126, 184, 186, 304, 305
Lawrence, John (Lord), 322-325
Lean, Joel, 253
Lemon, Elizabeth, 340
Lemon, Sir Charles, 200, 260, 261, 280, 285, 340
Leverrier, U. J. J., 287, 289
Lincoln's Inn, 236, 237
Lister, J. J., 260
Livingstone, Dr David, 228
London Library, 12, 125
London Magazine, 74
London and Westminster Review, 144, 159, 341
Louis Philippe, King, 229, 230
Ludlow, J. M., 238
Luther, Martin, 55, 76, 156, 243
Lyell, Sir Charles, 318

McCarthy, Sir Charles, 318
Macaulay, Zachary, 224
Macaulay, T. B., 222, 224
MacDonald, Margaret, 45
MacMahon, Marshal, 151
Madison, James, 20
Mahomet Ali, 203, 316
Martin, John, 284
Martineau, Harriet, 102
Masterman, C. F. G., 194
Maurice, Rev. F. D., 63, 70, 87, 116, 171, 193, 235-241, 284
Maurice, Mrs F. D., 87
Mayo, Katharine, 150
Melbourne, Lord, 301
Mendelssohn, Felix, 192, 201

Index

Index

Printed in Great Britain
by T. and A. CONSTABLE LTD
at the University Press
Edinburgh

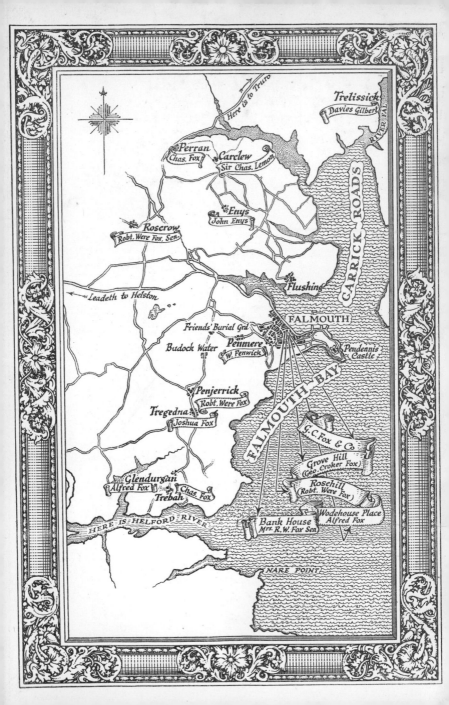